IMAGES
of America

ALOHA-REEDVILLE

ON THE COVER: Dairy cows graze near the barns and corrals on the David Hagg and Sons farm at Reedville in 1937. The farm exceeded the national record for butterfat production in 1936, for a herd of more than 50 cows. David and Augusta Hagg purchased acreage in 1890 next to Simeon and Amanda Reed's farm in Washington County, Oregon. For years, while developing their dairy, they cut and cleared timber from their land. By 1909, the Haggs were exporting milk and cream to Portland. Brothers Henry and Oscar Hagg became the second generation to manage the family business. Graduates of the Oregon Agricultural College, now Oregon State University, they applied scientific methods to maximize the farm's efficiency and profitability. Dairy stock was selected based on production records and beet pulp, instead of silage, used for winter feed. Henry and Oscar were dairy industry leaders and founding members of the Aloha Grange. Henry championed agricultural education and research throughout Oregon. Oscar was president of the Oregon Dairymen's Association, director of the Oregon Dairy Council, and a dairy marketing specialist with the Oregon State University Extension Service (9969-2961 Alfred A. Monner © Historic Photo Archive.)

IMAGES
of America

ALOHA-REEDVILLE

Janel Josephson

ARCADIA
PUBLISHING

ISBN 978-0-7385-9952-6

Published by Arcadia Publishing
Charleston, South Carolina

Printed in the United States of America

Library of Congress Control Number: 2012950717

For all general information, please contact Arcadia Publishing:
Telephone 843-853-2070
Fax 843-853-0044
E-mail sales@arcadiapublishing.com
For customer service and orders:
Toll-Free 1-888-313-2665

Visit us on the Internet at www.arcadiapublishing.com

To the people of Aloha-Reedville:
May your stories of courage, ingenuity, and
determination continue to inspire.

Contents

Acknowledgments 6
Introduction 7
Donation Land Claim Patent Holders 10
Donation Land Claims Map 11
1. Early Settlement 13
2. Hazeldale 17
3. Perkins Corner 31
4. The Reed Farm 41
5. Reedville 51
6. Huber 101
7. Aloha 105

ACKNOWLEDGMENTS

This book is a compilation of accounts and artifacts generously and thoughtfully shared with the author by Marcia Morrison Buck, Art Bullis, Stella Dimeo Casey, Cindy Cole, Chris Bierly Cullen, Bryce and Laurene Coleman, Scott Daniels, Judy Donovan, Kathleen Imlay Eames, Walt Eames, Karen Eubanks, Cathy Foster, John Foster, Susan Foulkes, Judy Goldmann, Lisa Gomez, Carolyn Thayer Guinther, Kevin Harrington, Winn Herrschaft, Roy Janssen, Preston Janssen, John Keith, Susanna Schappert Keith, John and Phyllis Kirkwood, Patricia Kliewer, Ann Koppy, Sally and Steve Kramer, Sue Lambing, Steve Larrance, Susan Leatherman, Virginia Mapes, Tom Maurer, Victoria McCurry, Frances Meier, Christine H. Messing, Adam Mikos, Deb Nystrom, Casey Parks, Ray Pitz, Nita Rinehart, Ruth Roberts, Thomas Robinson, Scott Rook, Joe Santoro, Nancy Santoro, Marcia Schonlau, John Tyner, Rick Van Beveren, Gay Walker, Laura E. Wilt, and Diane Woff.

INTRODUCTION

The story of Aloha or Aloha-Reedville, an unincorporated community in Washington County, Oregon, began nearly 10,000 years before the first pioneers of European descent arrived on the Tualatin Plains, one of the oldest agricultural centers in the western United States.

Throughout the Willamette Basin of the Pacific Northwest, the Kalapuya people established tribal territories distinguished by language. The Northern Kalapuyan band, called Tualatin, Faladin, or Alafati, lived near the Tualatin River. They built permanent, plank houses grouped into small villages and seasonal shelters near hunting and gathering sites. Alafati fished for salmon and trout and navigated rivers and streams in dugout, cedar log canoes where they harvested camas root, later processed and stored for food and trade. They gathered nuts, seeds, berries, tarweed, and filberts, and used slash burning methods to expand prairies to hunt and trap bear, deer, and elk along with birds and small game.

Following exploration of the Pacific coast in the 17th century, Capt. Robert Gray, on his second voyage from Boston to China, sailed inland up the Columbia River in 1792. The overland Lewis and Clark Expedition of 1804–1806 was followed by the creation of Fort Astoria in 1811, the first permanent American settlement on the Pacific coast. The Treaty of 1818 resolved competing claims to the region and established an international boundary at the 49th parallel.

The Hudson's Bay Company, one of the world's oldest commercial corporations, built Fort Vancouver, their Columbia District headquarters, at the confluence of the Willamette and Columbia Rivers in 1825. A trading outpost and supply depot, it was near Sauvie Island and Tualatin Valley farms, where wheat, produce, and dairy products were produced for export and trade. First settled by former Hudson's Bay Company employees, American "mountain men," missionaries and overland immigrants, the bountiful, northern Tualatin Plains contained some of the best farmland on earth: 50,000 acres of open, grassy prairie. In 1841–1842, agricultural enclaves emerged at West Tualatin Plains, today's Forest Grove and Columbia, now Hillsboro.

In 1842, the number of European descendants in Oregon Country, south of the Columbia River, was estimated at 102 American citizens and 63 British or French Canadians, mostly former Hudson's Bay Company employees. A provisional government was elected in 1843 to provide a centralized legal system, common defense, and temporary constitution to four districts: Champoeg, Clackamas, Yamhill, and Tuality. The Organic Laws of Oregon granted no-cost territorial land claims—up to 320 acres for unmarried individuals and 640 for married couples willing to improve the land.

The Tuality District, which encompassed today's Washington County, spanned the distance from the Willamette River to the Pacific Ocean and the northern boundary of the United States to the Yamhill River. By 1845, the Tuality District population was large enough to form a centralized government, including a sheriff, a treasurer, and three county judges with probate and administrative authority.

Philip and Sarah Harris and their extended family left Ohio and migrated west in 1845. After surviving guide Stephen Meeks's cutoff on the Oregon Trail, they settled on the Tualatin Plains, near the Tualatin River. Unlike the northern plains, claims closer to the river were likely to include a combination of hillsides, draws, swales, canyons, dense forests, and bottom land that overflowed. The family formed a church and post office, and shuttled passengers, freight, and livestock across the Tualatin River on rafts fashioned from cedar logs.

Nathan and Mary Robinson's family left Ohio for Oregon Country in 1846. They registered a territorial land claim on the Tualatin Plains, adjacent to Plains-Falls road. Their farm, known for award-winning apples and an early subscription school, is the site of the town of Reedville. The farm east of the Robinson's was owned by Andrew Jackson Masters and his wife, the former Sarah Jane Jenkins, who migrated from Kentucky in 1843. Between the two land claims, a road led south to Hazeldale, and Harris Ferry, and north to the Tualatin Plains and Willamette Falls.

The Masters farm shared a common boundary with a 900-acre claim registered to James H. McMillen. Originally from New York, McMillen signed onto a wagon train in 1845 in Missouri that included Phillip Harris, Benjamin Cornelius, Lawrence Hall, and Solomon Wheeler, all future neighbors on the Tualatin Plains. In Oregon Country, McMillen worked as a millwright and built the first bridge in the western United States. In 1850, he purchased Richard Torney's claim adjacent on the Plains-Falls Road.

The Donation Land Claim Act of 1850 designated 320 acres of free land to unmarried white male citizens 18 or older, and 640 acres to married couples who arrived in the Oregon Territory before 1850. Arrivals from 1850 to 1854 were eligible for half that amount. Claimants were required to live on and cultivate the land for four years before owning it outright. The law was one of the first in the United States to allow married women to hold property in their own name.

In 1856, the Confederated Bands of Kalapuya, a population reduced to about 433, ceded the entire Willamette Valley in exchange for resettlement on a series of reservations.

That same year, James McMillen mortally wounded A.J. Masters by gunfire near the Plains-Falls Road. He was tried, acquitted in self-defense, and sold his farm shortly thereafter to Jacob and Jemima Wheeler, and cattlemen Richard S. Perkins and Arthur H. Johnson, British immigrants and owners of a Portland meat shop. Over time, they acquired 1,400 acres in Aloha-Reedville.

Portland entrepreneur Simeon Gannett Reed and his wife, Amanda, purchased the Robinson farm in the 1860s. It was one of 17 commercial farms managed by the Ladd and Reed Farm Company, which was co-owned by Reed and twice Portland mayor William S. Ladd. In 1866, Reed became president of the Oregon Central Railroad. Two years later, a short-line railroad connecting Portland with Forest Grove was completed west of Beaverton as far as a railroad depot on the Reed farm. It 1871, it was the site of the largest single importation of the finest animals and purest blooded livestock ever introduced to Oregon or the Pacific coast.

Motivated by a desire to improve livestock herds and the regional economy, Reed employed expert breeders and agriculturalists and encourage the use of scientific methods to analyze and improve production and experiment with seeds, crops, irrigation systems, and steam-powered farm equipment.

By 1874, Reed's attention turned to Shorthorn cattle and Standardbred trotting horses. Extensive equestrian facilities were constructed, including a circular barn and an enclosed, half-mile harness racing track. Reed gained a reputation as a livestock breeder and cattleman, participated in exhibitions and the state fair, and joined the American Shorthorn Breeder's Association and Oregon Agricultural Society. The Reed's Washington County farm, a short train ride from their residence in Portland, was a popular destination for family, friends, business associates, and prospective buyers.

Although he could afford to privately finance agricultural experimentation, Reed expected the venture to yield a reasonable profit. In 1875, he restricted the scope of operations. By 1883, farm affairs were handled almost exclusively by Martin Winch, Reed's nephew and business agent who planned to sell all the livestock except work animals, put every available acre into grain production and develop what remained into real estate tracts. In 1887, Reed's railroad interests were acquired by the Southern Pacific Railroad.

The town of Reedville was platted in 1889. By 1891, the first dairy of any consequence in Washington County was operational on the Reed farm. In May 1892, when the Reeds relocated to Pasadena, California, the farm became part of a corporation.

Ladd served as president of the Board of Regents at the Oregon Agricultural College in 1892, now Oregon State University. When he died in 1893, his partnership with Reed was dissolved. Simeon Reed died in 1895. Amanda Reed inherited her husband's estate, including the Washington County farm and an interest in the Ladd and Reed Farm Company.

In 1901, east of Reedville, the Perkins farm was sold to the Standard Corporation. They subdivided and, operating as the Shaw-Fear real estate company, sold parcels in Beaverton Reedville Acreage, the Pasadena of Old Oregon. Potential buyers could choose between stump and timberland for $150 an acre or cleared land for $200.

Amanda Reed died in 1904. Her will named 11 heirs and more than 12 charities as beneficiaries and endowed a board of trustees to establish a Reed Institute. After extensive research, they founded Reed College in Portland, on the old Crystal Springs Farm, a site donated by the Ladd family.

By 1907, Jacob and Jemima Wheeler's land was divided into parcels by David Wheeler, who helped Silas, Hawley, and Julius Buck build the S.N. Buck & Sons store in 1908 on Wheeler Avenue, today's Southwest 185th Avenue.

Southern Pacific converted their branch steam railway to electricity in 1910. It was leased to the interurban Red Electric streetcar line, which connected depots at St. Mary's, Huber, Aloha, Tobias, and Reedville to Portland's Union Station. In 1912, the Bucks opened the Aloha branch of the US Post Office.

Tualatin Valley Highway, two-lane, concrete road for automobiles between Portland and Hillsboro, was installed by the Oregon State Highway Department in 1918. The Red Electrics discontinued operations in 1929.

After meeting on the second floor above Buck's Market, volunteers built the Aloha Grange building in Wheeler Avenue in 1932. By 1934, grain farming and dairying constituted the largest source of farm income in Washington County.

In 1955, the Oregon State Highway Commission awarded contract no. 4499 to the Porter W. Yet Company to increase Tualatin Valley Highway to four lanes of traffic between Beaverton and Reedville, a distance of 4.69 miles.

The 1962 Columbus Day storm damaged dozens of structures in the Aloha-Reedville area. Some were never repaired and later destroyed.

In 1971, Beaverton School District No. 48 opened Aloha High School on the site of the former Kinnaman dairy, Southwest 185th Avenue and Kinnaman Road.

By of the turn 21st century, the historic villages of Huber, Hazeldale, and Perkins Crossing disappeared into the growth of the nearby Aloha community. On Highway 10 near Farmington, a modern Harris Bridge was erected, dedicated to the early pioneer and his contribution to public works.

Aloha-Reedville Donation Land Claim Patent Holders

Barton: Edward and Hannah H. Barton, originally from Ohio, arrived in Oregon Country in August 1851. They registered their land claim on February 25, 1852. Barton was a Washington County commissioner from 1855 to 1857. One of the early members of the Reedville school district, he later manufactured carriages in Portland.

Comfort: Edwin B. and Elvira Holland Comfort settled a 632-acre claim in 1853.

Cooper: Perry and Nancy Cooper claimed 320 acres in 1853 on the northwest side of present-day Cooper Mountain, which was mapped as early as 1852.

Ellerson: David and Annie Elizabeth Lord Ellerson settled a claim in 1852 which included the site of today's Hazeldale School and a diagonal section of Farmington Road.

Graham: John and Matilda Graham established an irregular-shaped claim 1853. The western boundary was at today's Southwest 185th Avenue, between Johnson Street and Baseline Road.

Masters: Andrew Jackson and Sarah Jane Jenkins Masters settled in 1850 following a shipwreck near Astoria in 1849. Their claim was located between today's Southwest 198th and 209th Avenues. In October 1854, McMillen shot Masters and was later tried and acquitted.

McMillen: Capt. James H. McMillen, a native of New York, traveled to Oregon by ox team. He arrived on October 25, 1845, and was a millwright at Willamette Falls until the spring of 1849. After traveling to the California gold fields, he returned and purchased Richard Torney's claim on the Plains-Falls Road.

Merrell: Charles G. and Margaret DeVoe Merrell settled 640 acres in 1850. Their claim was exactly a surveyed square mile or section. Part of the Jenkins Estate, near present-day Southwest Farmington and Grabhorn Roads, was built in the southeast corner of the Merrell claim.

Reid: James H. and Sarah Jane Reid registered their claim in 1851. It was the site of the intersection of the Plains-Falls and Harris Ferry Roads, later known as Perkins Corner.

Robinson: Nathan and Mary Dorland Robinson registered a claim on July 12, 1847. The eastern boundary was today's Southwest 209th Avenue, formerly Kinnesswood Avenue. The western boundary was today's Southwest 229th Avenue, once Churchley Road.

Smith: Issac W. and Mary Smith certified their land claim July 20, 1851, in the area between modern day Blanton and Johnson Streets, and 178th to 198th Avenues. In partnership with Captain John Couch of Portland to move emigrants down the Columbia River by boat, Smith also served in the provisional government in 1845. In 1854, he was assistant engineer on the Pacific Railroad surveys and explorations along the southern route of a proposed transcontinental railway.

Torney: Richard K. Torney registered the very first donation land claim in the Aloha-Reedville area. It transferred it by quit claim deed to James H. McMillen on February 18, 1950. McMillen paid $5,000 for the land. Witnesses to the sale were A.L. Lovejoy and F.W. Pettygrove. The claim was described in number of chains (66 feet or 22 yards), between swales, fir and oak trees.

White: Richard and Caroline White arrived in Oregon Country in 1844. The claim, certified 1850, was. located between present day Baseline Road and Southwest Johnson Street. The western boundary was 219th, formerly Reedville Road.

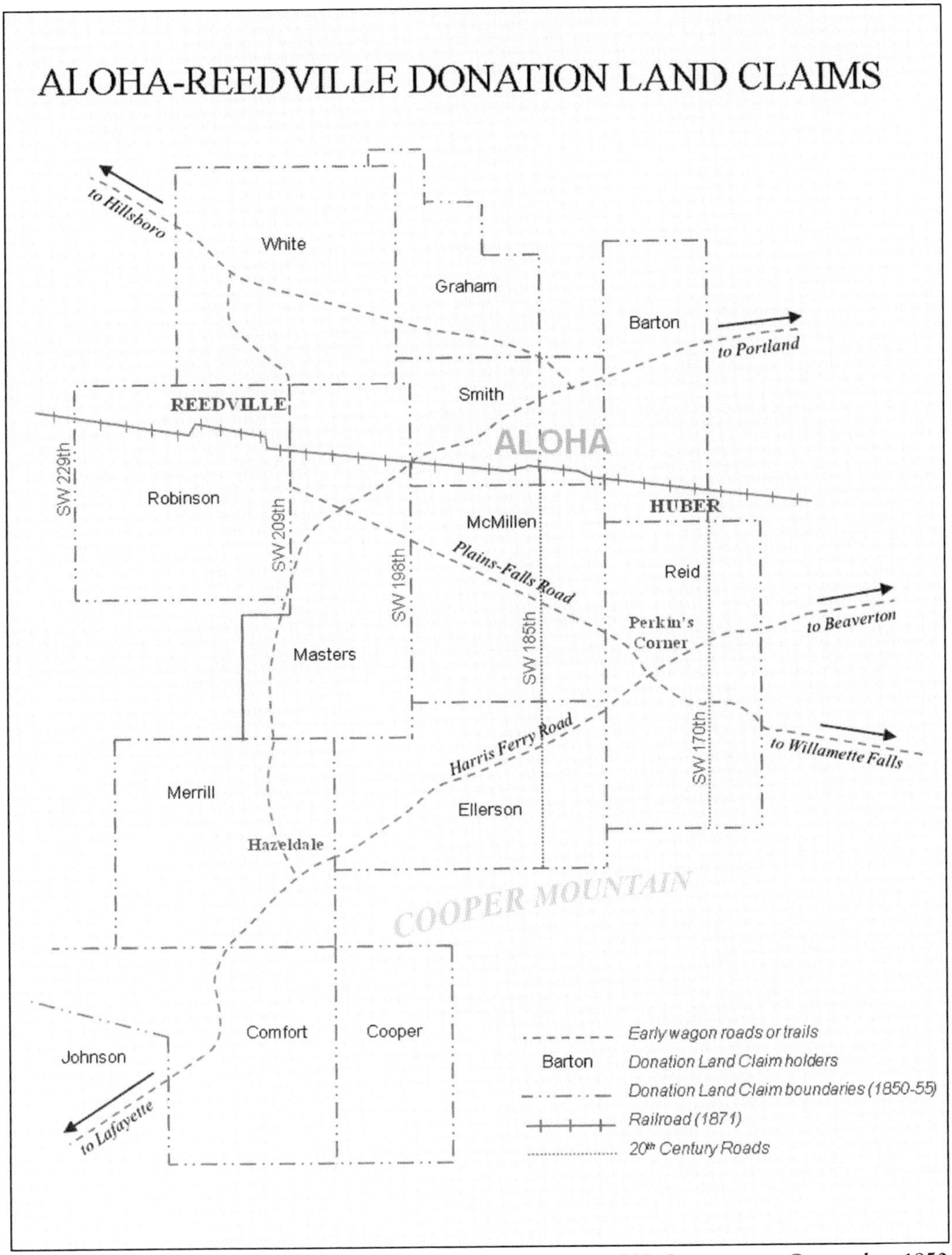

The Donation Land Claim Act of 1850 was enacted by the US Congress in September 1850 to promote homestead settlements in the Oregon Territory, the present-day states of Oregon, Washington, Idaho, and part of Wyoming. It granted 320 acres, free of charge, to white male citizens 18 or older, and 640 acres to married couples that arrived in the Oregon Territory before December 1, 1850. For settlers that arrived after 1850, until 1854, the law granted 320 acres. To own the land outright, claimants were required to live on the land and cultivate it for four years.

One

Early Settlement

In 1845, Phillip and Sarah Harris and their children, including daughter Jane and her husband, Hiram Johnson, arrived in Oregon Country. Originally from Ohio, they joined a group of 3,000 wagons that included Benjamin Cornelius, Lawrence Hall, and Solomon Wheeler. All would establish territorial land claims on the Tualatin Plains, one of the oldest agricultural regions in the western United States.

East of the Tualatin River, the family formed a church, started a post office, and, along with a handful of other ferry operators, including Dr. Brown, Peter Scholls, and the Boones, Sulger, and Noland families, shuttled passengers, livestock, and supplies on rafts made of cedar logs. A permanent, wooden ridge on what was then the road to the early settlement of Lafayette was built by Phillip Harris.

The Harris Ferry was near the geographic center of what is today's Washington County and the Plains-Falls Wagon Road, a key route for commercial activity between the wheat farms of the Tualatin Valley and the milling and shipping center at Willamette Falls. Today, a section of that road has been preserved as Southwest Kinnaman in Aloha-Reedville.

In 1848, the California Gold Rush intensified demand for Oregon timber and surplus farm products, exported from ports on the Willamette and Columbia Rivers. After St. Helens carved a road to the Tualatin Plains in 1850, the Portland & Valley Plank Road Company formed in 1851 to build the "canyon" road, a trail covered or "planked" with wood. After nearly a decade, the road was completed. A seasonal and treacherous passage, it emerged as the shortest distance between the Tualatin Valley and the nearest deepwater port.

Logs, cattle and farm products were transported throughout the region by steamship and barge during the 1860s. The Tualatin River Navigation & Manufacturing Company formed in 1871 to develop a continuous navigable waterway between the Tualatin Plains and the Willamette River. Before the first canal was completed in 1872, the Oregon and California Rail Road Company extended a short line railroad west of Beaverton that connected the Tualatin Plains to Portland.

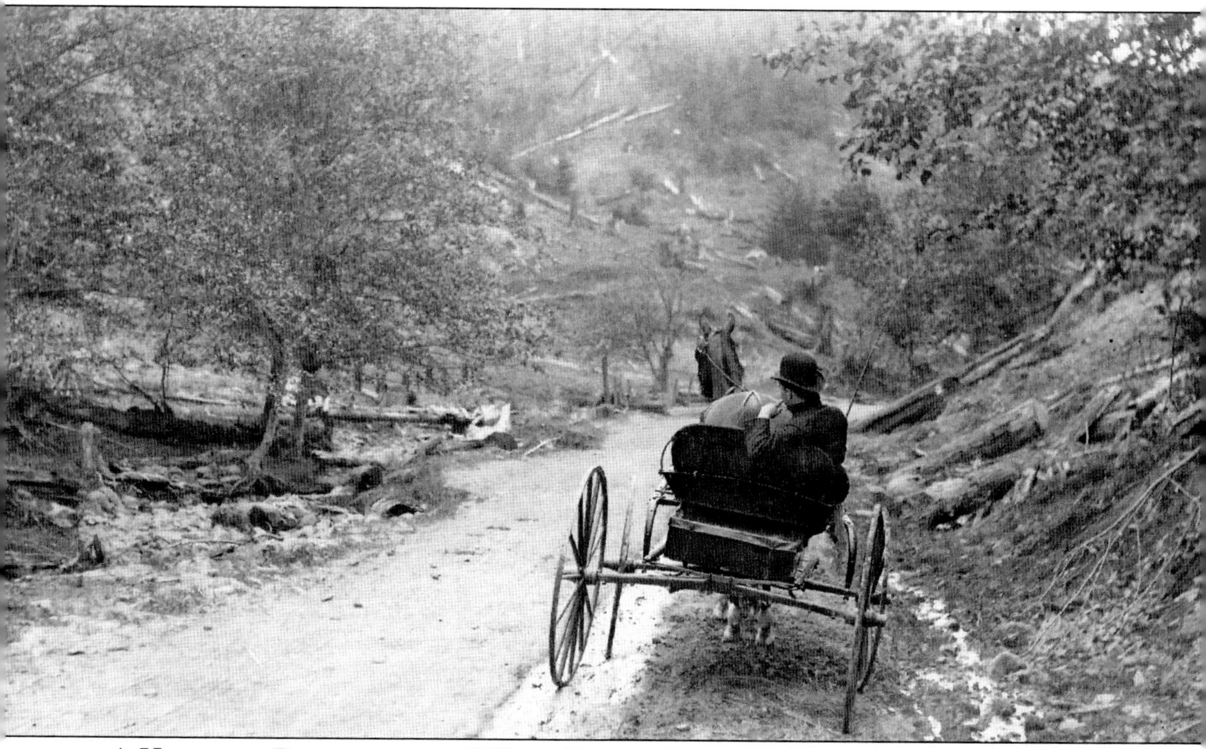

A Horse and Buggy around 1850 on Canyon Road. Timber and farm products from the Tualatin Valley were transported over the Tualatin Mountains to Portland, bound for markets in San Francisco, New England, London, and beyond. Passable roads were essential to commerce and the economy; in the early 1850s, the territorial government chartered the Portland & Valley Plank Road Company to improve existing roads and build new ones. The first project was Canyon Road, which was surfaced with wood planking or corduroy. The road was started in 1851, but the endeavor quickly went bankrupt. Public subscriptions and toll fares revitalized the project in 1855. Completed by 1860, Canyon Road was still a time-consuming and treacherous route. (Oregon Historical Society, No. bb009713.)

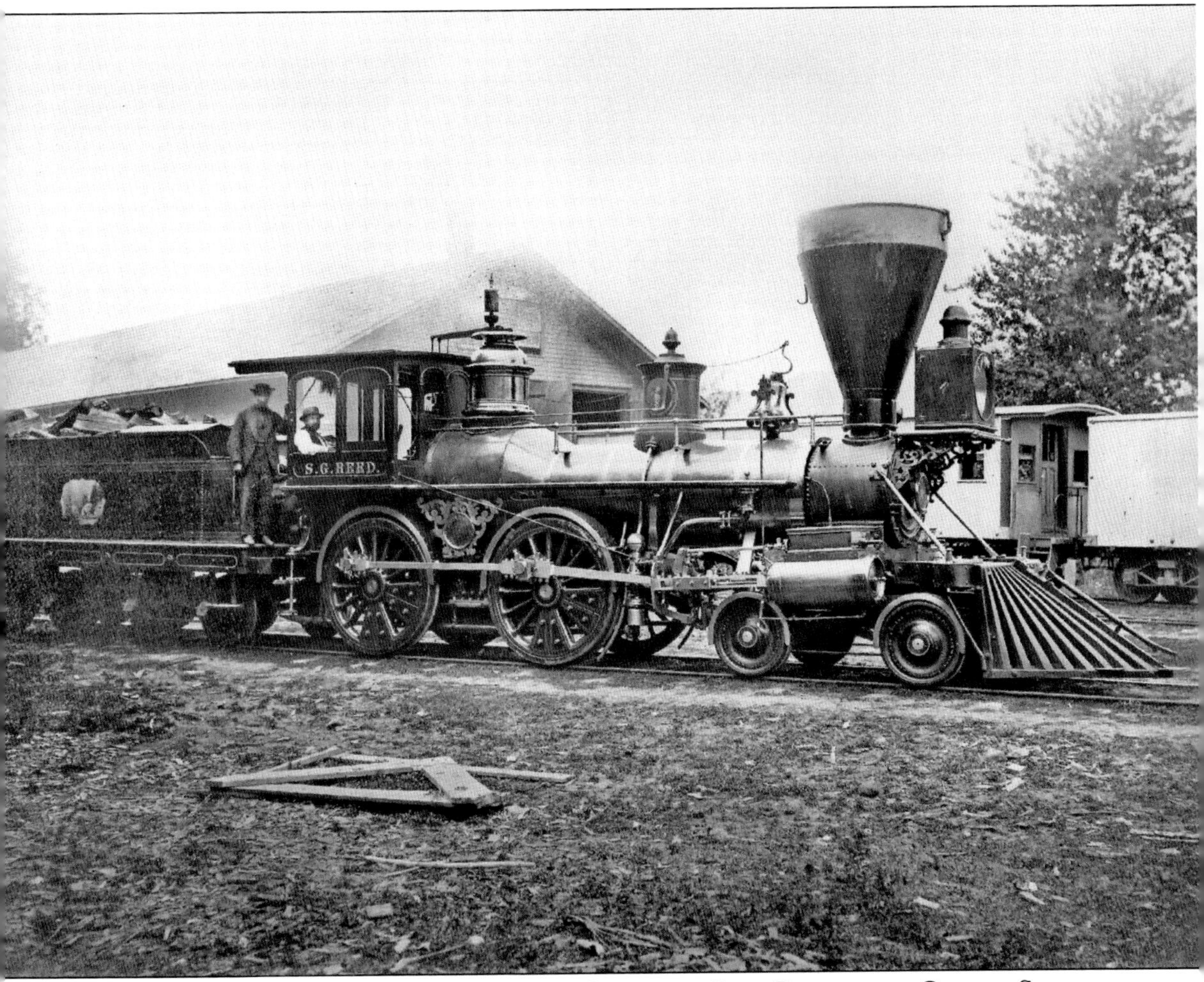

The *S.G. Reed* Steam Locomotive at Lower Cascades, Once Part of the Oregon Steam Navigation Company. The locomotive was named for Simeon Gannett Reed, one of the company's owners. The business was incorporated in the late 1860s by Reed, William S. Ladd, Capt. John C. Ainsworth, and others. In 1862, their holdings increased to include existing portage tramways on the north and south banks of the Columbia River. The company was reorganized in 1866 as the Oregon Central Railroad. In 1871, a railroad that extended past Beaverton toward Forest Grove was used by the Ladd and Reed Farm Company to import blooded livestock to a railroad depot on the farm owned by Simeon and Amanda Reed in Washington County. In the early 1900s, the depot was an important commercial center for Tualatin Valley farmers. (Photograph by Carlton E. Watkins; courtesy of Oregon Historical Society, No. bb009718.)

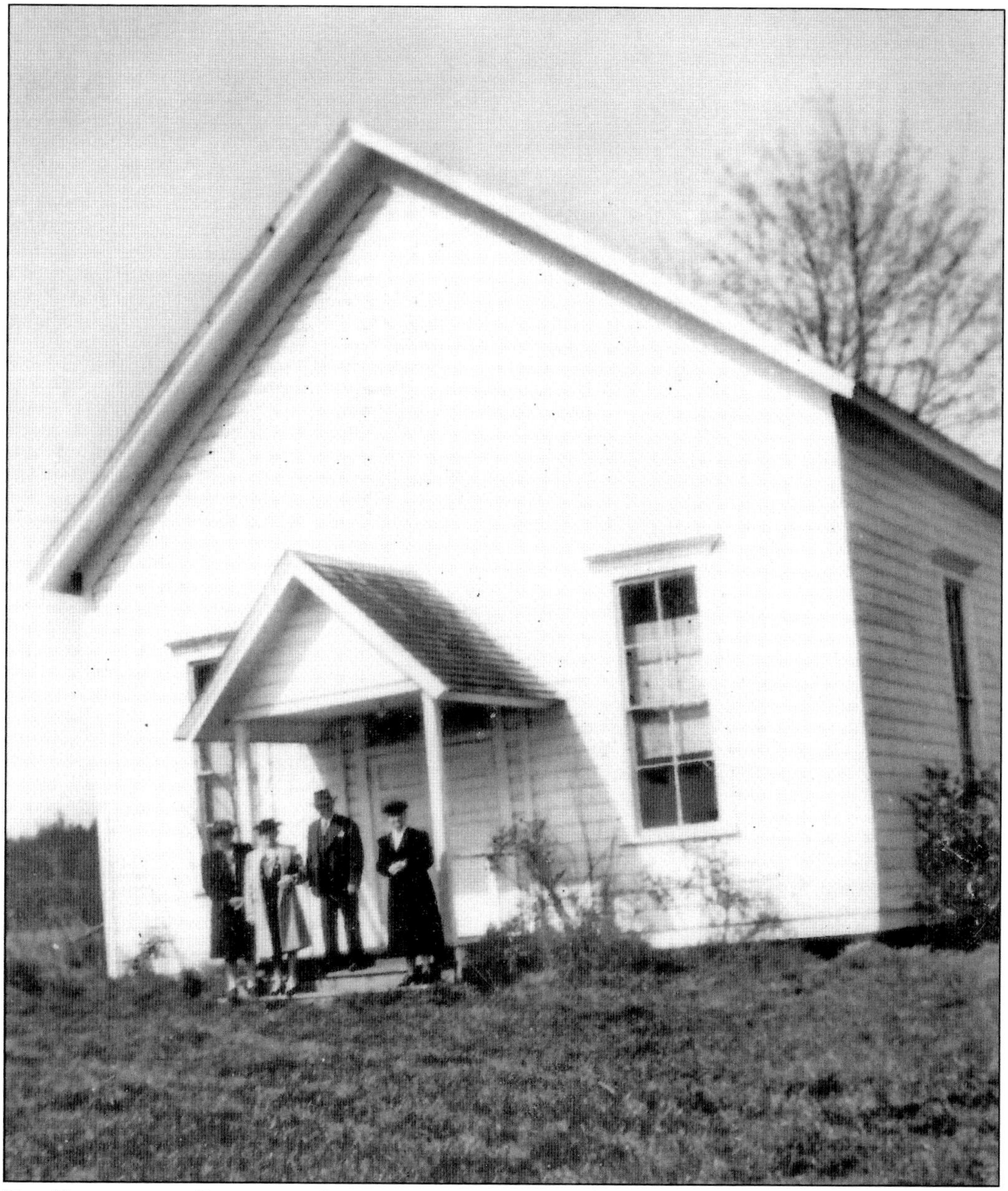

The Farmington Christian Church around 1922. The first church at what was then Harris Ferry was formed in the 1840s in a settlement associated with Phillip and Sarah Harris. Located near today's village of Farmington, the Harris family operated a ferry. Felix and Abram Landess arrived in 1847. By the 1850s, in addition to a church, there was a post office in the small community. Other early settlers included John Griffin, James H. Rice, and John N. Richey. The Comfort, Merrell, and Cooper families established donation land claims near Hazeldale and the intersection of present-day Southwest 209th Avenue and Farmington Road. In the early 1900s, Farmington was known as Twin Oaks. Now a modern Harris Bridge spans the Tualatin River near the original settlement (Oregon Historical Society, No. bb009712.)

Two

HAZELDALE

The families of Abraham, Felix, and John Landess; John Richey; and Nathan and Mary Robinson were among a group of 25 wagons that arrived in Oregon Country in 1846 and claimed land on the Tualatin Plains near Harris Ferry. The Robinsons' claim was adjacent the Plains-Falls Road. As early as 1847, it was the site of an early subscription school. Along the eastern border of their acreage, now Southwest 209th Avenue, a wagon road connected the Plains-Falls Road to Hazeldale, Harris Ferry, and the road to Lafayette.

South of the Robinson farm, Charles and Margaret DeVoe Merrell; David and Annie Elizabeth Lord Ellerson; and Edwin and Elvira Holland Comfort settled land claims in 1851 and 1852. Perry and Nancy Cooper registered a donation land claim in 1953 on the northwest slope of what is now Cooper Mountain.

By the 1870s, Austrian immigrants Alovis and Justina Gassner cultivated 1,400 fruit trees on their 60-acre farm south of the Harris Ferry Road. Hazeldale School District 60 was established in 1882 on what is now Southwest Farmington Road.

George Washington Miller, born in Catawba, North Carolina, immigrated to Oregon with his wife, the former Mary Alice Smith, in 1892. In 1898, they purchased an 85-acre farm near Hazeldale, where they raised nine children.

Bruno and Annunciata Santoro, Italian emigrants who entered the United States at Ellis Island, purchased a 20-acre farm in 1910 from John and Anna McNew. Originally, the land was mostly forest except for about an acre. Their purchase included a small house with a well on the back porch, a straw shed, and a chicken coop.

The one-room Hazeldale school building was moved and enlarged in 1911 after a fire in the nearby store.

From 1912 to 1916, Ralph and Belle Jenkins developed Lolomi, their 68-acre estate on the former Merrill donation land claim. In 1976, the property was purchased and renovated by the Tualatin Hills Park and Recreation District. It was listed on the National Register of Historic Places in 1978.

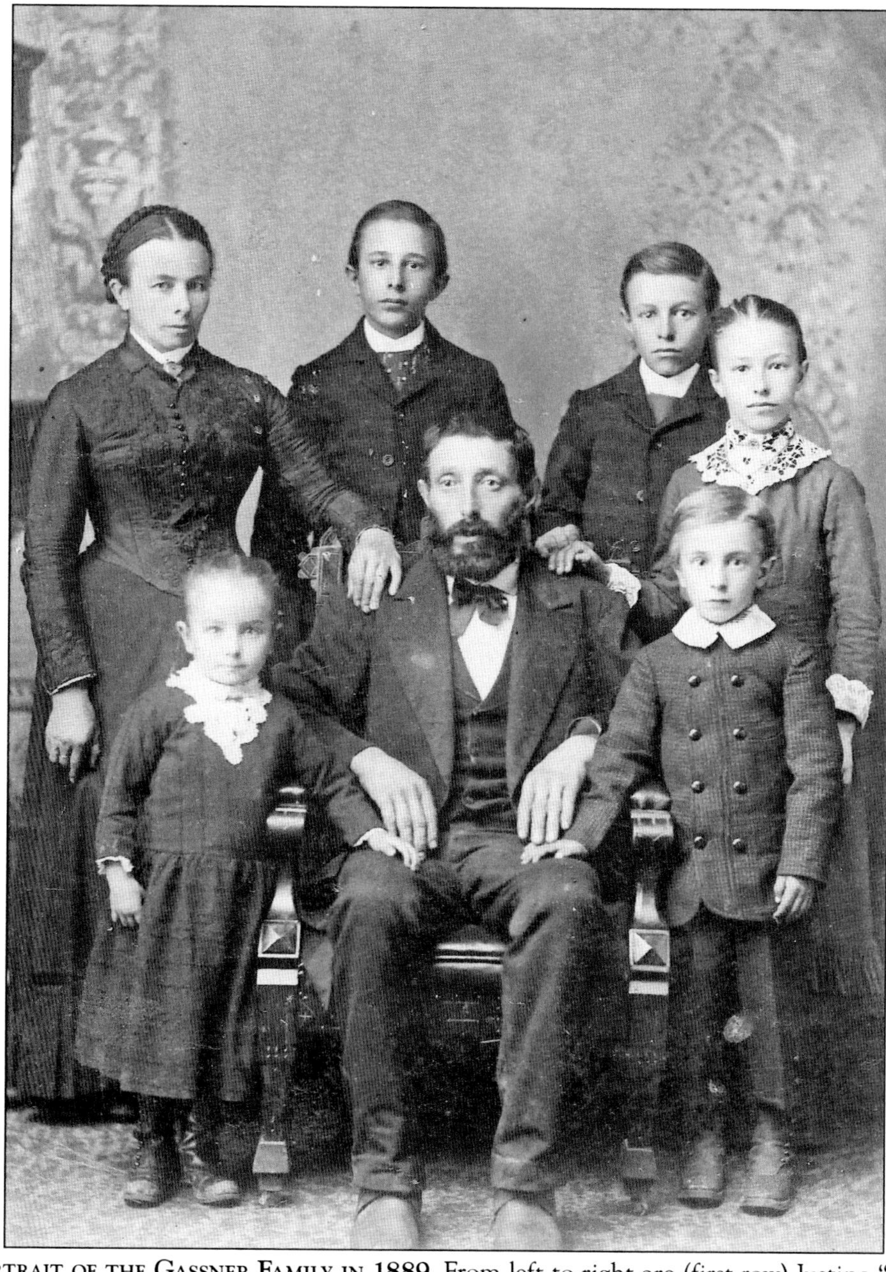

A Portrait of the Gassner Family in 1889. From left to right are (first row) Justina "Babe," Alois Sr., and Julian; (second row) mother Justina (Lampert), Xavier Antoine "Tony," Alois Jr. "Diz," and Carolina. Alois Gassner Sr. was born in Austria on December 15, 1847. He apprenticed as a stonemason before immigrating to the United States in 1869 and lived in Detroit, Michigan, and Freeport, Illinois, before living briefly in California in 1870. The Gassners relocated to Portland, where Alois Sr. worked at various jobs. He made sausage, drove an ice wagon, sold wholesale liquor, and built streets and sidewalks before relocating to Washington County. In the early 1800s, Gassner developed a 60-acre farm near Hazeldale, where he cultivated an orchard of nearly 1,400 fruit trees. The children attended Hazeldale School and St. Mary's of the Valley. (Miller and Gassner families.)

Carolina and Julian Gassner. Carolina (left) wears a bathing gown and Julian Gassner (right) a wool swimsuit in Seaside, Oregon, in 1910. Seaside, population 1,600, was Oregon's first beachfront resort. More than 10,000 tourists visited annually in the early 1900s. (Miller and Gassner families.)

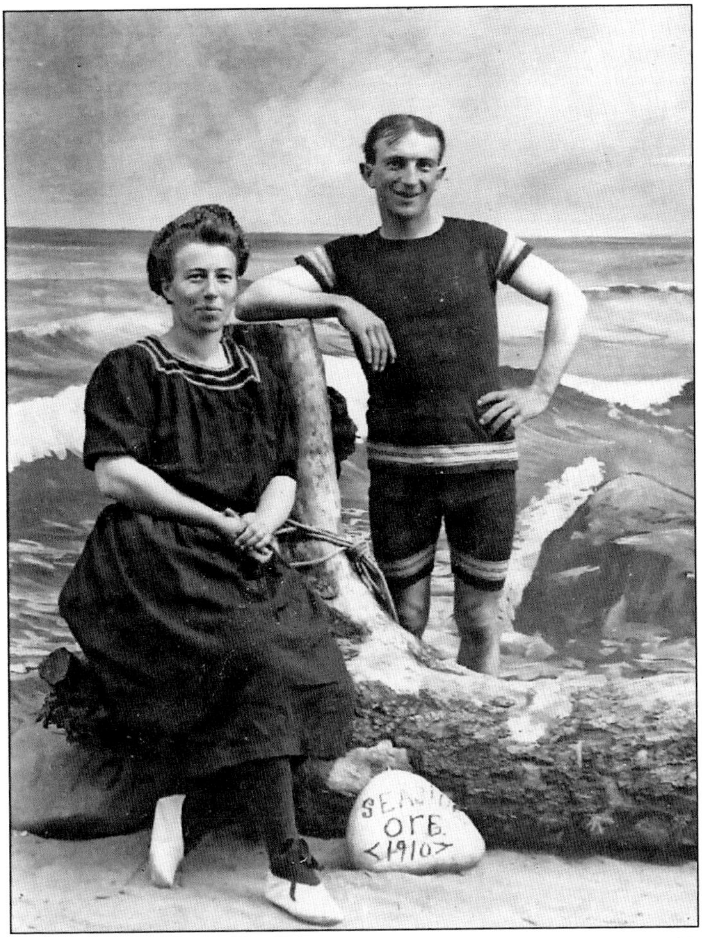

Hazeldale School Students, 1898. From left to right are (first row) Laura Miller, Orphea Morton, Mary Miller, Maud Morton, Clem Kemmer, unidentified, brother, Wilkes girl, Georgia Miller, sister; (second row) Willard Fleck, May Halterman, unidentified, Joe Kemmer, unidentified, Lillie Curtis, Jake Kemmer, Justina Gassner, and Julius Gassner; (third row) unidentified, Anna Morton, Dora Miller, and Pearl Taylor. (Miller and Gassner families.)

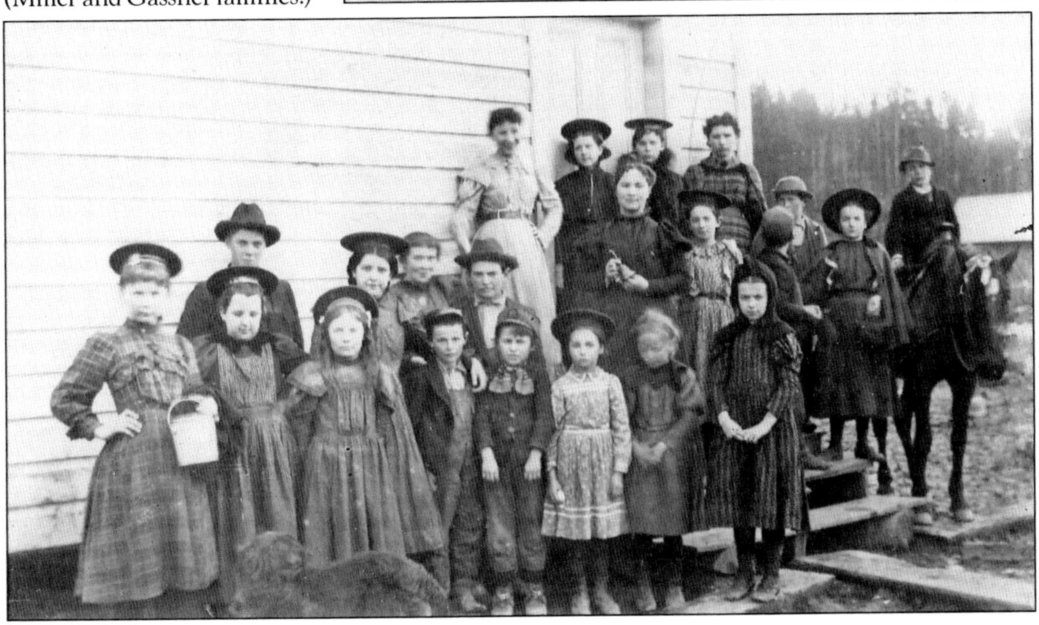

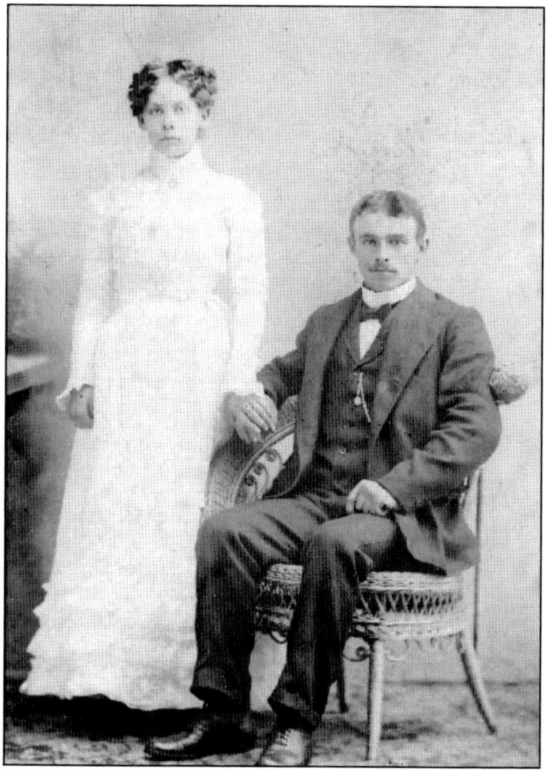

THE WEDDING PHOTOGRAPH OF ALOIS "DIZ" GASSNER AND DORA LEE MILLER. They were married on October 17, 1900, and lived in Reedville. Both of their families lived near Hazeldale. Dora, the daughter of George and Alice Miller, was born in North Carolina. Gassner was born in Portland in 1877. (Miller and Gassner families.)

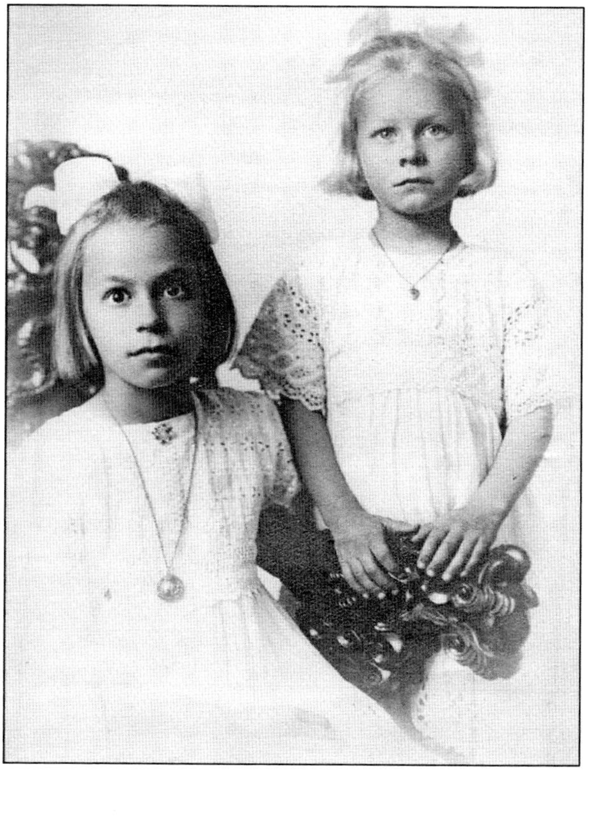

HILDA GASSNER (LEFT), BORN DECEMBER 28, 1901, AND ETHEL GASSNER (RIGHT), BORN FEBRUARY 28, 1907. Daughters of Alois "Diz" Jr. and Dora Lee Miller Gassner, the girls were the grandchildren of Alois and Justina Gassner and George and Alice Miller. They attended St. Mary's of the Valley. (Miller and Gassner families.)

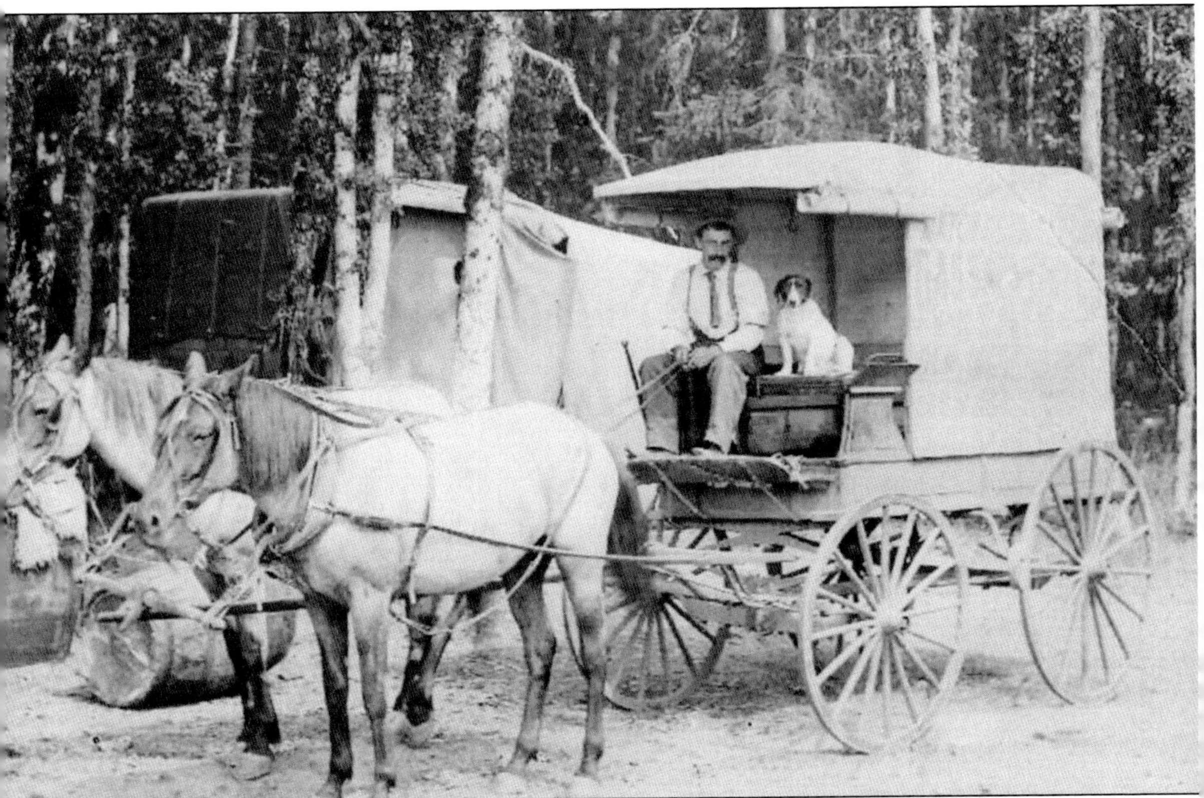

Alois "Diz" Gassner is pictured around 1909 on the seat of the Gassner-Taylor Store's delivery wagon in Reedville. Brothers Xavier Antone "Tony" and Alois "Diz" Gassner Junior and their brother-in-law William Taylor, who was married to the former Carolina Gassner, were proprietors of a general merchandise store in Reedville. They sold produce, meat, notions, shoes, and other items. Tony, a graduate of St. Michael's Business College in Portland, married Vronie Bany. Diz established a dairy of his own at age 23 which he sold six years later when he briefly lived in Seaside, Oregon. He was affiliated with the Catholic Order of Foresters and the Modern Woodmen of America, Silverleaf Camp, No. 8193, at Reedville. The Gassner-Taylor store, constructed by the Reedville chapter of the Order of the Lions, was located on the corner of what was Main Street, now Southwest 214th Avenue (Miller and Gassner families.)

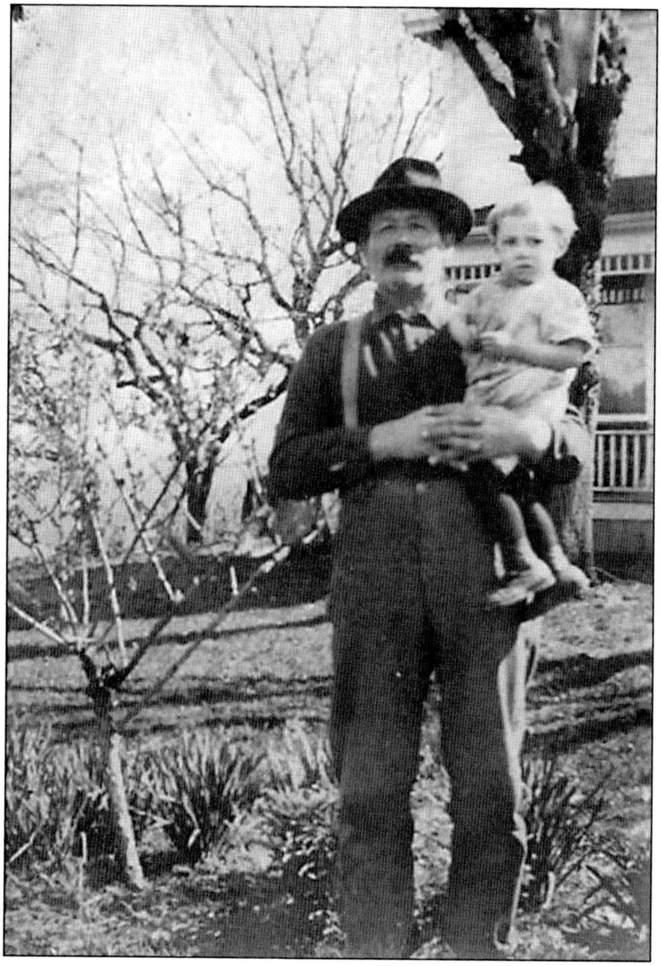

George Washington Miller is pictured around 1910 holding one of his grandchildren. Born in Catawba, North Carolina, Miller was married to the former Mary Alice Smith. They had 10 children. Daughter Dora Lee married Alois Gassner Junior. Miller owned 85 acres on Cooper Mountain. The Miller farm was located south of today's Farmington Road, in the vicinity of today's Miller Hill Road. George was the son of Wesley and Minerva (Deal) Miller. He was a member of the Modern Woodmen of America fraternal organization, belonging to Reedville Camp No. 8193. The image below looks north from Miller Hill in 1947 (Both, courtesy of Nita Rinehart.)

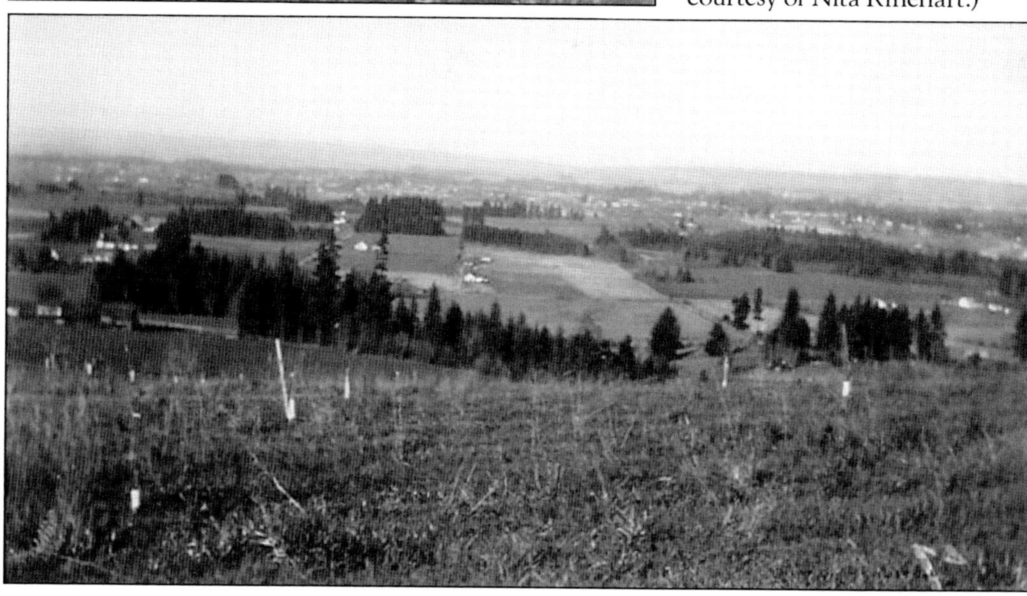

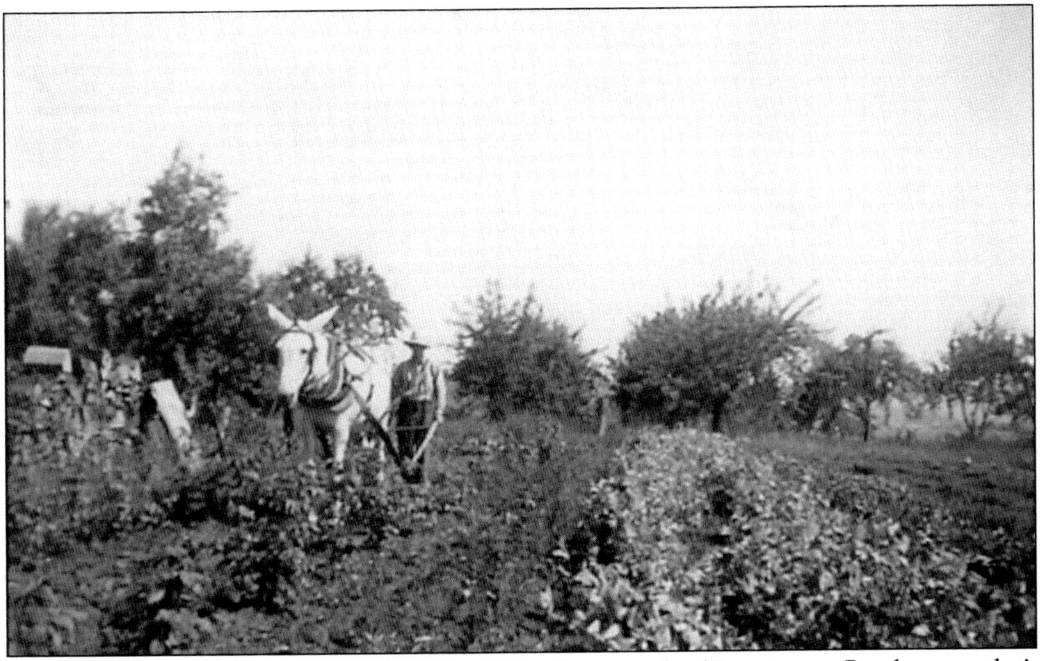

Thomas A. Miller, plows with a mule on the Miller farm, south of Farmington Road, near today's Miller Hill Road. Born May 7, 1894, he was the 7th of 10 children born to George Washington Miller and Mary Alice Smith. The Miller children attended the Hazeldale School (Courtesy of Nita Rinehart.)

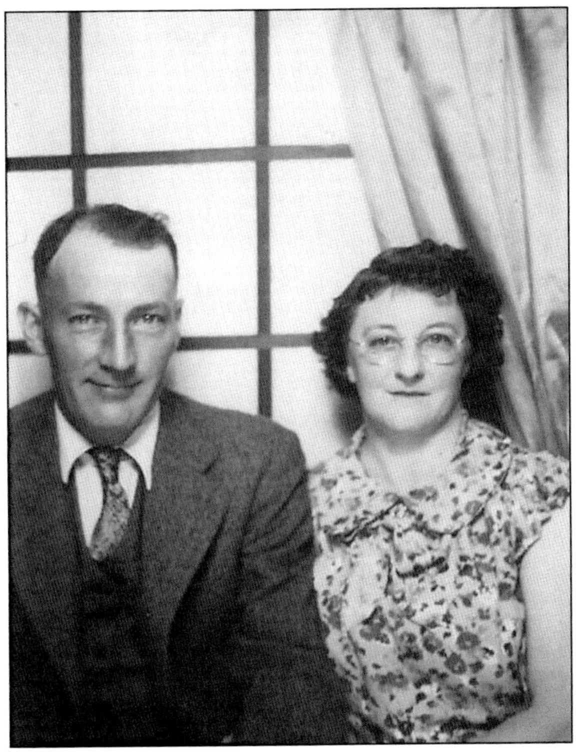

Thomas Miller is pictured with his wife, the former Hazel Danforth. Their children were named Virginia, Margaret, Ruth, and Jean. They lived on acreage in the vicinity of today's Miller Hill Road, south of Farmington Road. George Washington and Mary Alice Miller originally acquired the property in 1901. (Courtesy of Nita Rinehart.)

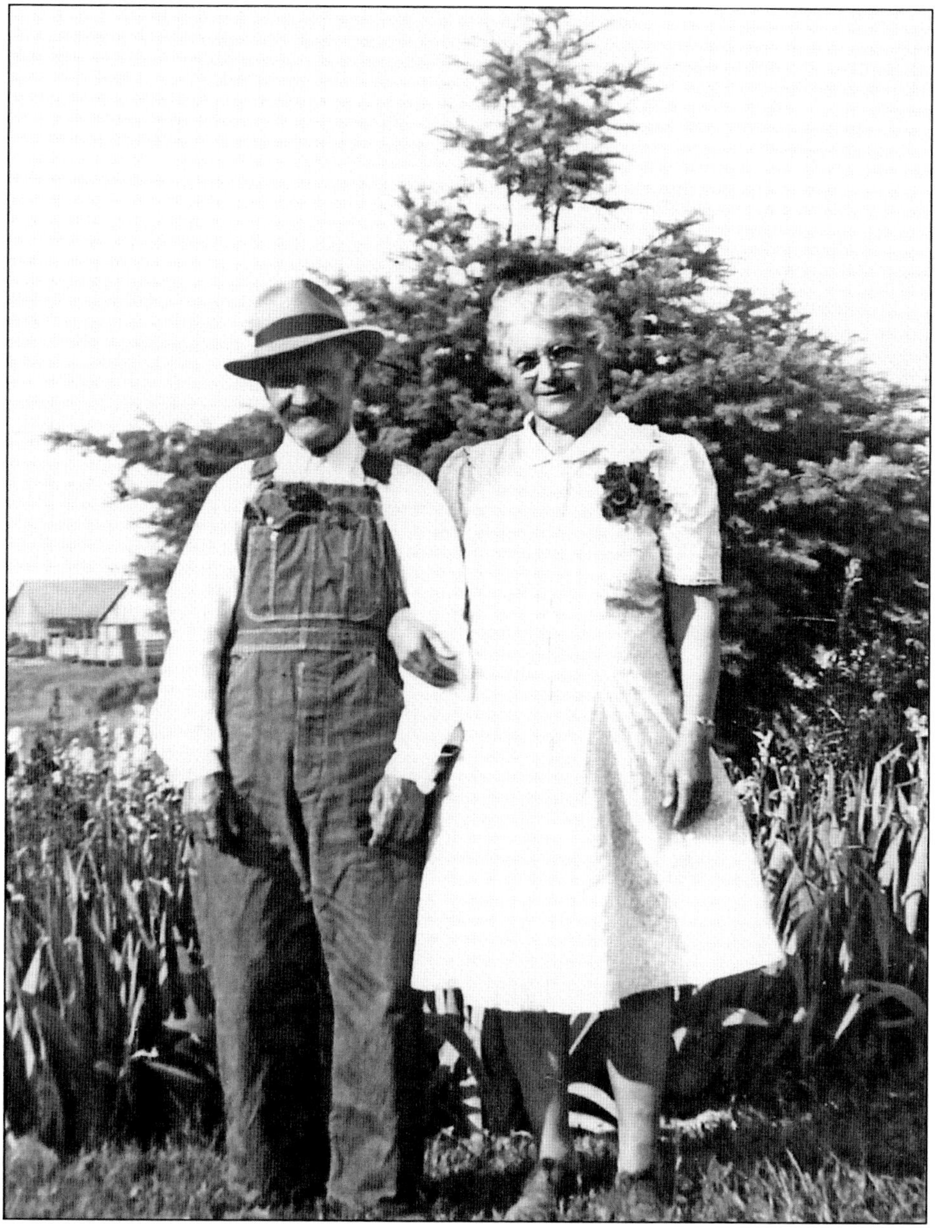

HAZELDALE RESIDENTS BRUNO (LEFT) AND ANNUNCIATA SANTORO (RIGHT). The couple is pictured at a party on June 22, 1944 to celebrate their 40th wedding anniversary, which had occurred on June 12. Both emigrated from Italy to the United States, arriving at Ellis Island. Bruno traveled on the ship *Bolivia* in 1896 and Annunciata on the *Prinzess Irene* in 1904. They came to Oregon and, after briefly residing in Portland, moved to Cooper Mountain in 1909. The next year, after traveling by foot to the historic Hazeldale store, Santoro learned of nearby farm for sale. In March 1910, he made a down payment of $100 on the 20-acre farm, and he paid the balance of the purchase price of $1,800 in August of that year to John and Anna McNew. In 2010, the Santoro family was honored by the State of Oregon and received recognition as a Century Farm because of their connection to the land and Oregon's rich agricultural heritage. (Santoro family.)

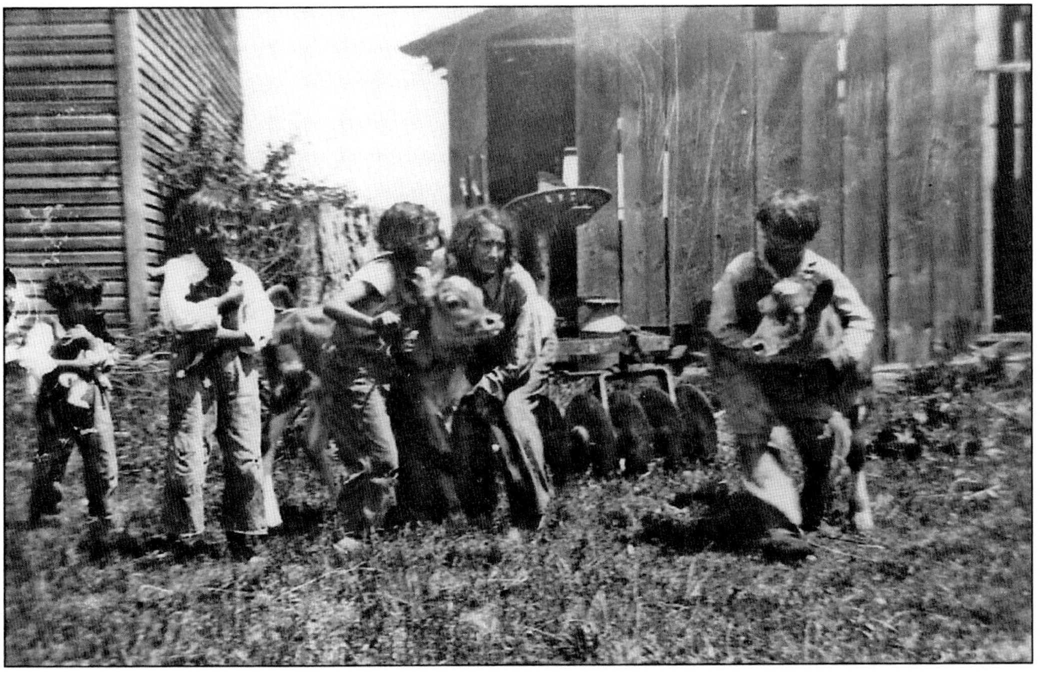

The Santoro Children. From left to right above, five of the 12 Santoro children, Rosie, Kate, Sue, Lee, and John, are pictured in front of the straw shed, one of the original farm buildings dating to before 1910. Other children not pictured include Joe, Rufie, Millie, and Mary. When the Santoros bought the land, it was heavily wooded. Only about one and a half acres of land was cleared where a small house, chicken coop, and the straw shed had been built. Both a 32-by-60-foot barn, added in 1916 by Mr. Bassett, and a residence built by his son Wayne Bassett are still in use today. The farm expanded again when two large chicken houses were added in 1921 and 1923 and a machine shed in 1941. A milk barn and milk house, constructed in 1945, are still in use today. Pictured at left, Bruno Santoro rakes hay with draft horses in the 1930s. (Both, Santoro family.)

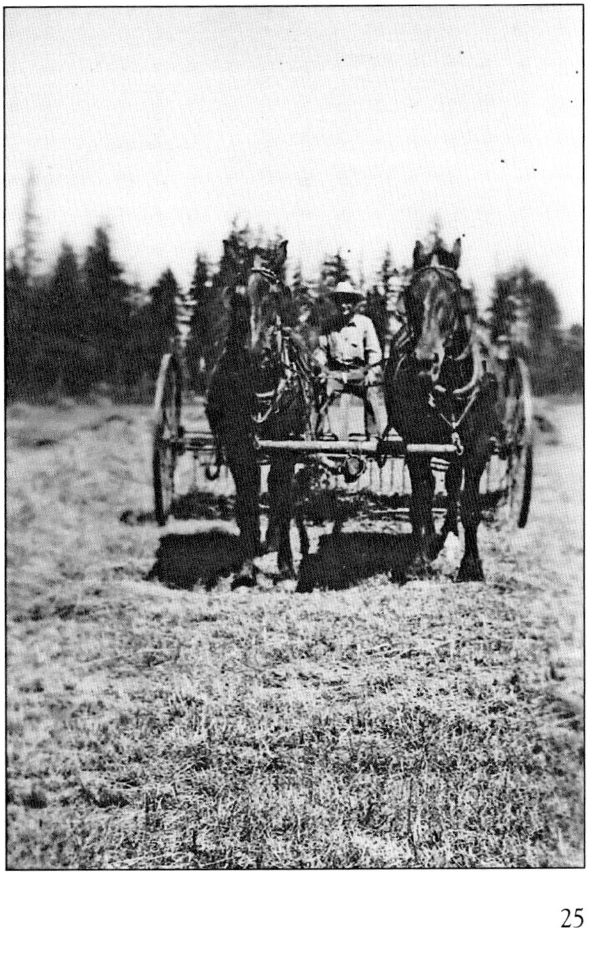

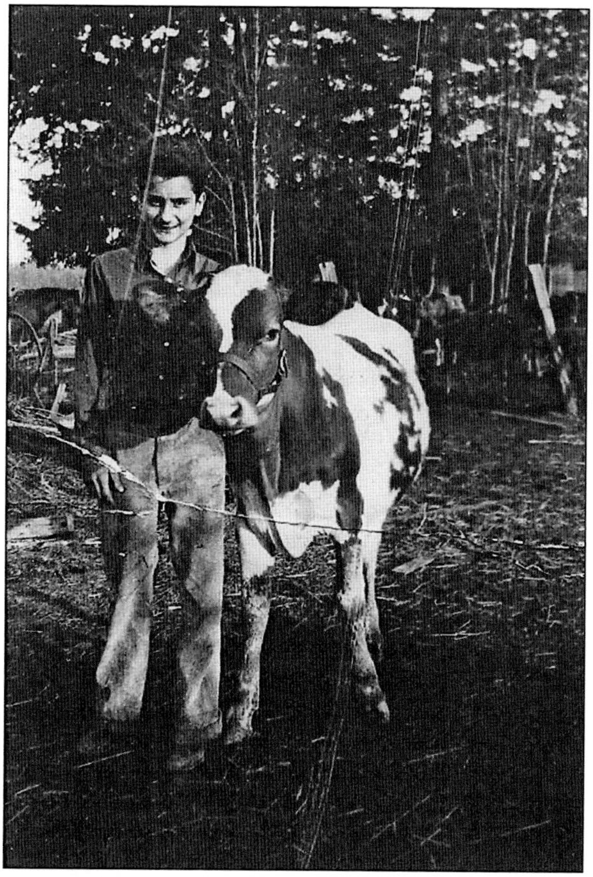

Fourteen-Year-Old Joe Santoro (Left) with His Six-Month-Old Calf Marietta, a Grand Champion Guernsey, 1936. In the early years, the Santoros had two workhorses, cows, hogs, and as many as 400 white Leghorn chickens on the farm. Eggs were sold on trips to Portland every Monday and Thursday. The family made Italian cheese, which was formed in baskets that were hand-woven by Bruno. The Santoros also raised raspberries, loganberries, strawberries, and filberts for sale. Below is an aerial view of the residence, barn, silos, and other farm buildings in the early 1950s. (Both, Santoro family.)

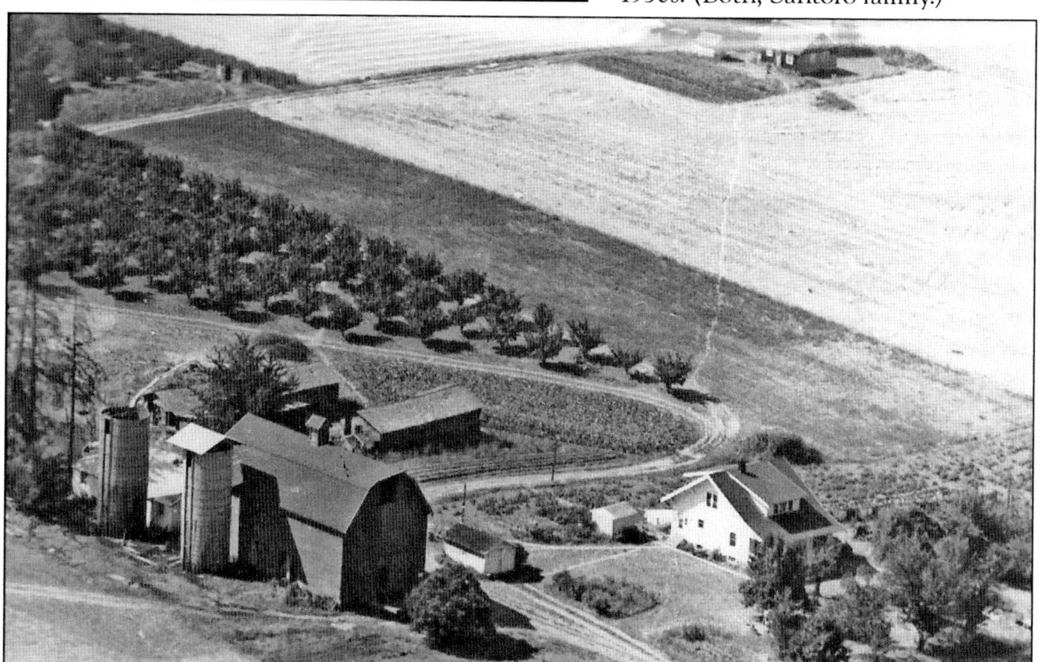

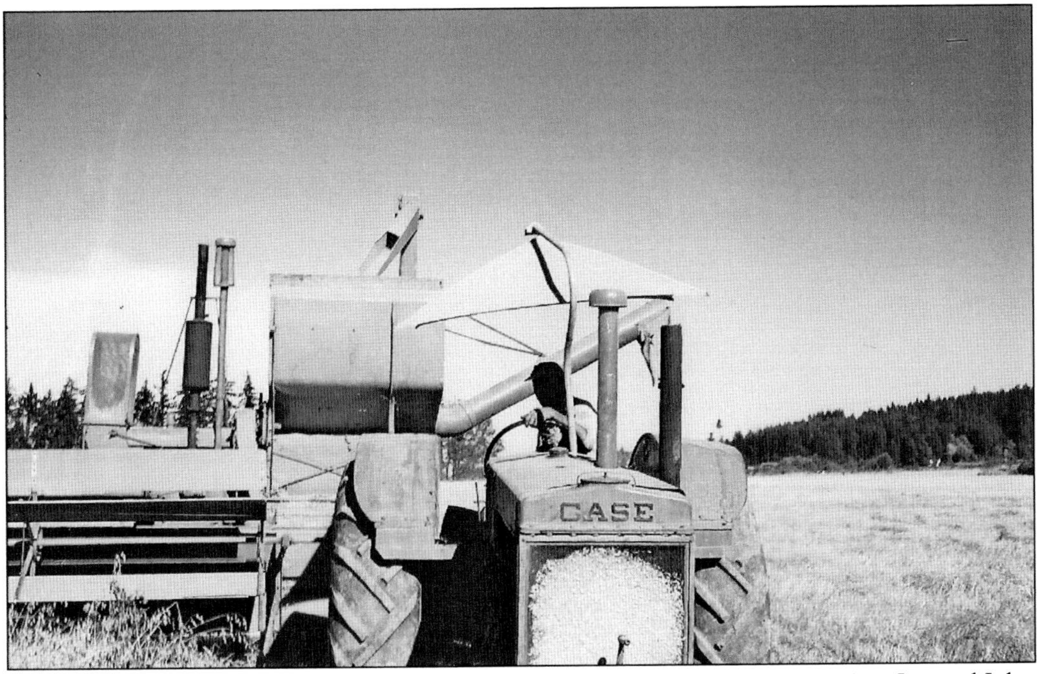

John Santoro (Above) behind the Wheel of a Case Combine, Early 1950s. Joe and John Santoro harvested hay for other farmers. It was a multi-step process involving cutting the seed heads when they were not quite ripe and the leaf was at its maximum. (Santoro family.)

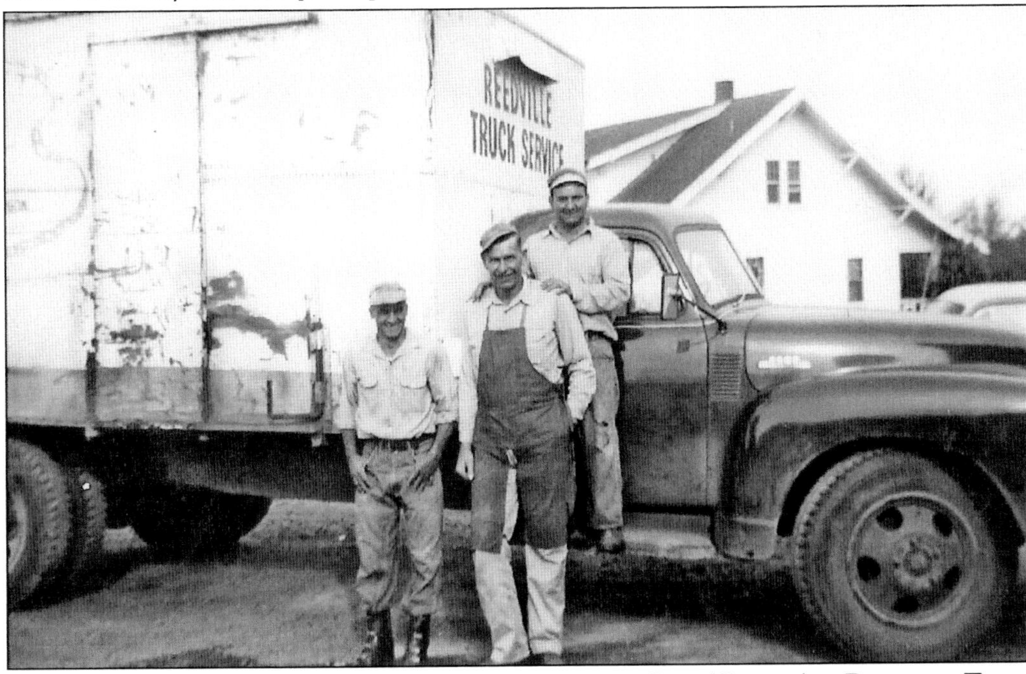

John (Left) and Joe Santoro (Right) Standing behind Slim (Center), a Reedville Truck Service Driver, 1950. The farm's first milk tank, installed in 1955, held 500 gallons. It was replaced by 750-gallon and 1,000-gallon tanks. The Santoros supplied Meadowland Dairy and Safeway stores. (Santoro family.)

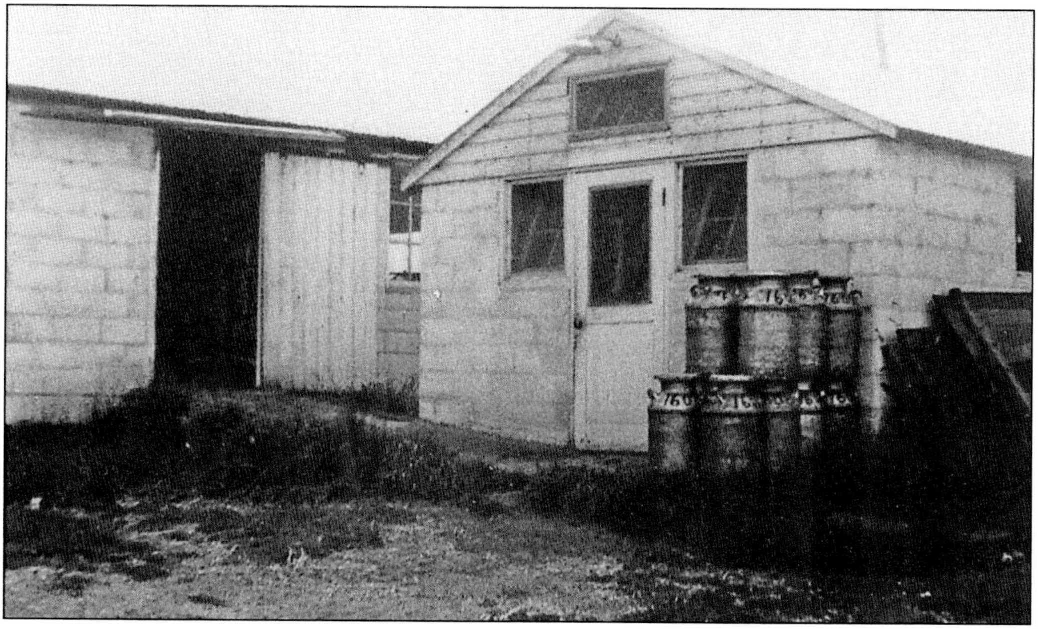

A Milking Shed (Above), Built in 1945, Still in Use Today on the Santoro Farm outside Reedville. In the five years after the shed was built, the farm's dairy herd increased from 20 to 85 head. A loafing shed (below) was added during 1951–1952. In 1960, a milking parlor with a 500-gallon tank was built. By the late 1960s, the tank size had been increased twice. Dairy products were sold to Meadowland from 1945 to 1955 and to Safeway stores from 1955 to 1977. In the 1970s, Washington County recognized three individual cows with the High Butterfat Award and the Santoro farm for High Herd Average for 670 pounds of butterfat. (Both, Santoro family.)

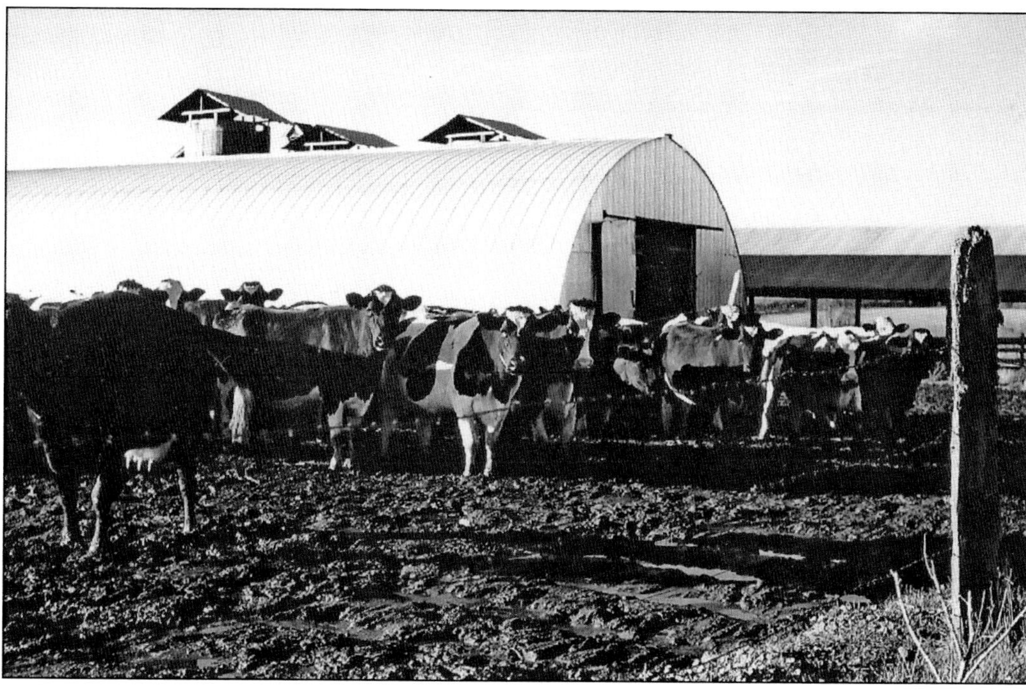

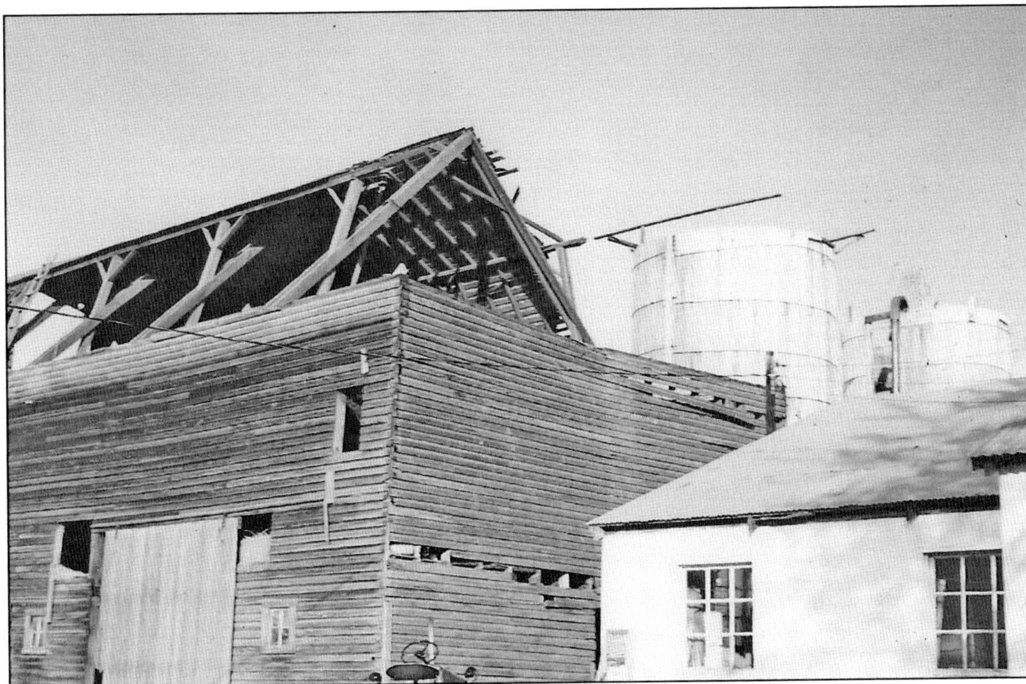

The Santoro Farm. The farm sustained extensive damage during the Columbus Day Storm in 1962. The barn roof and silos were damaged (above), and all the milk in the 1,000-gallon refrigerated holding tank in the milking parlor (right) was lost. The farm was without electricity for five days. (Santoro family.)

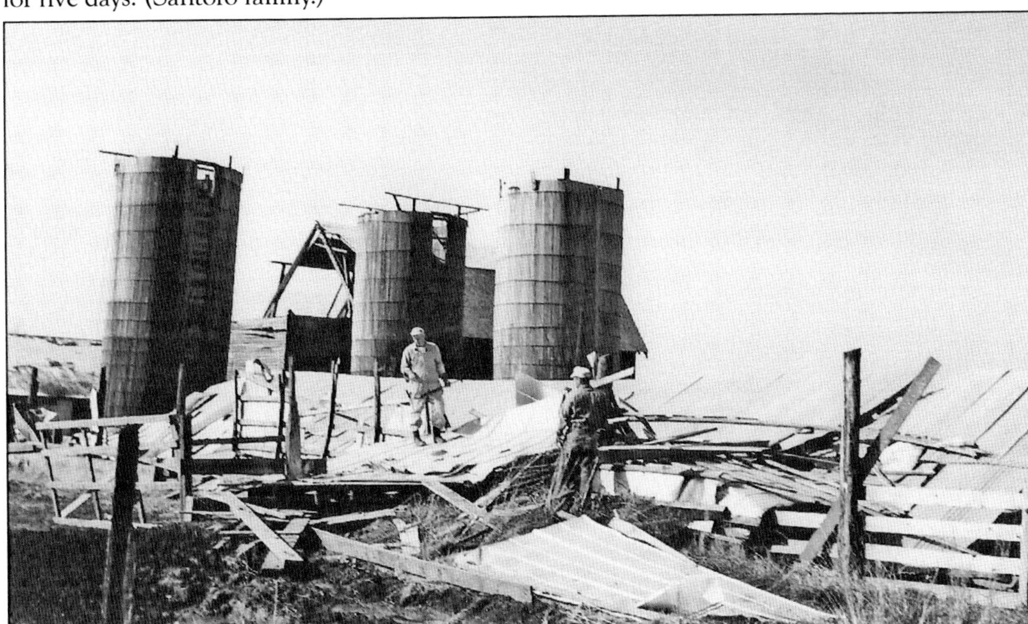

Storm Damage. A loafing shed and silos built during 1951–1952 were also damaged during the Columbus Day Storm. The silos were removed and replaced by a bunker in 1966. The original loafing shed, built in 1951, is pictured after the 1962 storm. It was later rebuilt and is still in use today. (Santoro family.)

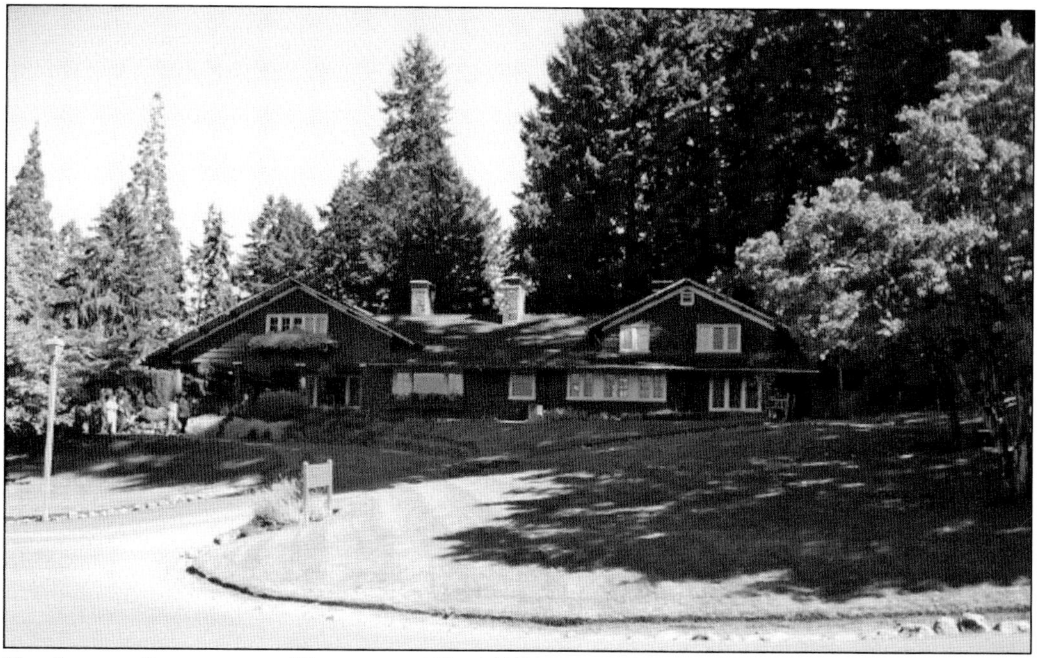

THE JENKINS ESTATE, NEAR HAZELDALE. The 14,500-square-foot residence (above), built beginning in 1913, was the home of Ralph and Belle Jenkins, who met at a riding stable on Canyon Road. They purchased 68 acres near today's Southwest Farmington and Grabhorn Roads and enhanced the property with gardens and equestrian facilities. The main house includes seven bedrooms, a full-length veranda porch, beamed ceilings, solid maple hardwood floors, ornate light fixtures and huge stone fireplaces. The grounds include a stable, carriage house, teahouse, reflecting pool and English-style gardens. Belle was the youngest daughter of Capt. John C. Ainsworth, who co-owned the Oregon Steam Navigation Company with Simeon Reed and William S. Ladd. She is pictured (below) on her horse Strawberry in 1918. (Above, photograph by the author; below, Beaverton Historical Society.)

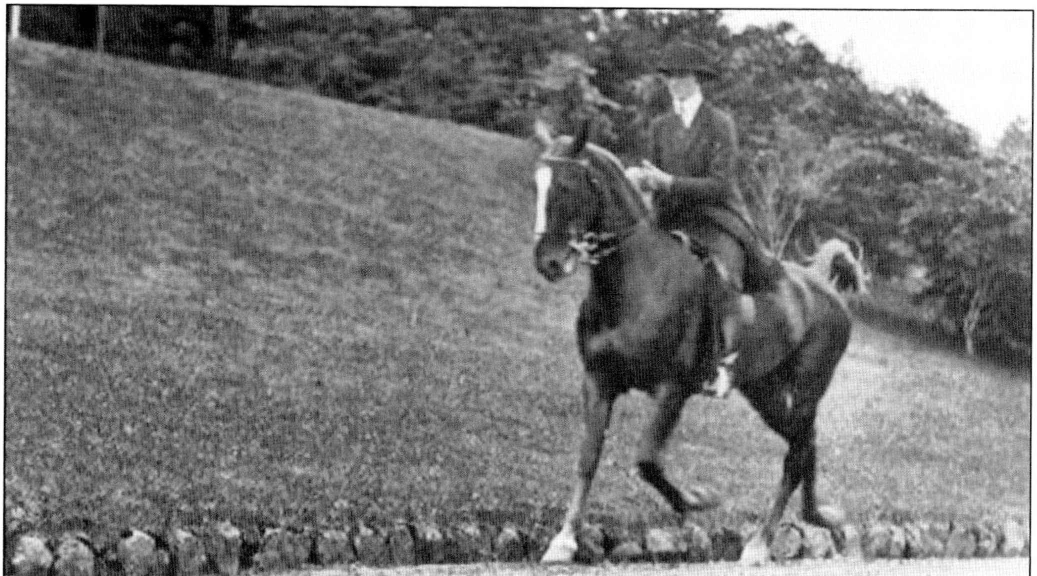

Three

Perkins Corner

In 1857, cattlemen and British immigrants Richard S. Perkins and Arthur H. Johnson, proprietors of a Portland waterfront butcher shop, purchased a 100-acre tract of land from James. H. McMillen. It was the first acquisition in what would become a 1,400-acre cattle ranch in Aloha-Reedvillle. The southeast corner of the property, which intersected the road to the Harris Ferry, was known as Perkins Corner.

Born in Bristol, England, in 1823 to a wholesale cattle merchant, Perkins immigrated to the United States in 1851. He joined Robert Perry's wagon train in Ohio and worked his way across the plains by driving four yoke of oxen. Perkins was of the original members of the Washington County Agricultural Society. He and his wife, Elizabeth, originally from Kentucky, had nine children. They built a five-bedroom residence in 1871 on what later became Southwest Rosa Road in Aloha. Lumber and huge cedar blocks for the foundation were transported by steamship on the Tualatin River. The house was demolished in 1985.

Jacob and Martina Huber emigrated from Switzerland in the 1880s. They claimed 160 acres southeast of Perkins Corner, where the family operated a dairy until the early 1930s.

At the turn of the 20th century, brothers Frank and Ernest Livermore operated a series of three sawmills and logged the northeastern slope of what is now Cooper Mountain. The first was Springwater Mill, located on their 280-acre property, near today's Southwest Rigert Road and 170th Avenue. The second mill, built in 1900, was closer to Southwest 185th Avenue. Their third and last mill, at Perkins Corner, produced building materials that they transported to Huber station for export on the rail or sold at the nearby F.W. Livermore Building Materials store.

The first Cooper Mountain school was built near today's Southwest 185th Avenue in the 1890s and relocated in 1912 at the site of the present-day school on Southwest 170th Avenue.

Throughout the second half of the 1900s, as Beaverton expanded west of Hyland Avenue, today's Southwest Murray Boulevard, an increasing number of what were once Perkins Corner farms transformed into suburban, residential subdivisions.

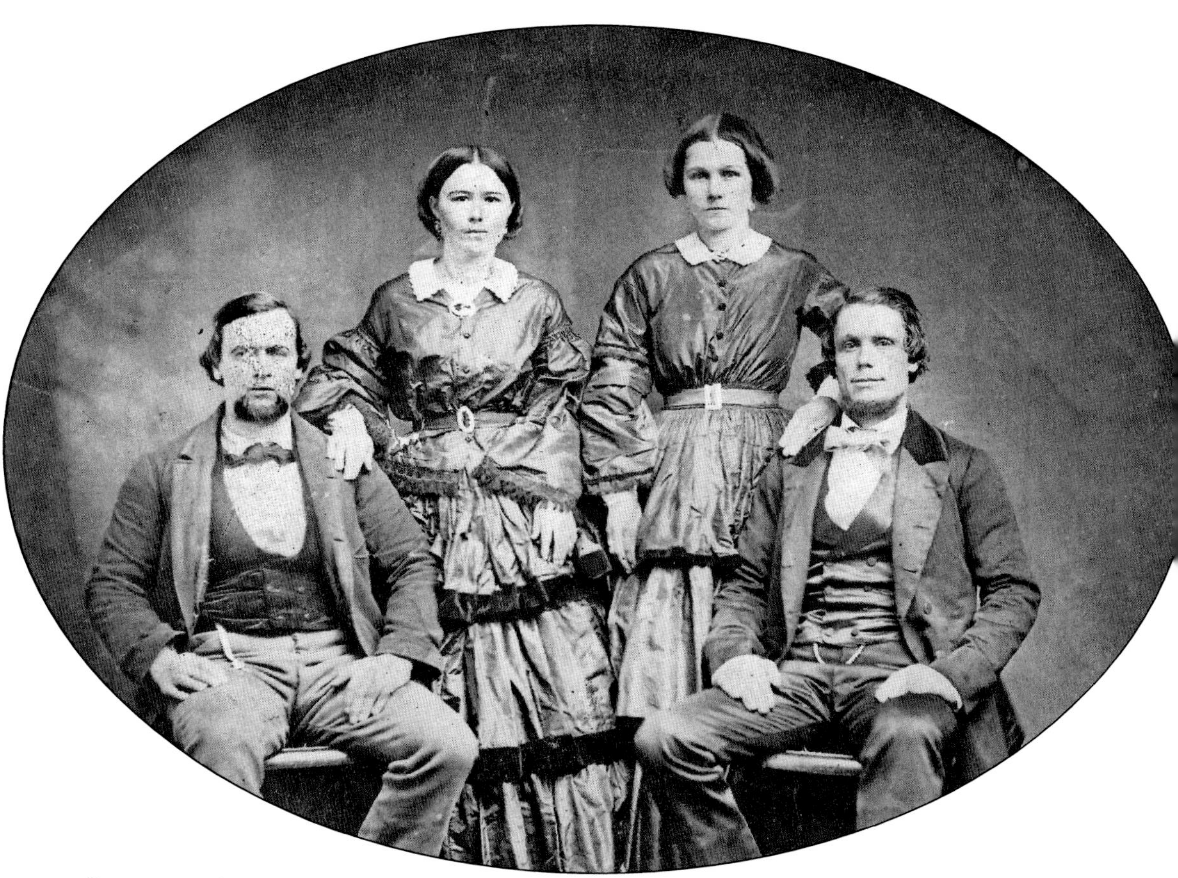

CATTLEMEN ARTHUR H. JOHNSON AND RICHARD S. PERKINS AND THEIR WIVES IN 1870. Johnson (left) and Perkins (right), Portland merchants, purchased a 100-acre parcel of farmland from James McMillen in 1856, later owning about 1,000 acres in the Aloha-Reedville area. Perkins was born in Bristol, England, in 1823. He immigrated to the United States in 1851 and joined Robert Perry's wagon train in Ohio. He worked his way across the plains by driving four yoke of oxen. Perkins met Johnson, also from England, after arriving in Portland. Elizabeth Perkins was from Kentucky. The Perkinses had nine children and built a five-bedroom residence on what later became Southwest Rosa Road in Aloha. Lumber and huge cedar blocks for the foundation were transported by steamship on the Tualatin River to Harris Bridge, today's Farmington. Built in 1871, the house was demolished in 1985. (Oregon Historical Society, No. bb010033.)

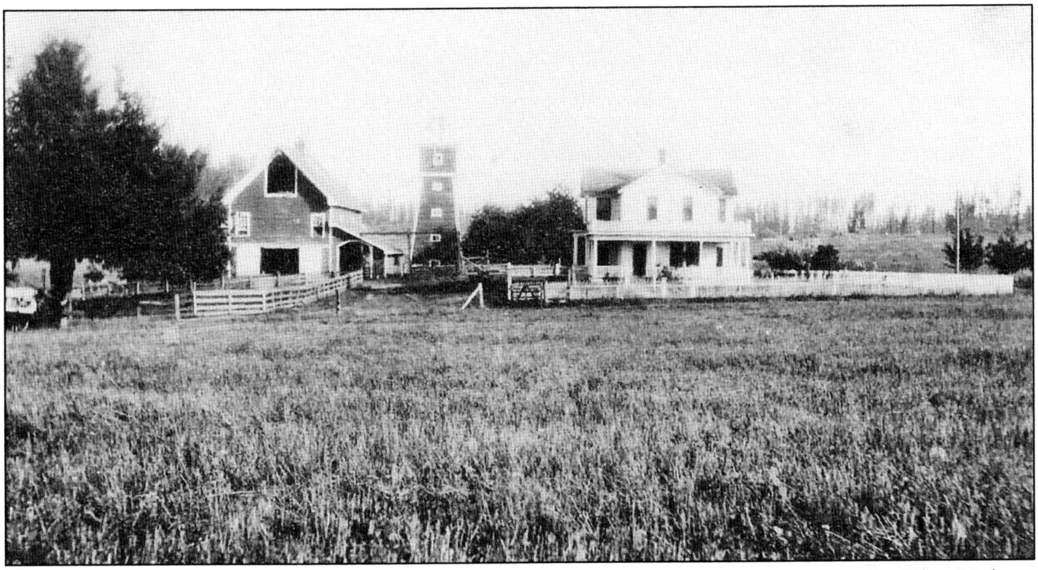

The Farm of Jacob and Martina Huber, Southeast of Perkins Corner. The Hubers stored hay in the barn at left. The windmill (center) operated a pump that brought underground water to the well. The Hubers emigrated from Aargau, Switzerland, in the 1880s. (Huber and Meier families.)

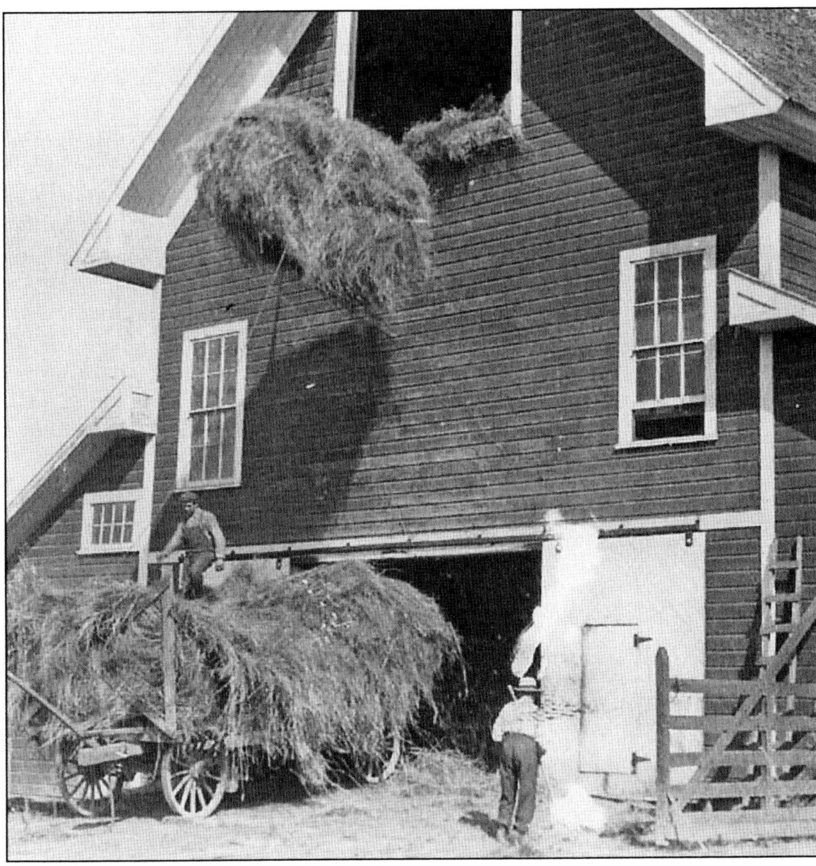

Lifting Loose Hay into the Barn's Second-Story Hayloft on the Huber Family Farm. After harvesting and drying, loose hay was lifted with a pulley and then dropped through holes or slots in the hayloft floor to feed livestock the family maintained for their dairy farm. (Huber and Meier families.)

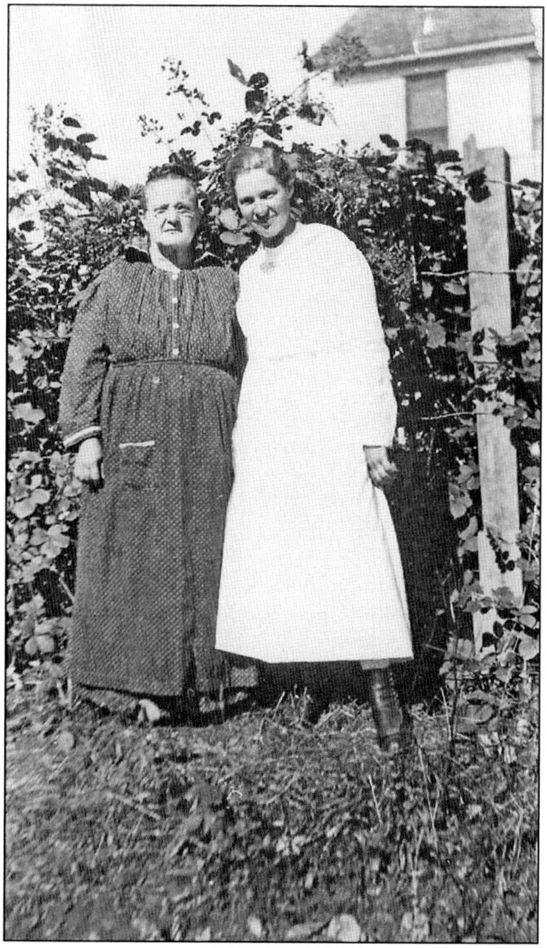

MARTINA AND EMMA HUBER, ABOUT 1920. Born in 1862, Martina immigrated to the United States with her husband, Jacob, in the 1880s. They settled in Washington County, where three children were born—Louise in 1890, John in 1895, and Emma (right) in 1897. Emma walked to school at St. Mary's School. Her sister Louise Huber (below) was a teacher at Cooper Mountain School in 1911 and 1912. Brother John Huber served as the school clerk in 1928. In the early 1900s, Jacob Huber cleared a trail from Perkins Corner north to what was then the Southern Pacific Railroad. (Both, Huber and Meier families.)

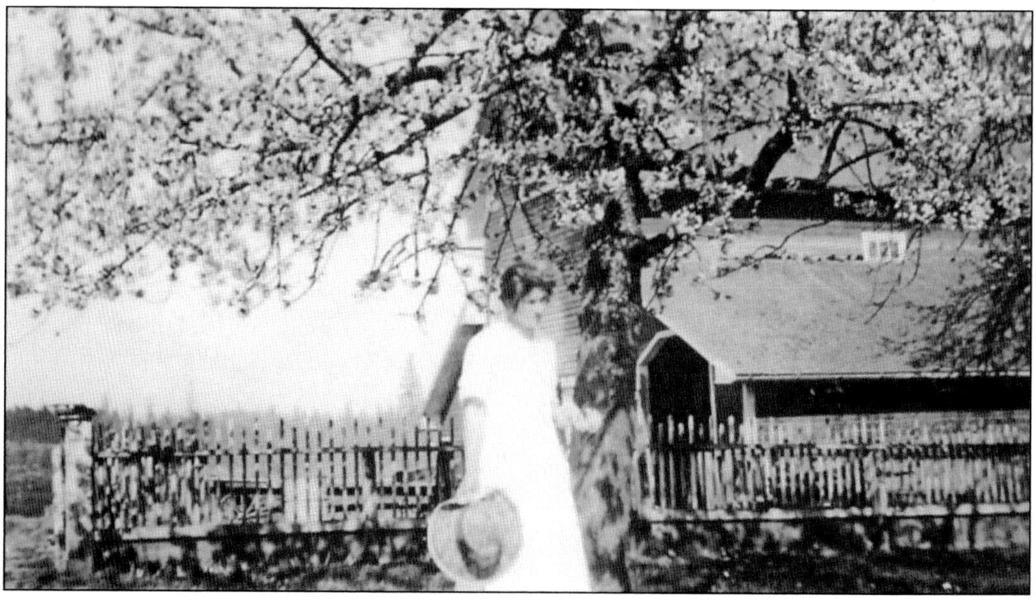

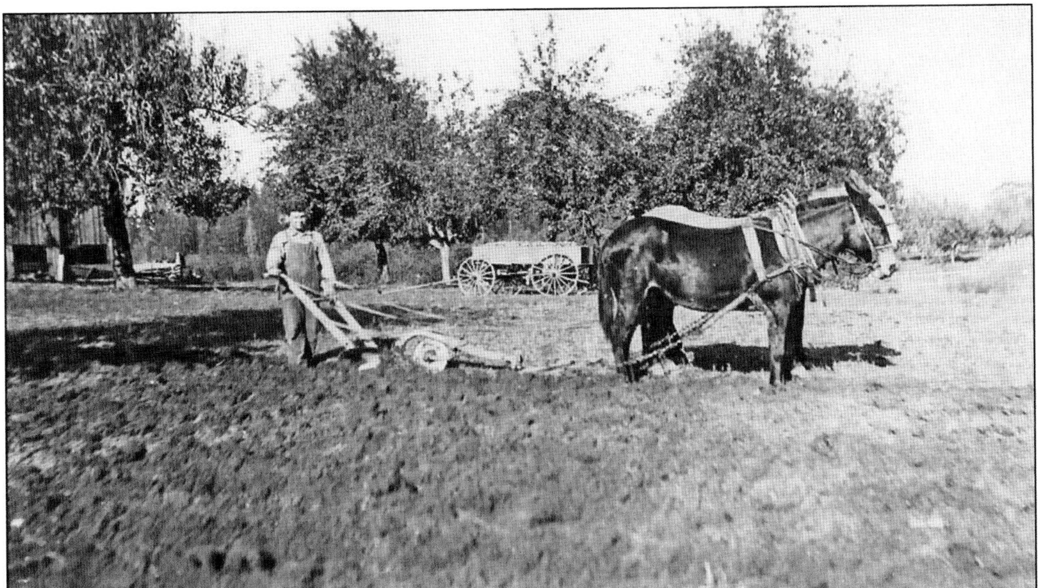

John Huber Using a Horse-Drawn Plow. After Jacob Huber's death in 1916, children John (age 21, pictured above) and Emma Huber (18) operated the family farm, which included a dairy. During World War I and the 1920s, John sold milk in Portland, transported in 10-gallon tins by horse-drawn wagon. (Huber and Meier families.)

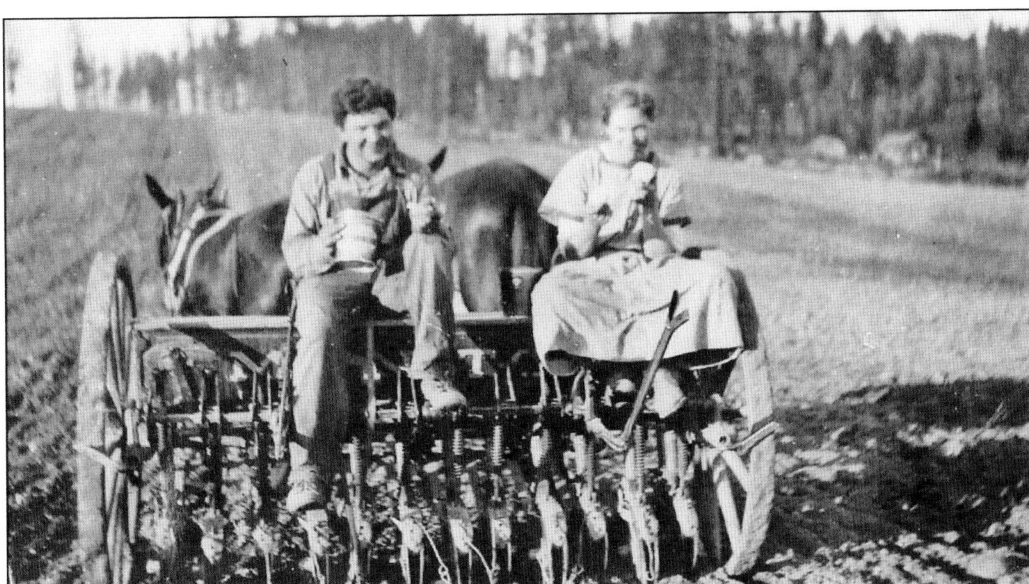

John Huber (Left) and Emma Huber (Right) Taking a Break on Their Acreage near Perkins Corner. In 1900, Washington County farmland peaked at 251,568 acres. In 1910, there were 2,871 farms and 107,919 acres of improved land. (Huber and Meier families.)

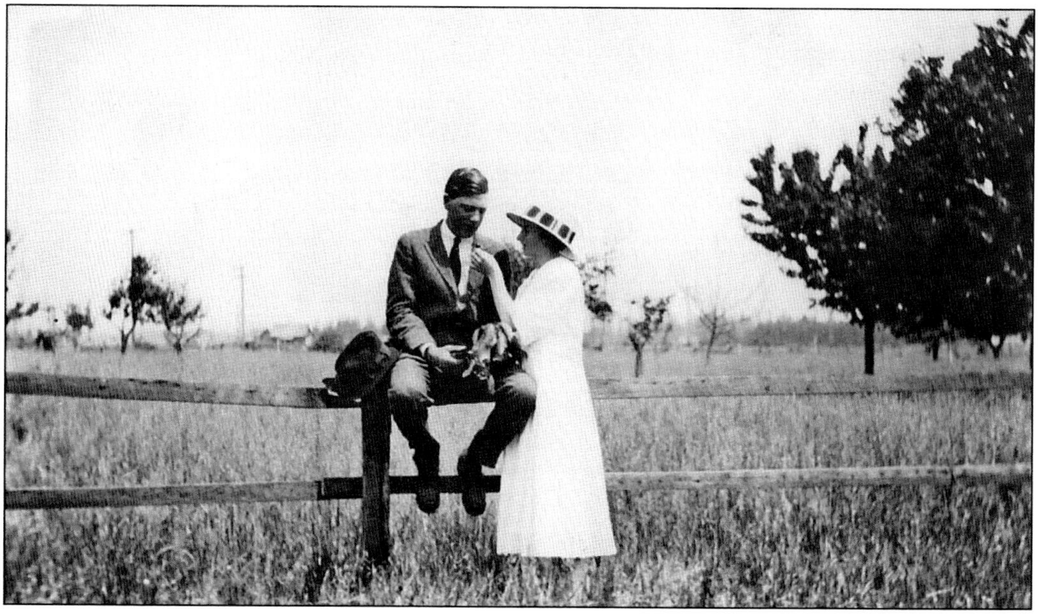

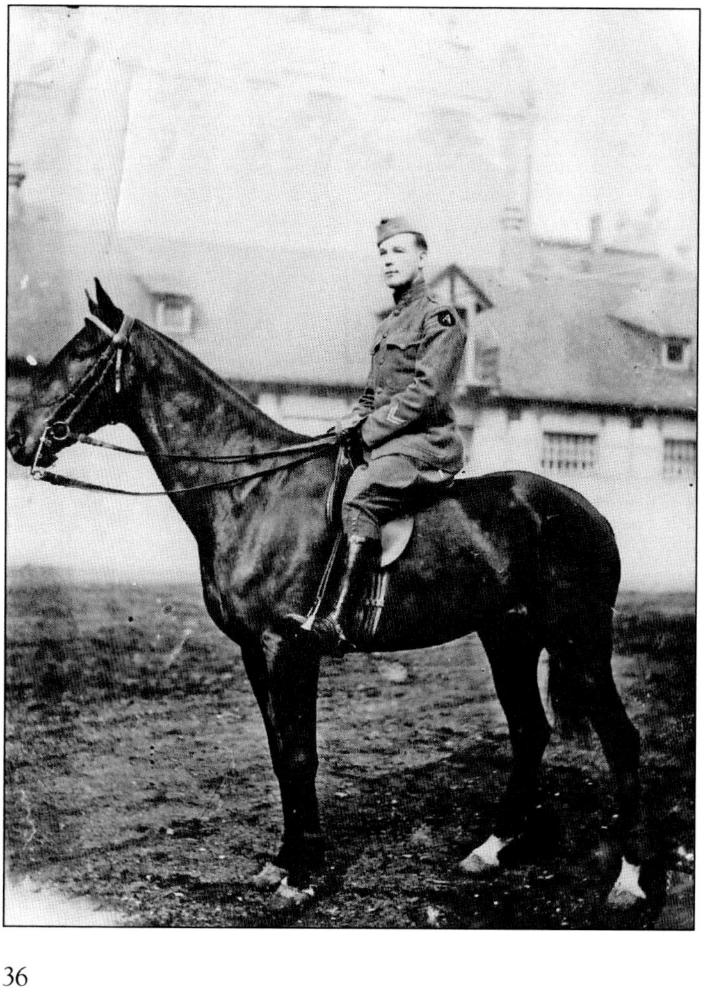

EMMA HUBER AND CARL MEIER. They married and moved to River Road near Hillsboro. The Meier children, born in the 1930s, were named Leona, Vernon, and Frances. The Huber and Meier families immigrated to the United States from the same region in Switzerland. (Huber and Meier families.)

CARL MEIER IN UNIFORM DURING THE WORLD WAR I ERA. After passage of the Selective Service Act in 1916, 2.8 million men were drafted. In 1918, the United States was sending 10,000 soldiers to France every day. (Huber and Meier families.)

The First of Three Sawmills Operated by Francis "Frank" W. and Ernest Livermore on Their 280-acre Property, Springwater, on Cooper Mountain. The mill operated between 1896 and 1897, when it was destroyed by fire. Mills used band saws 4 inches wide, 19 inches long, and 22 gauge in diameter. (Beaverton Historical Society.)

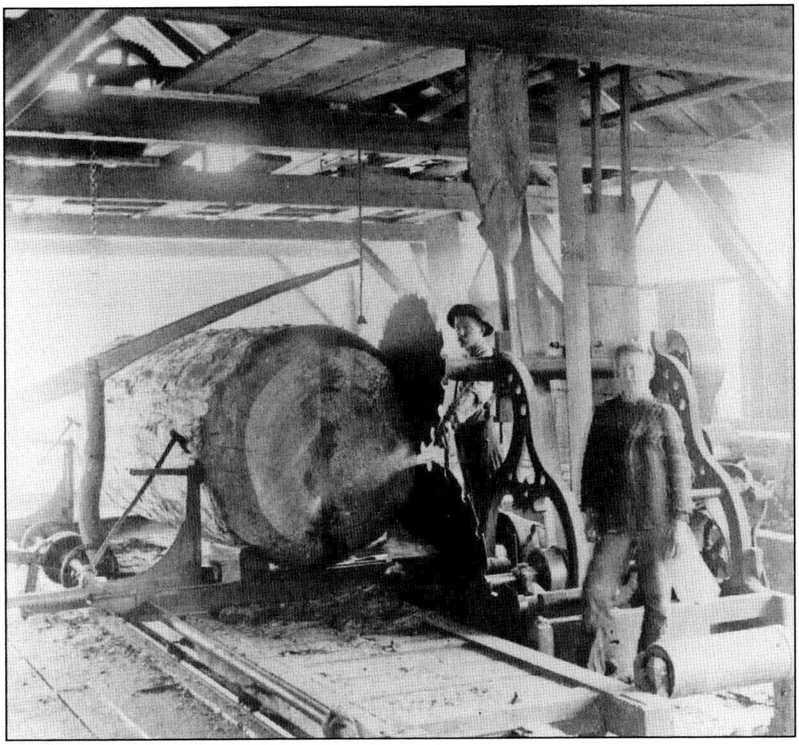

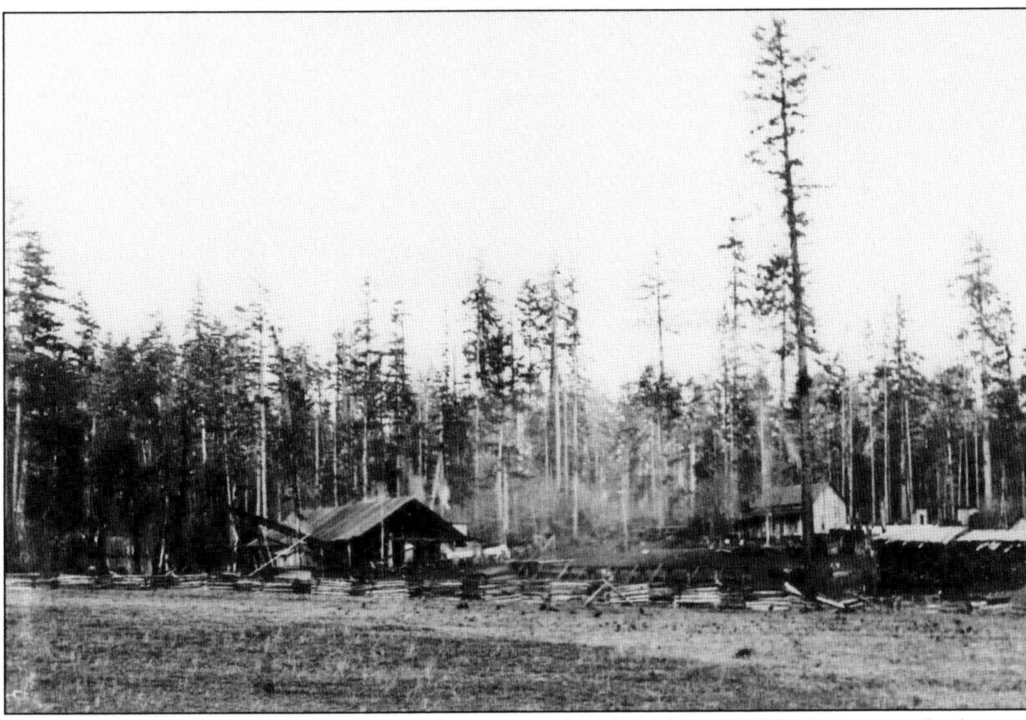

The Second Livermore Mill. Built in 1900 near today's Southwest 185th Avenue, it also burned to the ground. In the forest, fallers cut trees with axes or crosscut saws. Buckers stripped bark from the logs and sawed them into shorter lengths. (Beaverton Historical Society.)

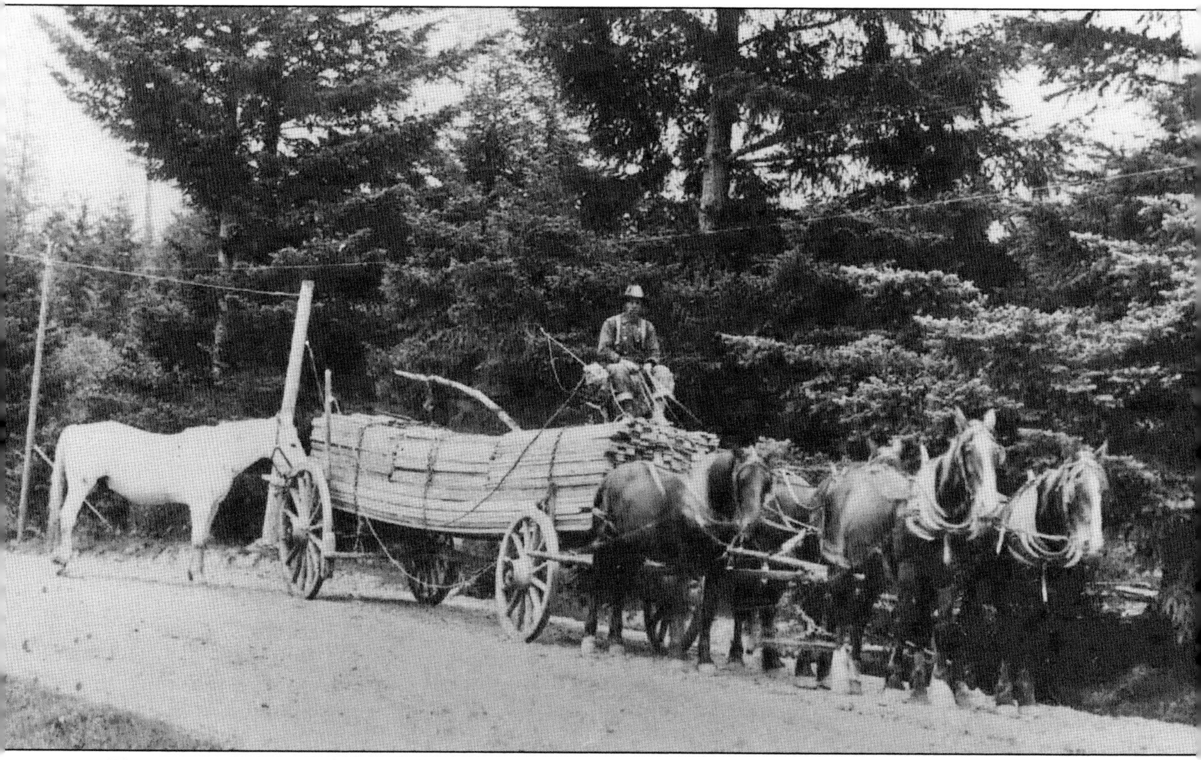

Transporting Lumber. Milled lumber was transported by horse and wagon from the third Livermore sawmill at Perkins Corner to the Huber station on the Southern Pacific Railroad. It was exported by train or sold at the F.W. Livermore building materials store. At the turn of the 20th century, Francis W. "Frank" and Ernest Livermore logged the northeast slope of Cooper Mountain and operated a series of three sawmills. The first, Sweetwater Mill, was located on their 180-acre farm near today's Southwest 170th and Hart Road. After it was destroyed by fire, a second mill operated closer to Southwest 185th. In 1890, there were 2,555 Oregonians working in the logging and log transportation industry and 1,962 working in sawmills. At the beginning of the 20th century, railroad expansion increased demand for wood products used for building tracks, bridges, stations, fences, and fuel to operate steam-powered locomotives. (Beaverton Historical Society.)

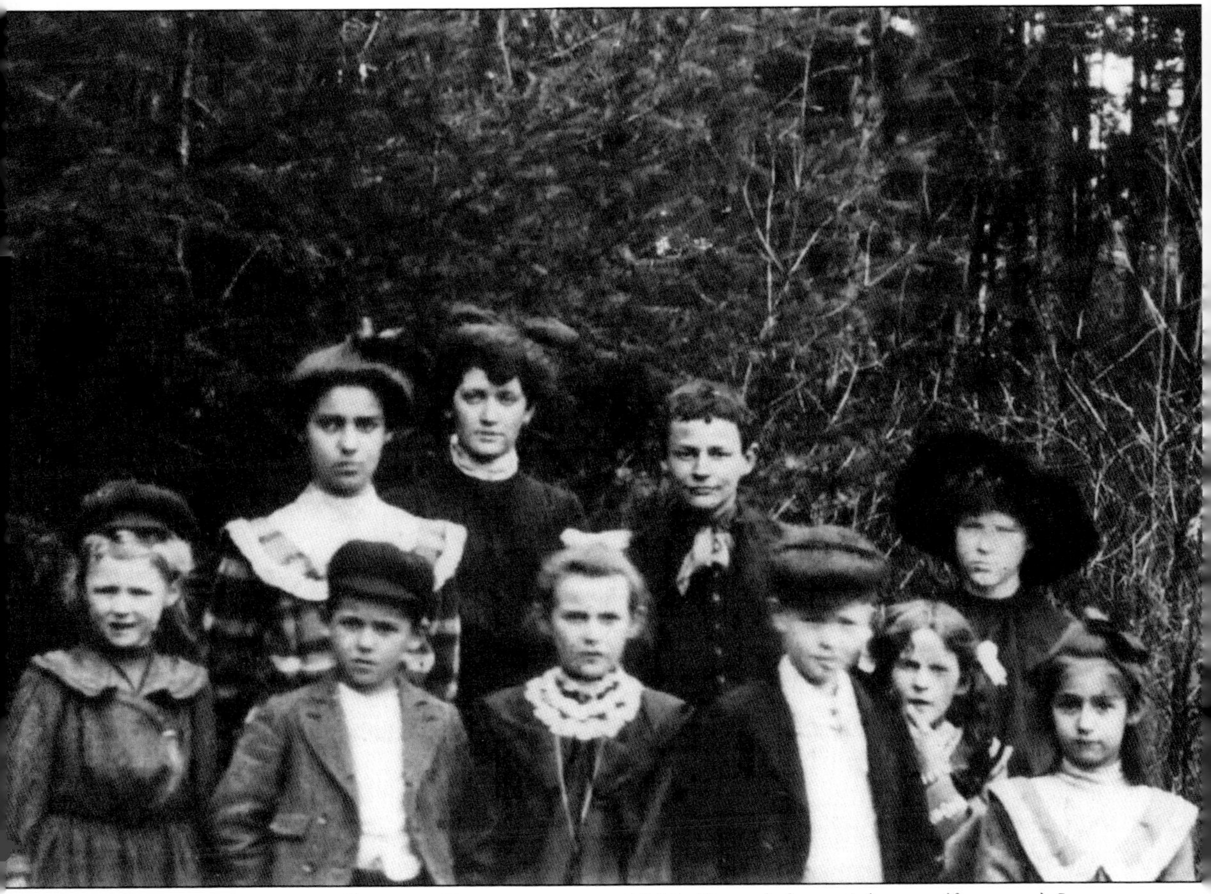

The Cooper Mountain School Class, around 1905. From left to right are (first row) Ivy Livermore, Clement "Clem" Kemmer, "Susie" Kemmer, Fred Reusser, Eva Kemmer, and Edna Reusser; (second row) teacher Ivy Peterson (second from left) and Bertha Reusser (far right). The original one-room school building, in operation until 1912, was located about two-thirds of a mile west of the current school site. In the early 1900s, the school was operated by nearby residents. Xavier Gassner served as school clerk from 1902 to 1909. John Huber was the clerk in 1928. Nick Kemmer, Alex Reusser, W.G. Grabborn, W.H. Hart, and Frank and Ernest Livermore were Cooper Mountain School Board members in the early 1900s. (Beaverton Historical Society.)

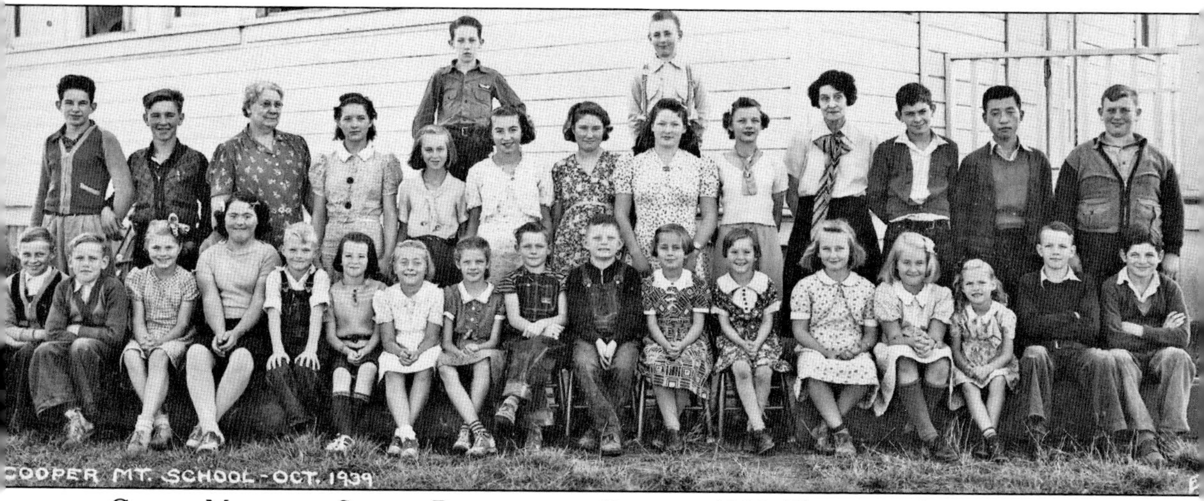

Cooper Mountain School Photograph, October 1939. The original Cooper Mountain School was west of the current site at Southwest 170th Avenue near Bany Road. In 1893, teachers included Maude Dant, Louise Huber, and Lena Grabhorn. In 1928, John Huber was the school clerk. In 1936, a second classroom was added to the Cooper Mountain School. Other improvements were made in 1949 and 1954. By 1957, there were three classroom teachers and a part-time music instructor. By the 1959–1960 school year, enrollment grew to 60 students. In 1967 and 1970, the building was remodeled and new construction completed on a modern, 18-classroom elementary school. By 1972, enrollment reached 403 students. Cooper Mountain District No. 94 was the 12th public school district to join Beaverton School District 48, in 1960. Earl E. Fisher, who went on to become mayor of Beaverton and a member of the Oregon State Legislature, was a teacher from 1918 to 1922. (Washington County Museum.)

Four

The Reed Farm

The Robinson land claim sold to Portland entrepreneur Simeon Gannett Reed and his wife, Amanda, in the 1860s. Reed, along with friend and business partner William S. Ladd, were investors in the Oregon Steam Navigation Company, Oregon Central Railroad, and other enterprises. They also co-owned the Ladd and Reed Farm Company, which managed the Reed farm and 16 other properties in Multhomah and Yamhill Counties.

In 1871, Reed traveled throughout North America and selected the finest pure-blooded cattle, sheep, hogs, and chickens for export to his farm. Sole proprietor of operations in the early 1870s, Reed employed professional farm managers and expert agriculturalists and encouraged experimentation with grasses, grains, irrigation systems, and steam-powered farm equipment. An enthusiast of the popular New England sport of harness-racing, he built a circular-shaped barn and covered, half-mile track north of the rail for his stable of trotting horses. Reed and his country showplace gained international notoriety for award-winning livestock. Sixteen miles from Portland by rail, the Reed farm was a popular destination for family, friends, and business associates.

In spite of Reed's financial investment, by 1875 the farm was not profitable. Cost-cutting measures were implemented. Over time, the quality of breeding herds deteriorated. By 1883, farm affairs were handled almost exclusively by Martin Winch, Reed's nephew and business agent, who planned to sell all the livestock except work animals, put every available acre into grain production, and develop what remained into real estate tracts. In 1889, the town of Reedville, located on Reed farm acreage north of the railroad, was platted for development.

Ladd died in 1891. His partnership with Reed was dissolved, and the Ladd and Reed Farm Company was incorporated. By 1891, the first dairy farm of any consequence in Washington County operated on the Reed farm.

The Reeds relocated to Pasadena, California, in 1892. Simeon died in 1895. Amanda inherited the entire Reed estate. She died in 1904. Her will, contested until 1909 by 11 heirs, designated multiple charities as beneficiaries and established the Reed Institute and, later, Reed College in Portland.

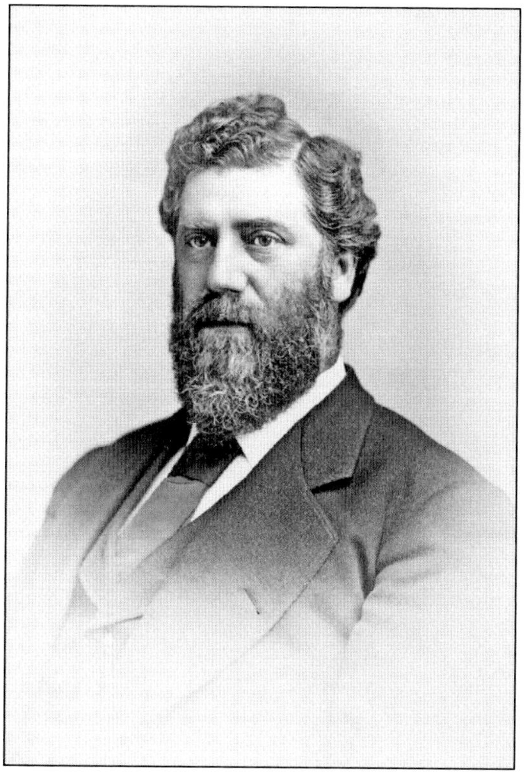

SIMEON GANNETT REED IN 1870. Originally from Massachusetts, Reed operated mercantiles in Sacramento and Rainier before working at the W.S. Ladd & Company in Portland. By 1871, Reed and his wife, Amanda, purchased the Robinsons' farm in Washington County. (Reed College Hauser Library Special Collections and Archives.)

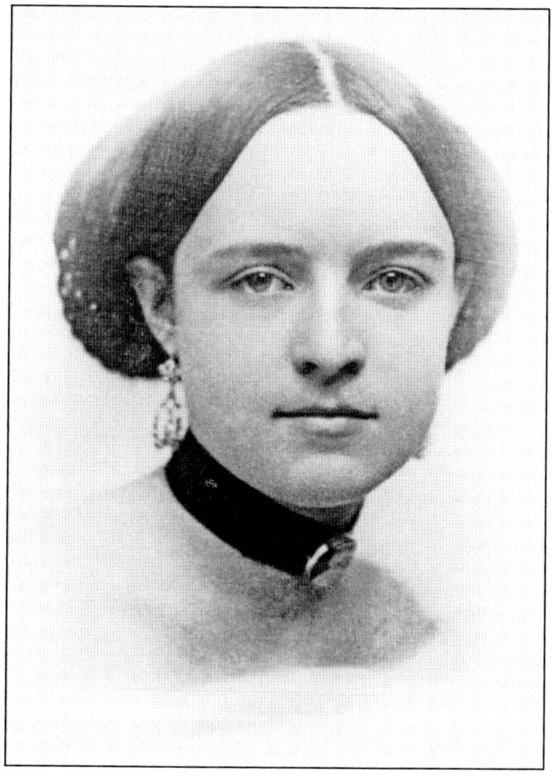

AMANDA WOOD, IN 1850, THE YEAR SHE MARRIED SIMEON REED. Born in Quincy, Massachusetts, in 1832, she left Boston in 1854 to move to Portland and join her husband, who was a prominent Portland businessman and entrepreneur. She made the journey with Caroline Ames Elliott, who was engaged to marry William S. Ladd. (Reed College Hauser Library Special Collections and Archives.)

William S. Ladd (Right). William Sargent Ladd sailed from New England for San Francisco, then Oregon Country in 1851. Twice mayor of Portland, he sold dairy and farm products from the Tualatin Valley at his mercantile. He co-owned the Oregon Steam Navigation Company and Ladd and Reed Farm Company with friend and entrepreneur Simeon Reed. (Oregon State Library.)

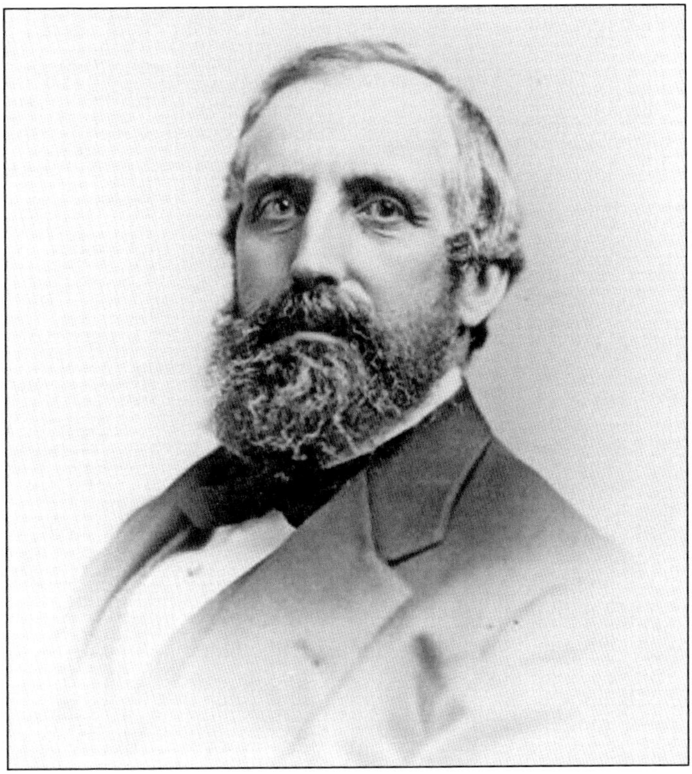

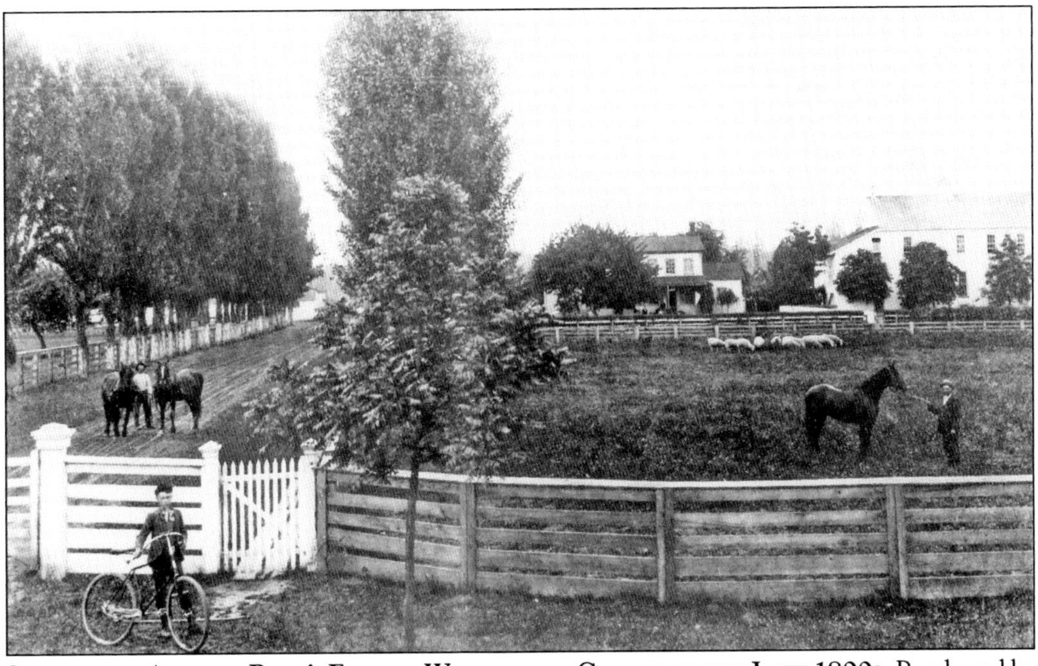

Simeon and Amanda Reed's Farm in Washington County in the Late 1800s. Purchased by Portland entrepreneur Simeon Reed and his wife, Amanda, from Nathan and Mary Robinson, this property was managed by the Ladd and Reed Farm Company as a livestock breeding operation. (Reed College Hauser Library Special Collections and Archives.)

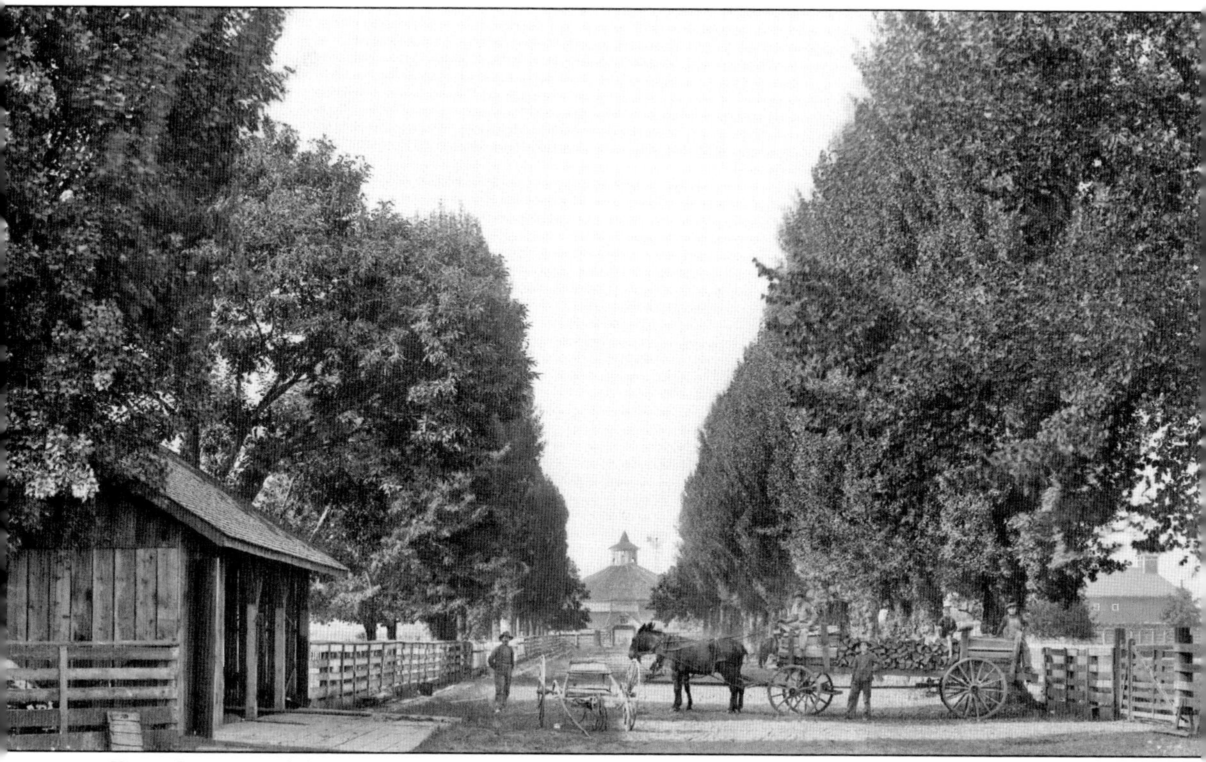

REED STABLES. Elaborate equestrian facilities on the Reed farm included the circular barn (center) that was built for Reed's stable of Standardbred horses. A covered exercise arena and half-mile harness-racing track was located north of the old Plains-Falls Road between today's Southwest 209th and 229th Avenues. In 1860, Reed became president of the Oregon Central Railroad, later the Oregon and California Railroad. In 1871, a short line railroad was built west of Portland. In 1871, Reed traveled throughout North America selecting and importing blooded Clydesdale draft horses, Shorthorn, Ayrshire, and Alderney cattle, Cotswold and Leicester sheep, and Golden Spangle Hamburg, Buff Cochin, Dark Brahma, and Gray Dorking chickens. (1205-B1 © Historic Photo Archive.)

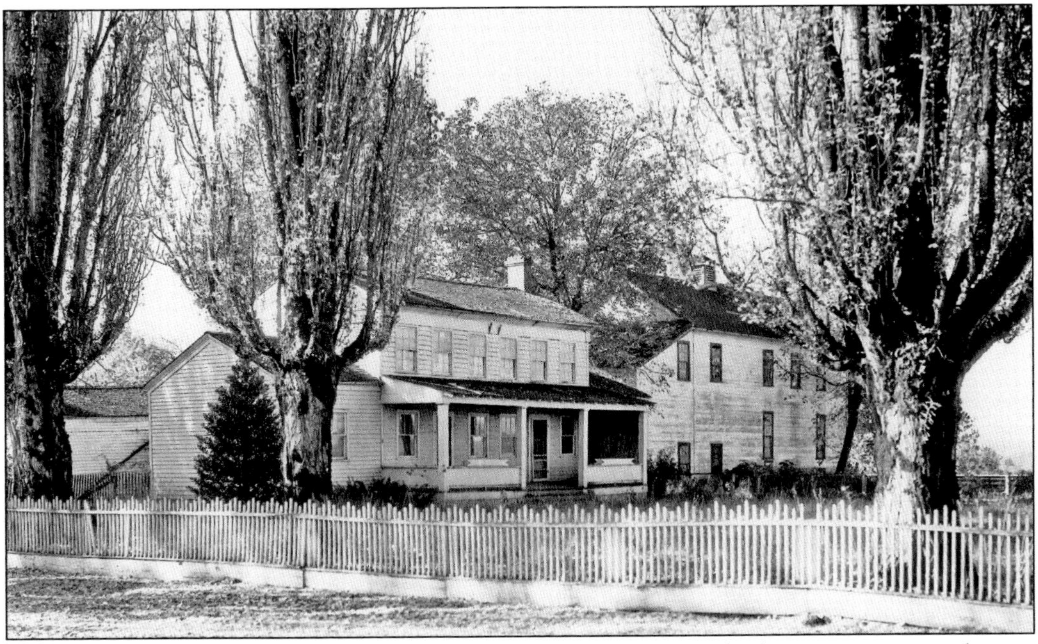

The Residence and Other Buildings on the Reed Farm. The historic two-story house, built in the mid-1800s, was constructed entirely of fir whipsawed onsite by pioneer carpenters. The residence was irreparably damaged during the Columbus Day Storm in 1962 and was later destroyed. (Reed College Hauser Library Special Collections and Archives.)

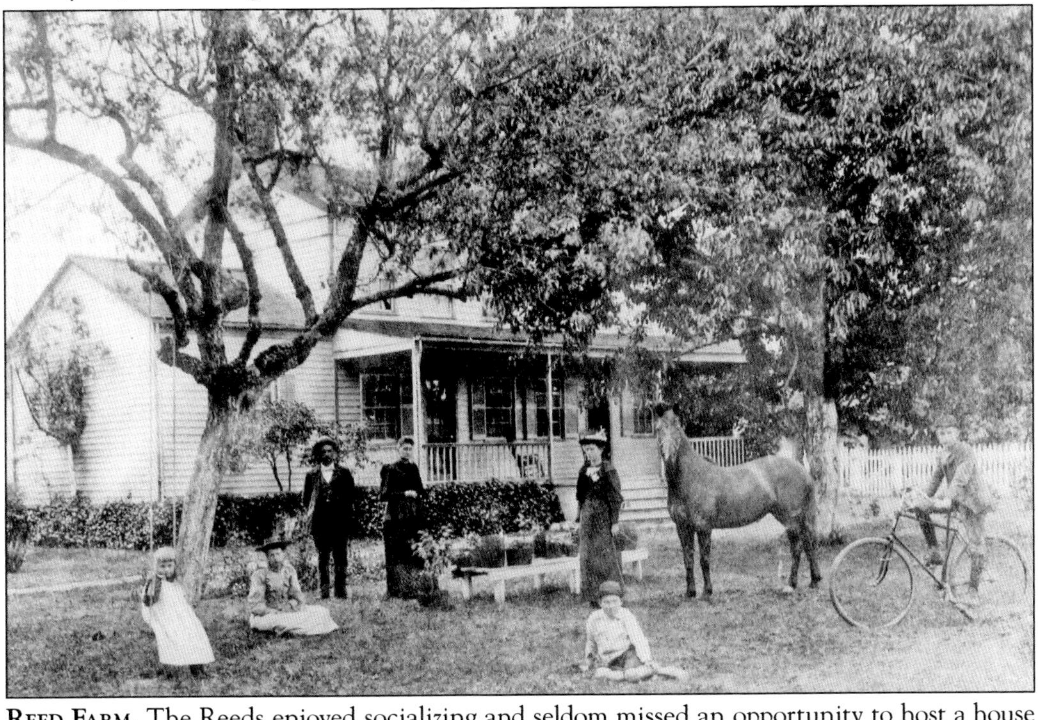

Reed Farm. The Reeds enjoyed socializing and seldom missed an opportunity to host a house full of visitors, especially young people. (Reed College Hauser Library Special Collections and Archives.)

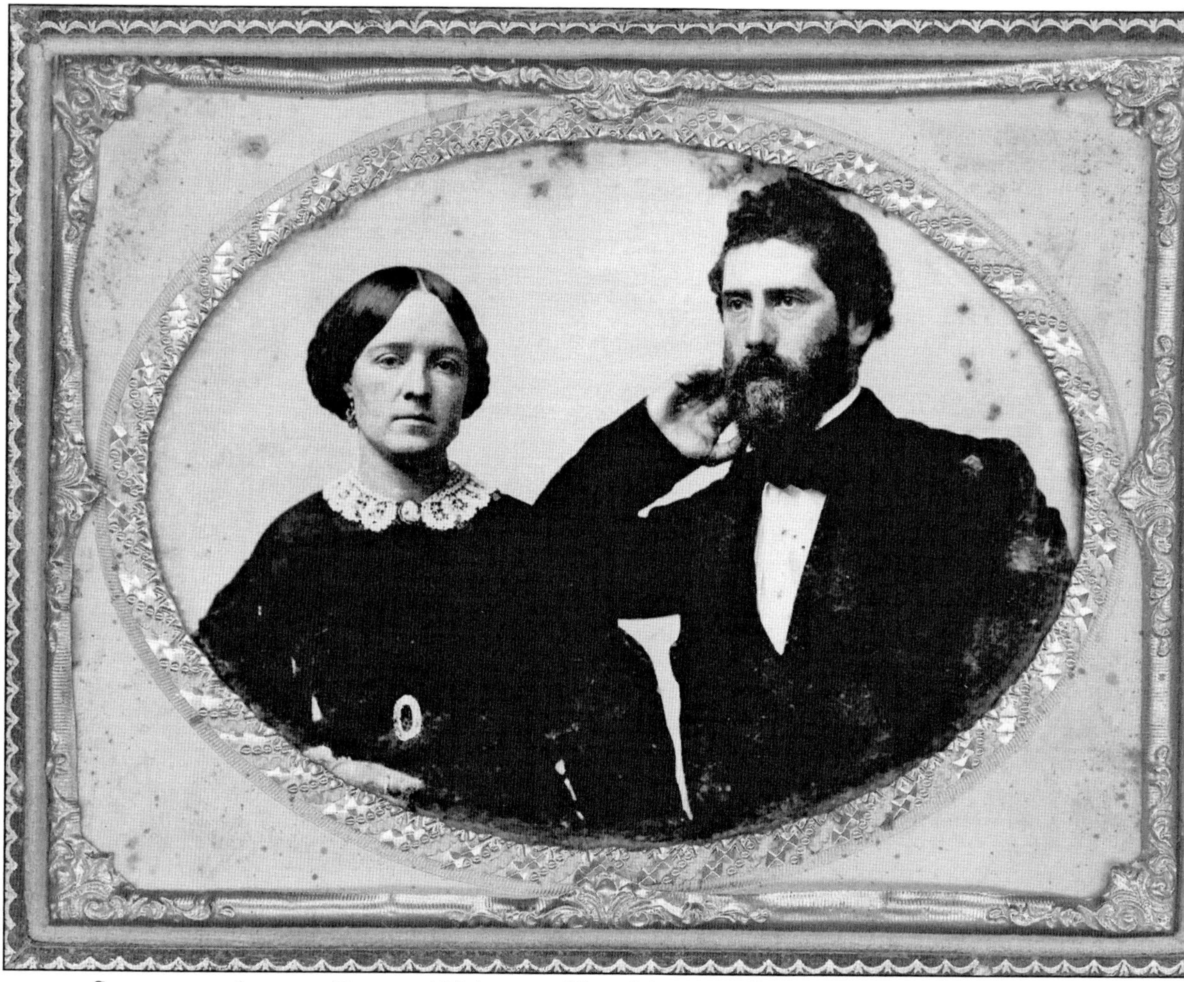

SIMEON AND AMANDA REED IN 1854, AFTER THEY MOVED TO PORTLAND FROM MASSACHUSETTS. In 1860, Reed invested in the lucrative Oregon Steam Navigation Company. By 1871, the Reeds acquired Nathan Robinson's farm on the Plains-Falls Road. After a railroad depot was constructed on the farm, Reed transported the largest private importation of livestock into the Pacific Northwest. He collaborated with expert agriculturalists and implemented innovative scientific management practices. Reed was president of the Oregon Central Railroad Company and Electric Railways of the United States, vice president of the Oregon Rail & Navigation Company and the Oregon Central Military Road Company, and affiliated with the Oregon Agricultural Society. Despite their resources, the Reeds lived modestly and generously supported cultural and philanthropic institutions. As early as 1875, they began to consider how to use their fortune in the interest of the public. (Reed College Hauser Library Special Collections and Archives.)

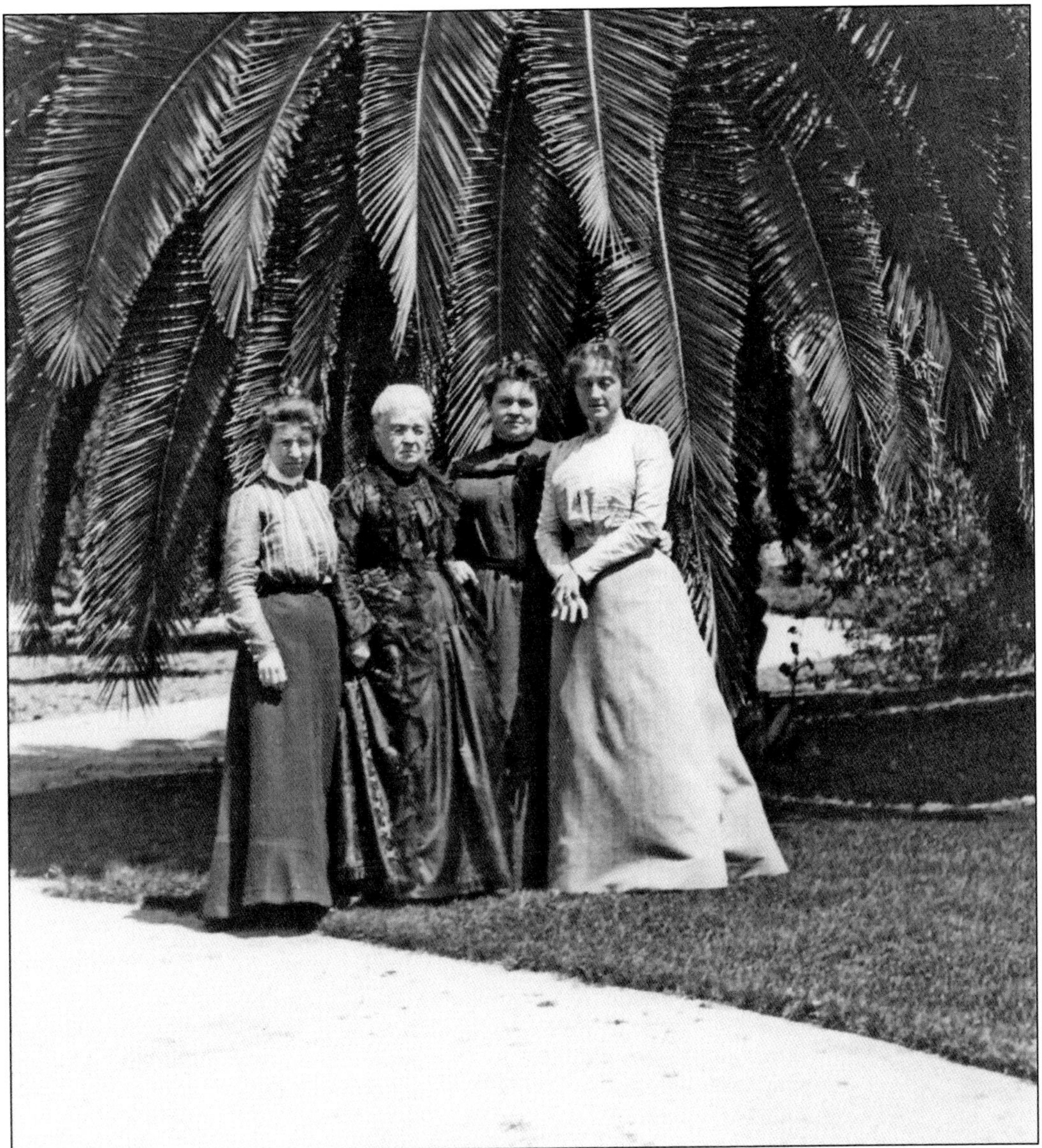

Amanda Reed (Second from Left), Wearing a Black Mourning Dress in Pasadena, California, around 1901. The Reeds moved to Pasadena in 1892. Simeon died three years later, in 1895. He was well remembered for his poise, good humor, and superlative hospitality. His will encouraged Amanda to devote a portion of their fortune for "a suitable purpose of permanent value." When Amanda died in 1904, her estate was bequeathed to foundations and charities and the Reed Institute (now Reed College), which began classes in 1911. The school was built in Portland on 40 acres of land deeded by the Ladd Estate Company. For decades, the Reed Institute and the Ladd and Reed Farm Company sold lots and blocks in Reedville to help subsidize the institution, which was founded "for the promotion of literature, sciences and art," as described in Amanda's will. (Reed College Hauser Library Special Collections and Archives.)

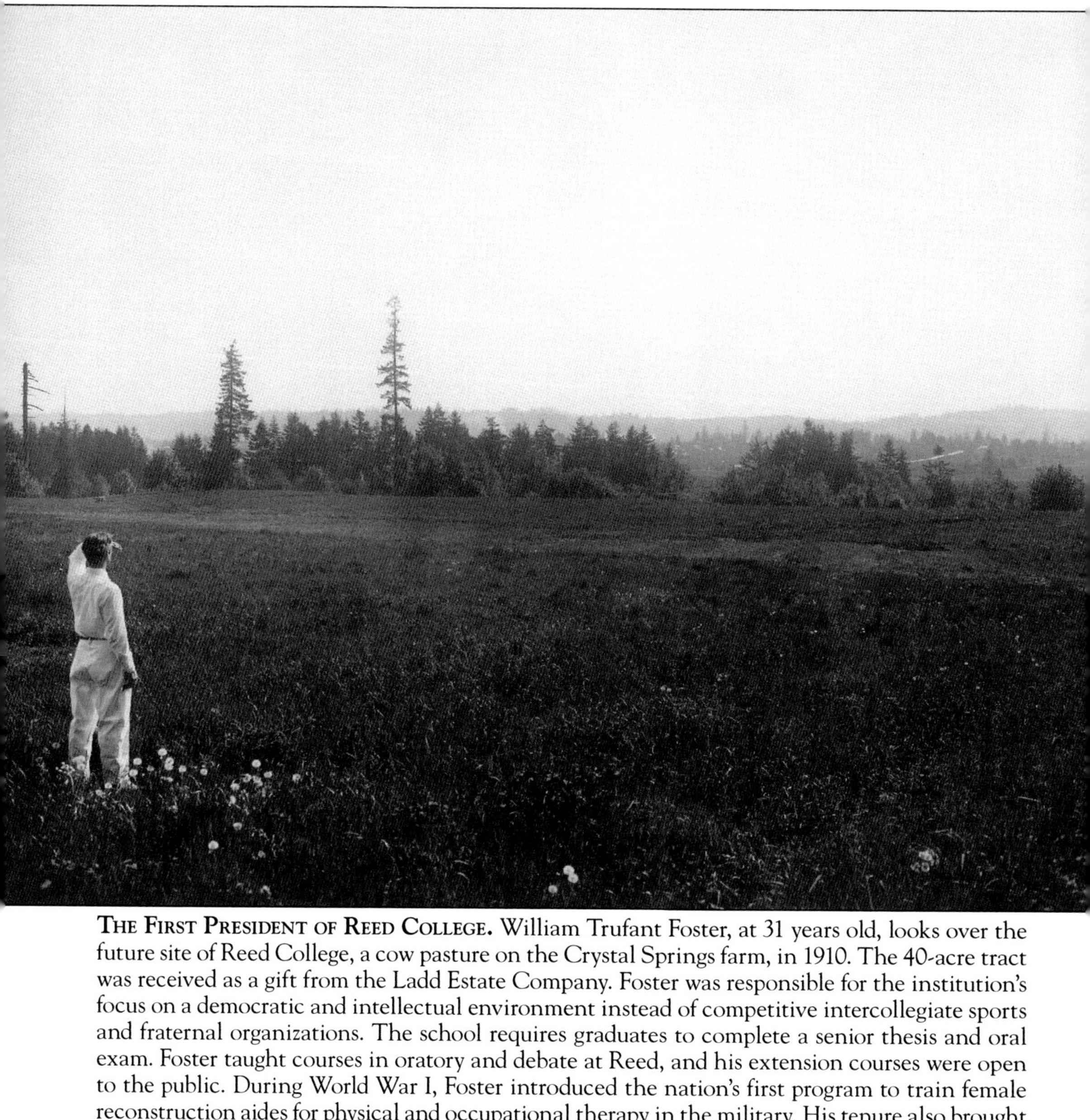

The First President of Reed College. William Trufant Foster, at 31 years old, looks over the future site of Reed College, a cow pasture on the Crystal Springs farm, in 1910. The 40-acre tract was received as a gift from the Ladd Estate Company. Foster was responsible for the institution's focus on a democratic and intellectual environment instead of competitive intercollegiate sports and fraternal organizations. The school requires graduates to complete a senior thesis and oral exam. Foster taught courses in oratory and debate at Reed, and his extension courses were open to the public. During World War I, Foster introduced the nation's first program to train female reconstruction aides for physical and occupational therapy in the military. His tenure also brought about an interest in simplified spelling, a technique that relies on speech sounds or phonetics. (Reed College Hauser Library Special Collections and Archives.)

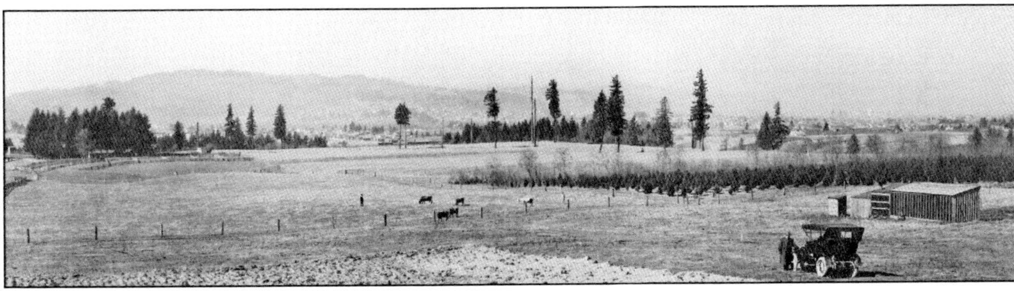

The Reed College Campus in Portland. In the foreground (above) in 1915 are the Great Lawn and part of Southeast Woodstock Boulevard. Eliot Hall and the Old Dorm Block are in the distance. One of the first campus buildings, the Old Dorm Block (below), is pictured during construction in 1912. It was inspired by old English manor houses. Gargoyles on the roof and above doorways emphasize the building's use for recreation and sleep. The design included a fully functioning sundial above the sally port or entrance. Many of the building's eight residence halls have fireplaces, balconies, and window seats. (Both, Reed College Hauser Library Special Collections and Archives.)

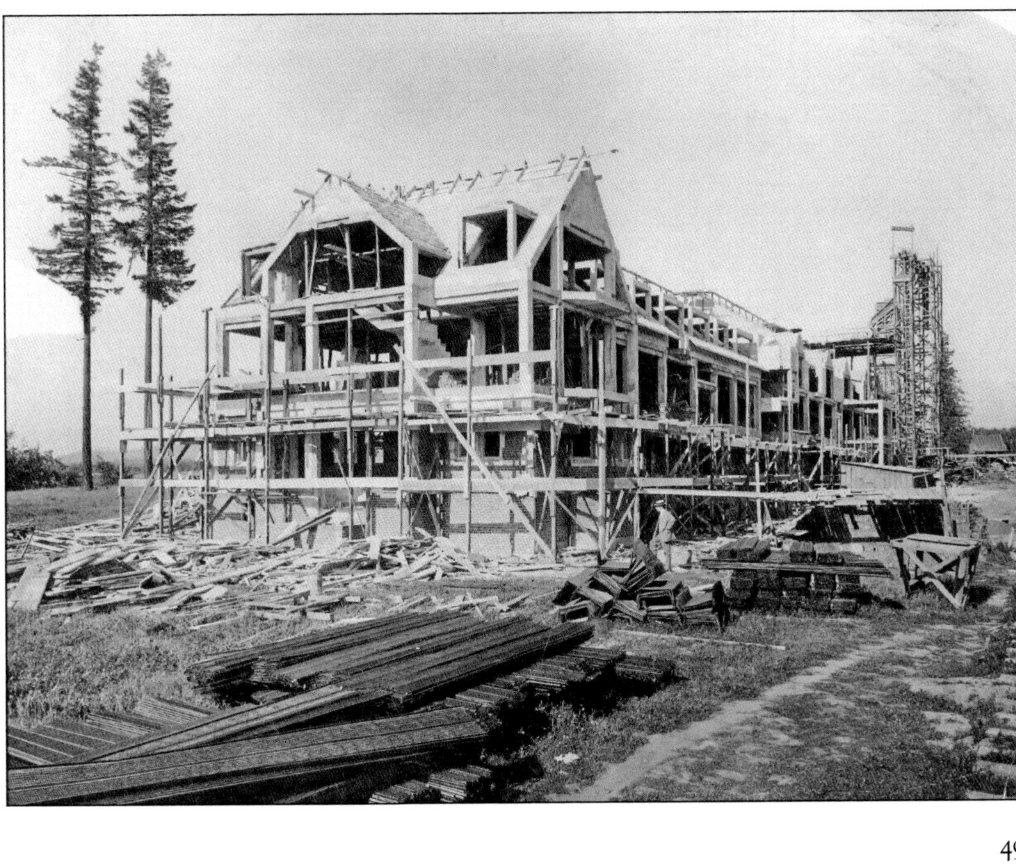

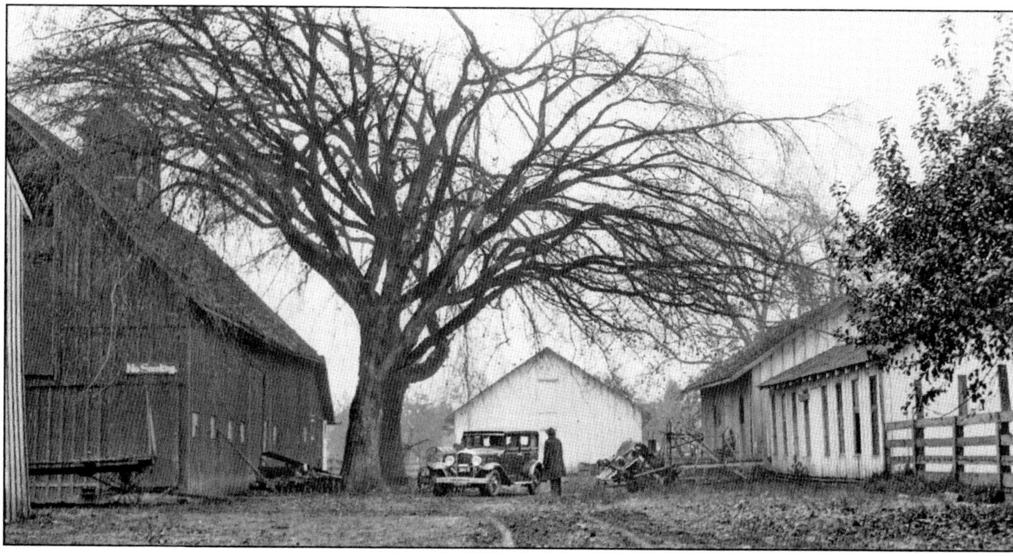

John D. Kelly. By the 1920s, Kelly owned the former Reed farm at Reedville (above). A Sylvan merchant, Kelly kept eight teams of horses to work the farm. He cultivated, harvested, and sold feed and seed to Tualatin Valley farmers. After Kelly retired in the 1930s, the farm became the property of his descendants. For decades, lots in the town of Reedville were sold by the Reed Institute and the Ladd and Reed Farm Company. A row of black walnut trees along the old Plains-Falls Road, on the west side of today's Southwest 209th Avenue (below), were planted by Nathan Robinson. (Above, No. 9904-G15 © Historic Photo Archive; below, photograph by the author.)

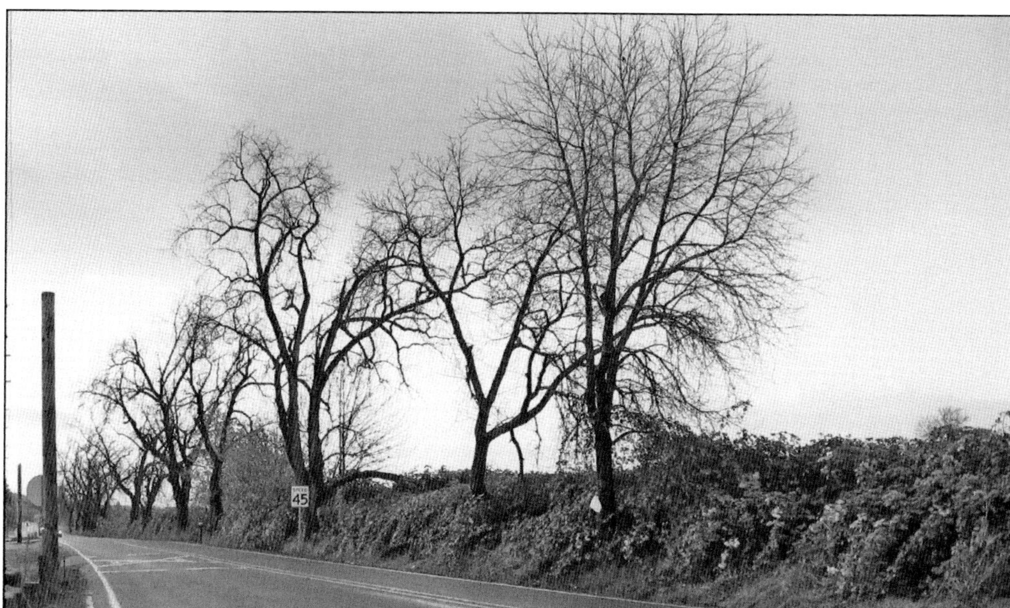

Five

Reedville

When the town of Reedville was platted in 1889, on Reed farm acreage north of the railroad, it included the original 1.5-acre site for a future school and church, deeded by Nathan and Mary Robinson in 1859, in the northeast corner of their farm. It sold to Simeon and Amanda Reed in the 1860s.

Managed by the Ladd and Reed Farm Company until the early 1890s, and the center of their livestock breeding operations, the farm employed laborers, managers and leading agriculturalists. Construction of a short line railroad in 1871 attracted loggers, railroad workers, and a new wave of European immigration. A post office opened in 1877, and by 1881 a feed mill was in operation near the railroad depot. The Reedville school was constructed in 1882 on the site first deeded by the Robinsons.

In 1887, Reed's railroad interests were acquired. David and Augusta Hagg purchased 160 acres adjacent to the Reed farm in 1890. The Imlay family opened the J.B. Imlay and Sons mill in the early 1890s next to the railroad. They lived in a nearby house built by Nils Oakerman.

At the turn of the 20th century, Reedville was a thriving commercial center. Mercantiles, saloons and fraternal organizations were built near the railroad depot where farmers throughout the Tualatin Valley brought timber, cord wood, grain and dairy products for export. The earliest residents included the Imlay, Oakerman, Dant, Allen, and Weisenback families.

After converting from branch steam to electricity, Southern Pacific leased their line as part of the Red Electric interurban railway. In 1918, Reedville's Front Avenue became part of Tualatin Valley Highway, a two-lane, cement road for automobiles. When the Red Electrics ceased operation in 1929, the Reedville railroad depot closed. In 1929. Tualatin Valley Highway was improved in 1933 by the Federal Emergency Relief Administration.

The Reedville post office operated until 1954. From 1956 to 1958, the Oregon State Highway Commission expanded the highway to four lanes. In 1962, the Columbus Day storm caused significant, sometimes irreparable damage to dozens of commercial and farm buildings.

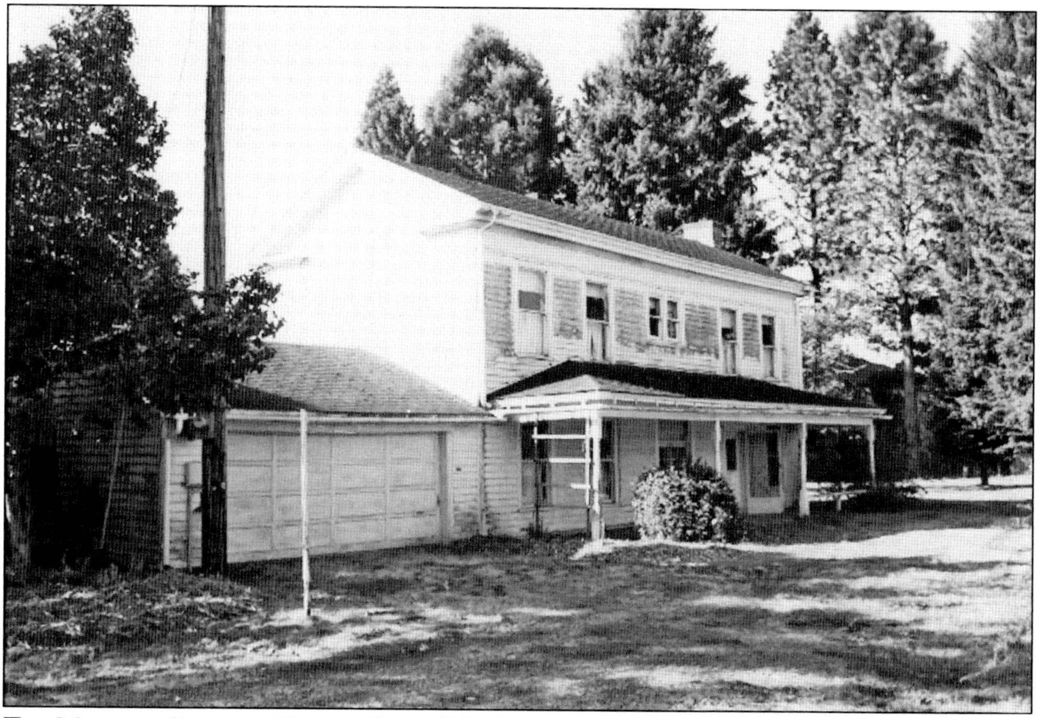

The Masters Century House. One of Washington County's oldest standing structures, the house is pictured as it looks today (above) on Southwest Kinnaman Road in Reedville. Built in 1853 on the Andrew Jackson and Sarah Jane Masters land claim, the structure's central rectangular section is fashioned in the Classical Revival style, with a low-pitched gable roof and boxed eaves, beams, crossties, and uprights milled from cedar logs. There is an enclosed porch on the east elevation and a bathroom attachment on the west. A one-story kitchen ell and woodshed extend south from the kitchen (below). Masters was born in Green County, Kentucky, in 1816. (Both photographs by the author.)

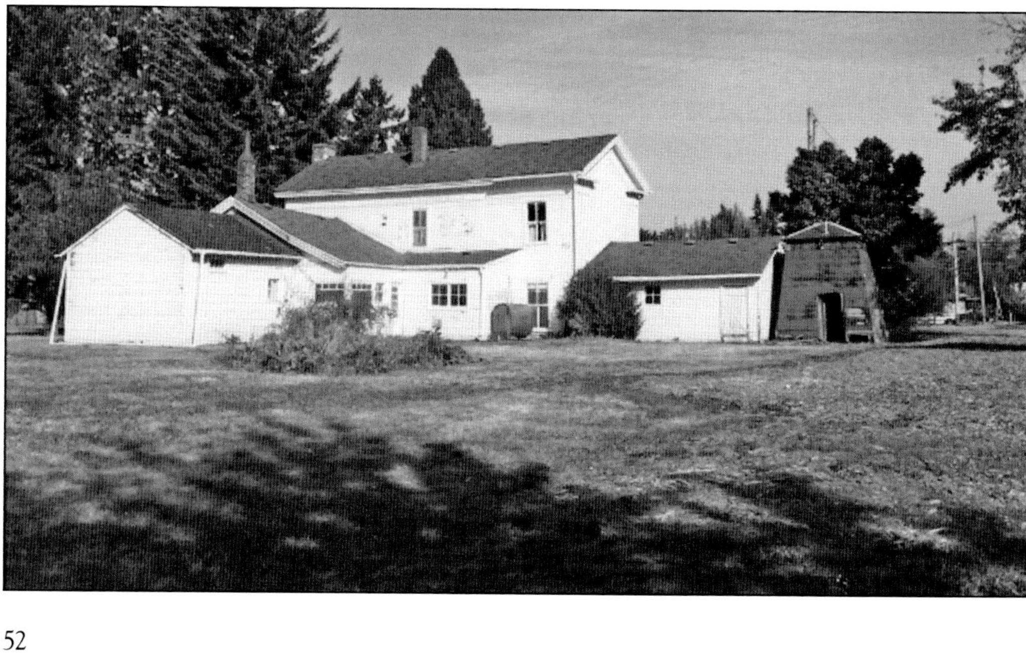

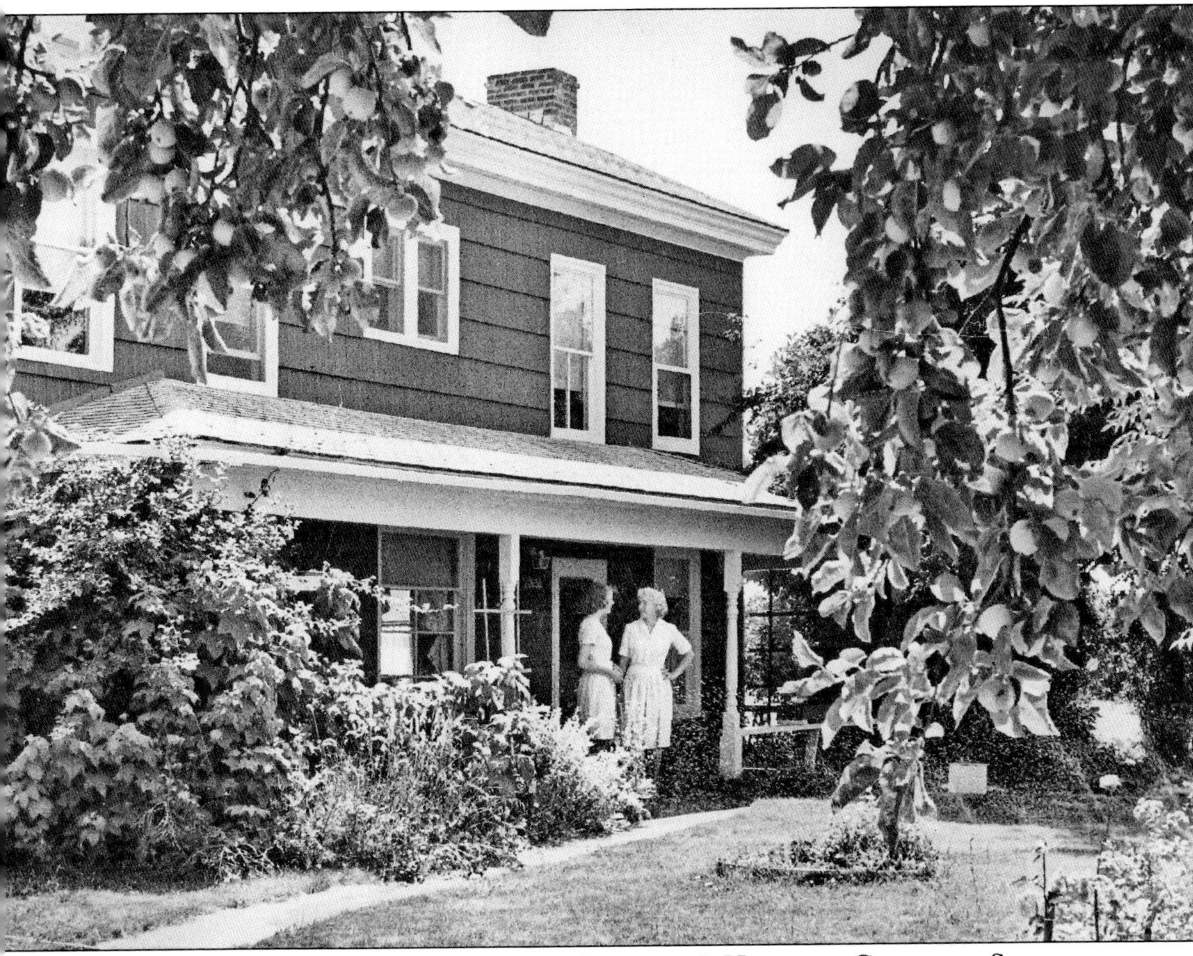

The Masters House in 1964, When It Was Owned by J. Hugh and Constance Stevens. The structure was built in 1853 for a cost of $6,000 by A.J. and Sarah Masters. Married in 1842, they settled in Washington County in 1850. In 1856, Masters was shot and killed by neighbor James McMillen in a boundary dispute on what the locals called Devil's Lane, near today's Southwest 198th Avenue. The Masters House was deemed a Century House in 1953 by Tualatin Valley historian Robert L. Benson and members of the Tualatin Valley Heritage Group. In the 1960s, the Stevens family replaced the original sill and stone foundation with concrete slab and removed machined shake siding. New weatherboards were installed in the 1970s. In 1983, Washington County designated the structure as an official cultural resource. (Oregon Historical Society, No. bb009715.)

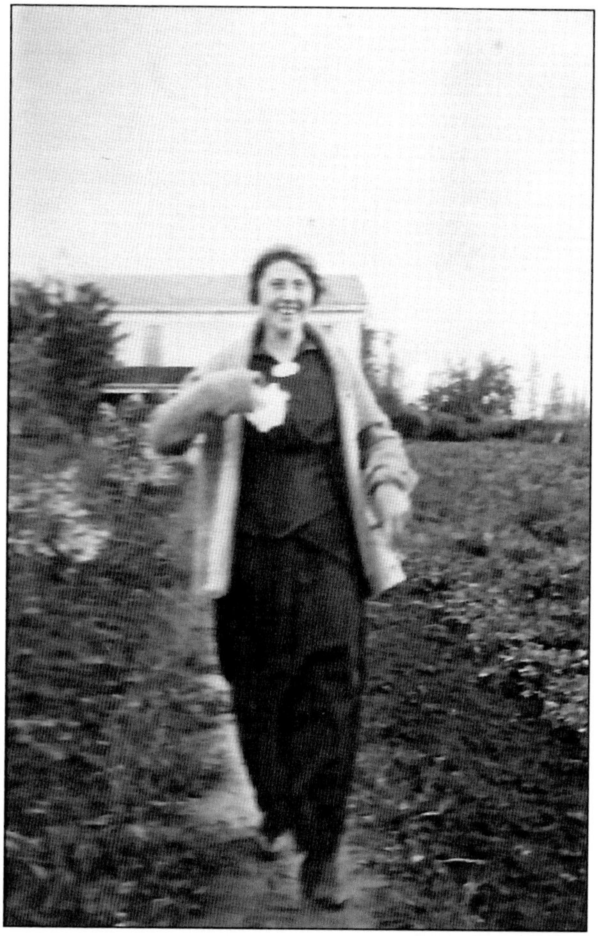

Ruth Swalley on the Front Path of the Family Home in the Early 1900s. The Swalleys lived in the former Masters House, on today's Kinnaman Road in Reedville, around 1900 to 1919. Ruth and Hazelle Swalley were the daughters of John Swalley, a Civil War veteran, and his wife, Eva. (Marjorie Denton Larrance family.)

John Denton (Center) and Ruth Swalley (Right) outside the Reedville Railway Depot around World War I. From 1918 to 1929, the United States Railway Administration consolidated and nationalized operations of four major express companies, including the Wells Fargo and Company, to ensure efficient operations during the war effort. Wells Fargo transported mail, parcels, money, and goods by rail. (Marjorie Denton Larrance family.)

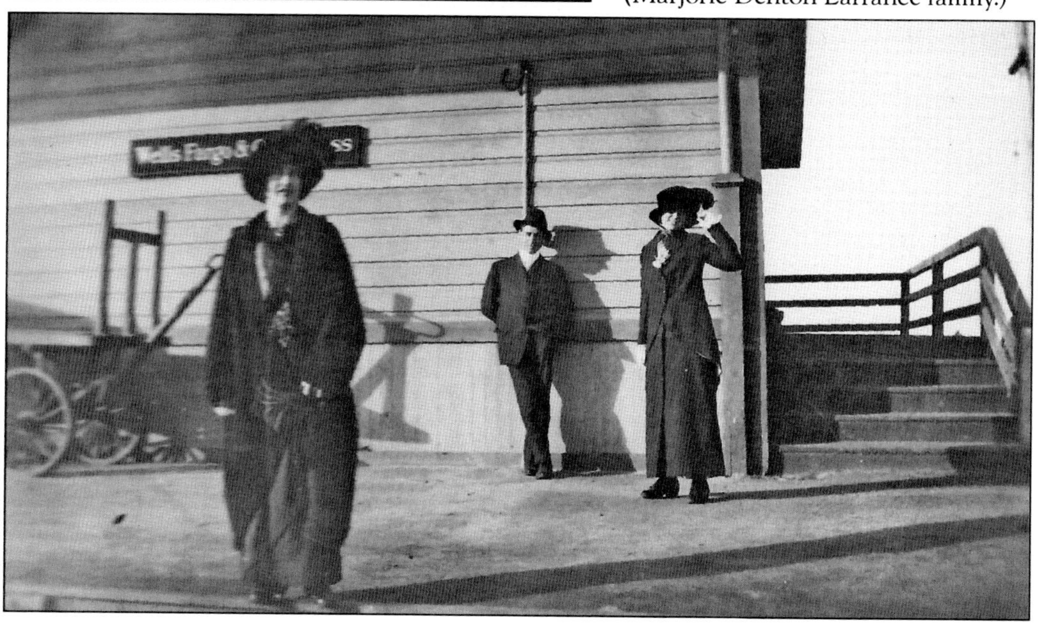

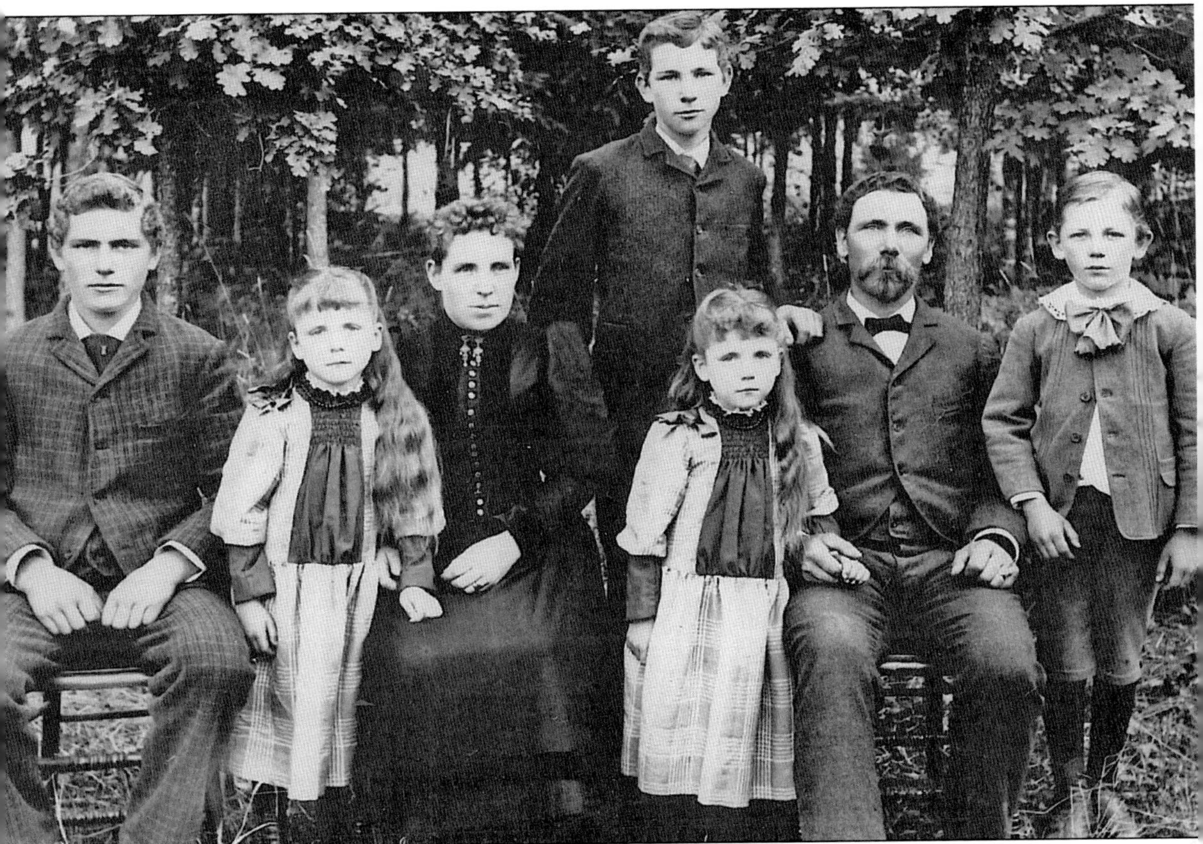

THE OAKERMAN FAMILY IN THE 1890S. From left to right are Edwin, twins Lena and Tina, Christina, Paul, Nils, and Arthur Cyril. Nils Peder Oakerman was born in Sweden in 1851. A carpenter, he immigrated to the United States in 1870, working briefly in construction in Kansas City, then on the railroad in Kansas and Missouri, carving ties with an axe. In 1872, Oakerman moved to Chicago to help rebuild the city after the Great Fire. He went to San Francisco in 1874 for a 10-month contract building the Palace Hotel. In 1876, he married Christina Olson. After Edwin was born, they moved to Portland, then to a 160-acre farm in Washington County in 1877. Son Paul was born in 1878, followed by Arthur Cyril in 1884 and twins Lena and Tina in 1888. The Oakermans joined Reedville Church in 1893. They moved to Beaverton in 1905. (Sally and Steve Kramer.)

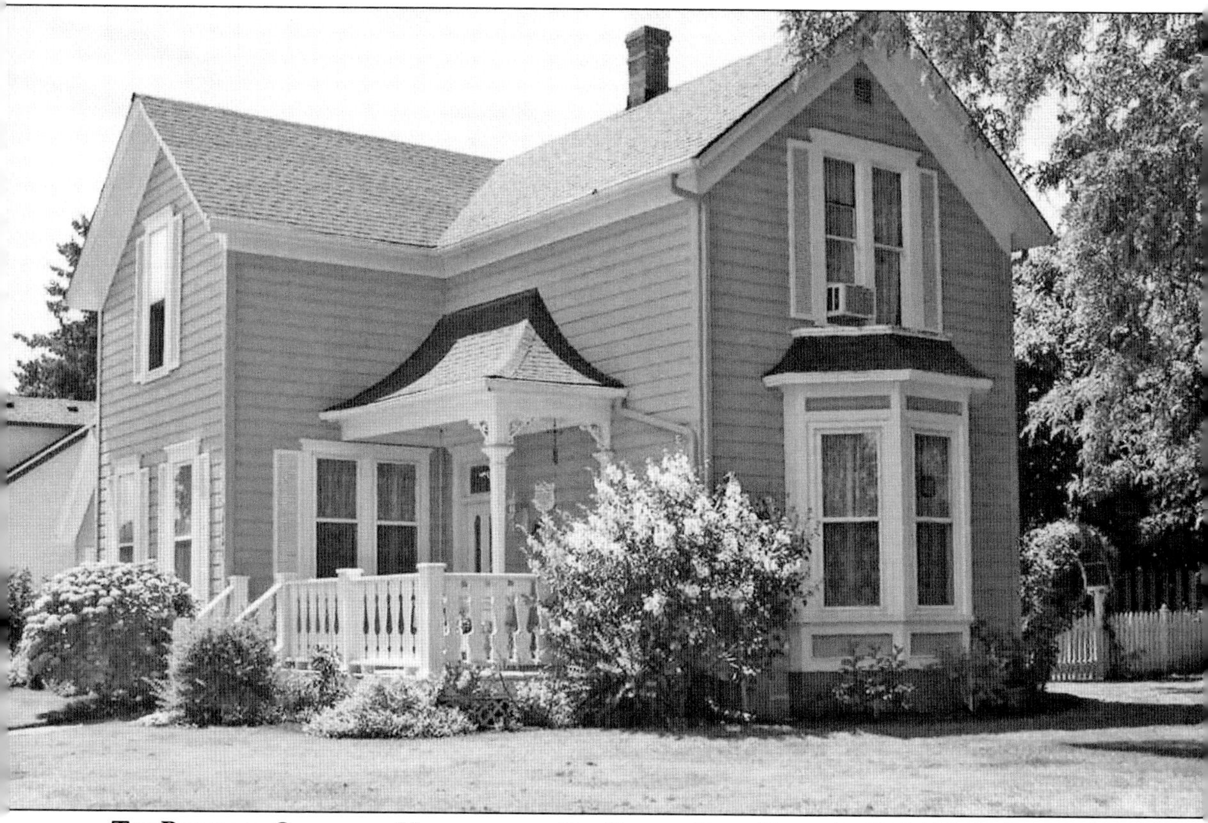

The Restored Oakerman House on the Old Plains-Falls Road. In 1887, Nils Oakerman built a house (above), facing the old Plains-Falls road. A carpenter and joiner, Oakerman purchased 100 acres of farmland for $700 from the family of Andrew Jackson Masters. The 1.5-story Rural Gothic–style residence is among the oldest standing in Washington County. The house was purchased in 1999 and restored by Sally and Steve Kramer, who installed a new electrical system, plumbing, exterior landscaping, and a perimeter foundation that took nearly a year to finish. They also gutted the kitchen and designed, crafted, and installed new cabinets. It took seven years to complete the work, most of which was done by the Kramers themselves. (Sally and Steve Kramer.)

The Millars. In 1905, when the Oakermans moved to Beaverton, Josiah (right) and Mary Ellen Robinson Millar (left) purchased the farm and residence. Millar, originally from Quebec, Canada, was born in 1856. He was the proprietor of Reedville and Twin Oaks mercantiles. The Millars' children were Grace "Gracie," William, and George Alfred. (Sally and Steve Kramer.)

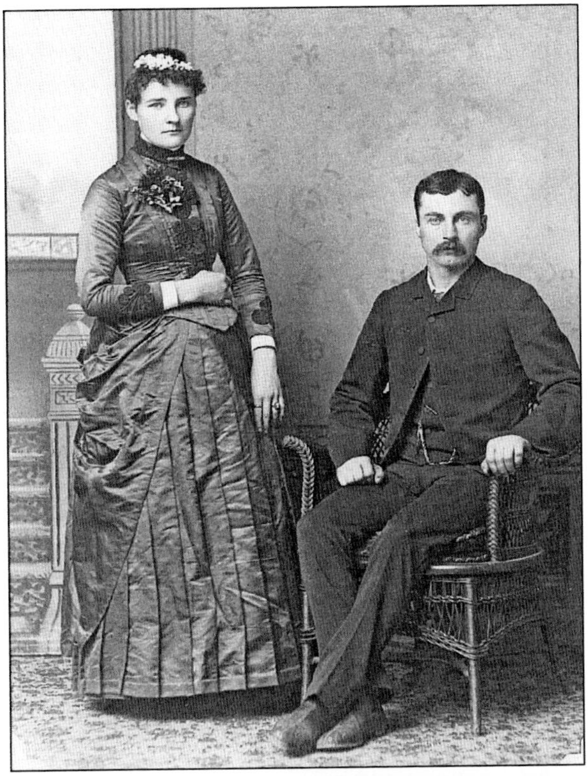

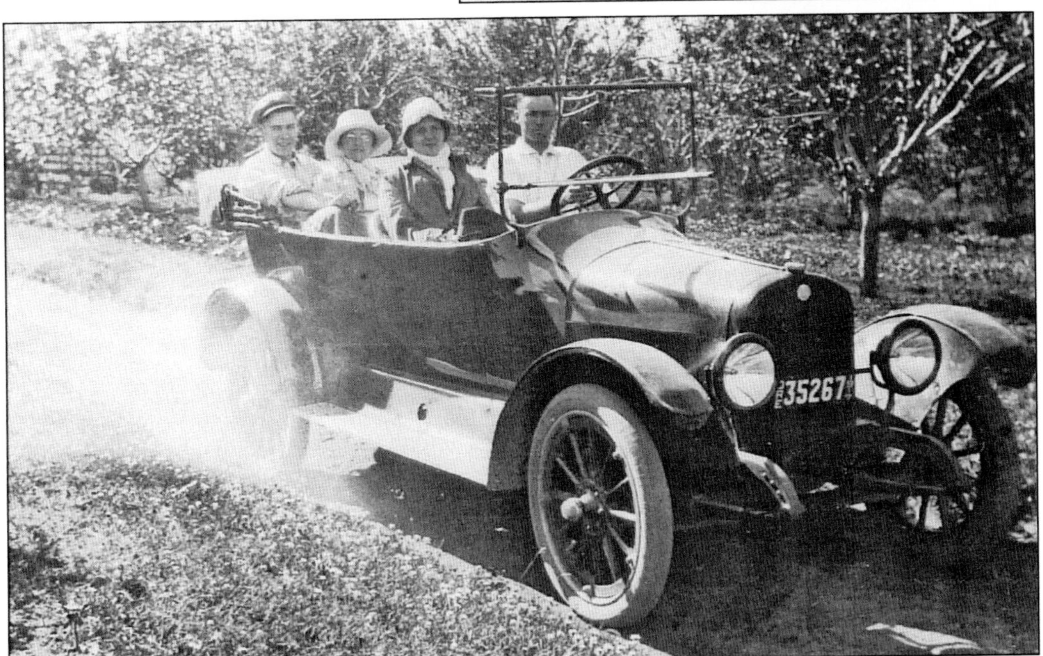

Alf and Hazelle Millar. George Alfred "Alf" Millar, at the wheel (right), and Hazelle Swalley Millar (second from right) ride in a 1916 Dort automobile in Hood River, Oregon. They were married on October 24, 1917. In the back seat are Peter Brandon (left) and Dolores George Brandon (right). (Sally and Steve Kramer.)

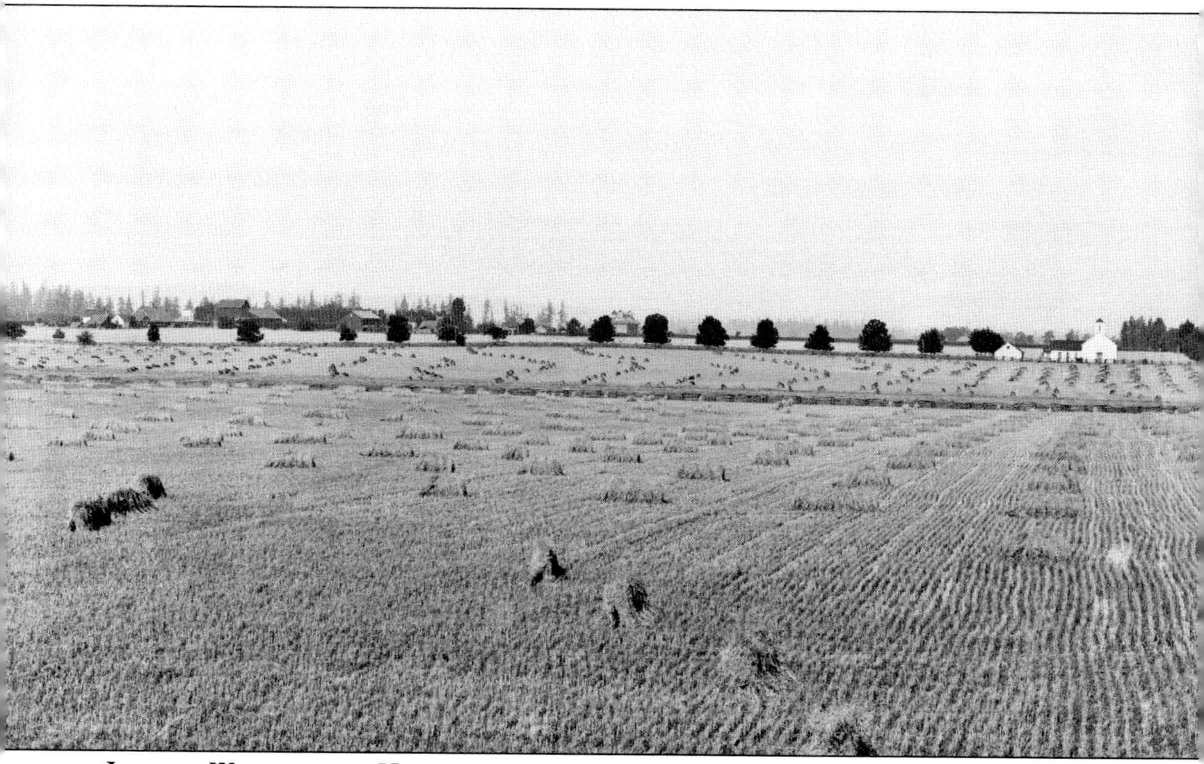

Looking West across a Hayfield at the Reedville Church (Right) and Buildings on the Reed Farm (Left). The historic second Reedville School (right) had a white, two-story belfry. A row of black walnut trees (center), planted by the first land claim holder, Nathan Robinson, distinguishes the eastern boundary of what was then the Reed farm (middle). In the background, the Reeds' covered two-story harness-racing track (center) was once located near today's Cornelius Pass Road. A warehouse and grain elevator (left) were acquired by James Burd Imlay in the early 1890s. Today it is the site of Harvey Marine, a boat manufacturing company. (1205-B2 © Historic Photo Archive.)

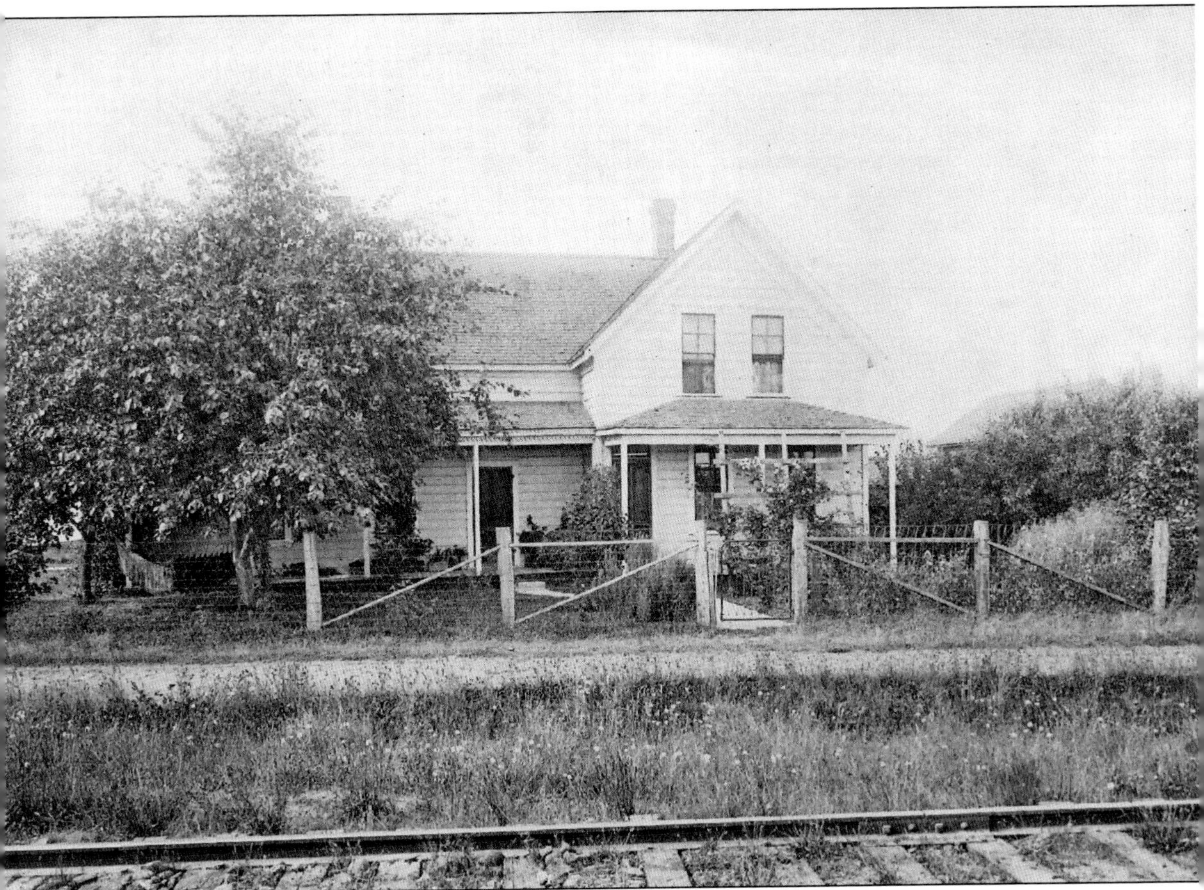

A Residence Belonging to James Burd "J.B." and Isabella Imlay and Their Family in Reedville. Originally from Scotland, the Imlays lived in Illinois then moved to the Glencoe area of Washington County, now North Plains, where J.B. worked at the Milne mill. In 1891, Imlay purchased an interest in a grain elevator owned by J.J. Morgan and Robert Imbrie on land that had been part of the Reed farm. He founded J.B. Imlay and Sons, a feed and seed store and mill. Imlay was also Reedville postmaster from 1897 to 1908, deputy assessor for Reedville and Beaverton townships, clerk of the Reedville School Board for 20 years, and a founding member of Reedville Presbyterian Church. The Imlay home was sometimes used as a temporary residence for traveling ministers and schoolteachers. The father of 10 children, Imlay was also a member of the Masonic Lodge. (Kathleen Imlay Eames.)

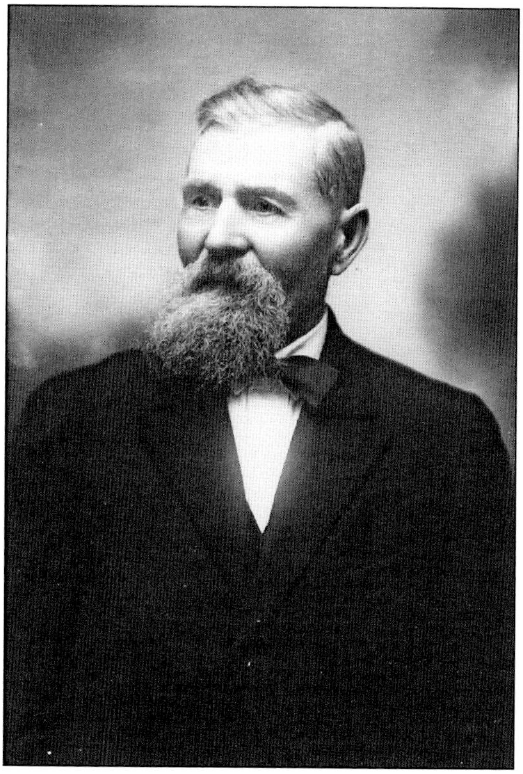

J.B. Imlay. Imlay was born in 1842 in Aberdeen, Scotland. He arrived in the United States in 1866, settling for a time in Illinois. In the early 1890s, he founded J.B. Imlay and Sons, a feed and seed company, located next to the rail in Reedville. (Kathleen Imlay Eames.)

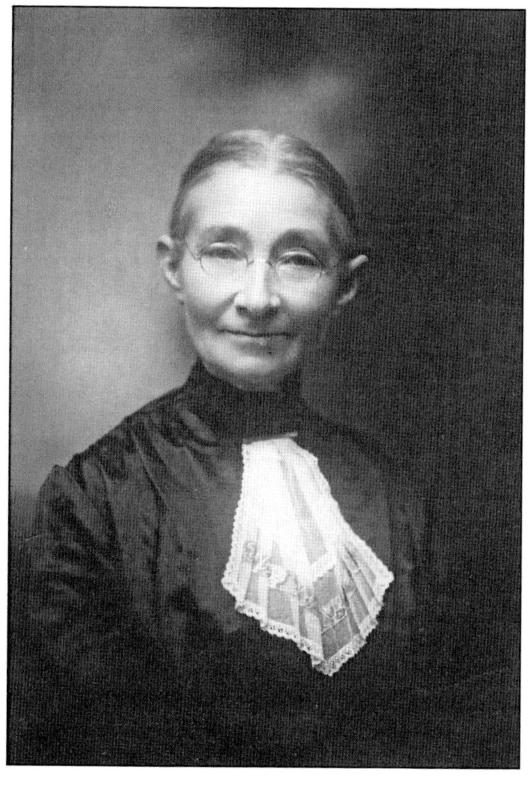

Isabella Thom Imlay. Isabella was born in Strichey, Scotland, on September 9, 1849. She immigrated to the United States in 1871 and married J.B. Imlay in 1879 near Morrison, Illinois. The Imlays arrived in Oregon in the 1880s. Isabella lived in Reedville until her death in 1938. (Kathleen Imlay Eames.)

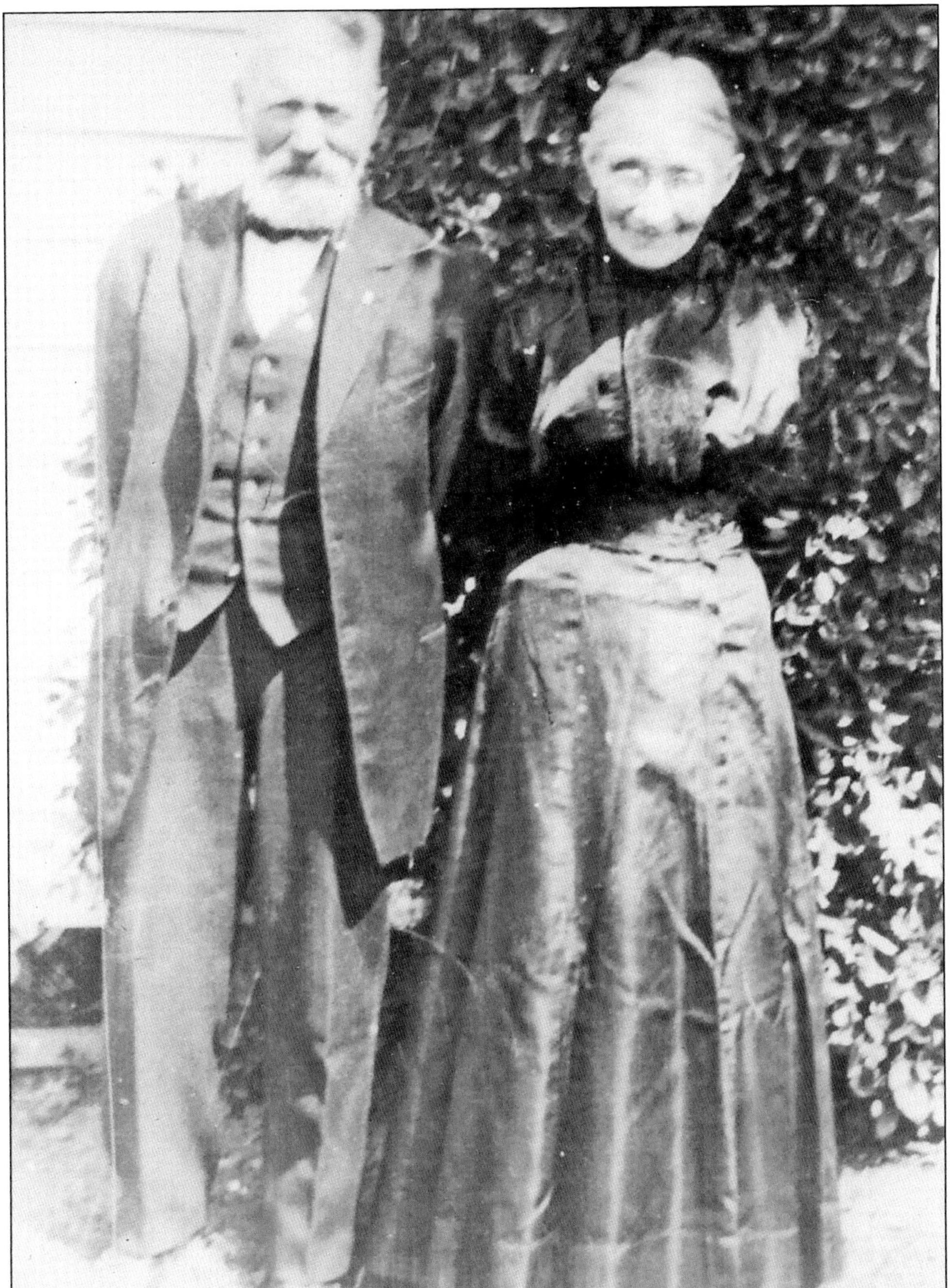

J.B. and Isabella Imlay in the Early 1900s. Imlay purchased a warehouse and began operating a gristmill in Reedville around 1891. The company sold and poultry and dairy feed and provided custom grinding and mixing services. One of the largest and most efficiently operated businesses of its kind in the Pacific Northwest, the J.B. Imlay and Company won many awards and ribbons at the Washington County Fair and the Pacific International Live Stock Exposition. From 1933 to 1956, Charles "Charlie" Imlay was proprietor of the Reedville mill. He also operated Imlay's Home Town Hardware store in Aloha until 1968. (Kathleen Imlay Eames.)

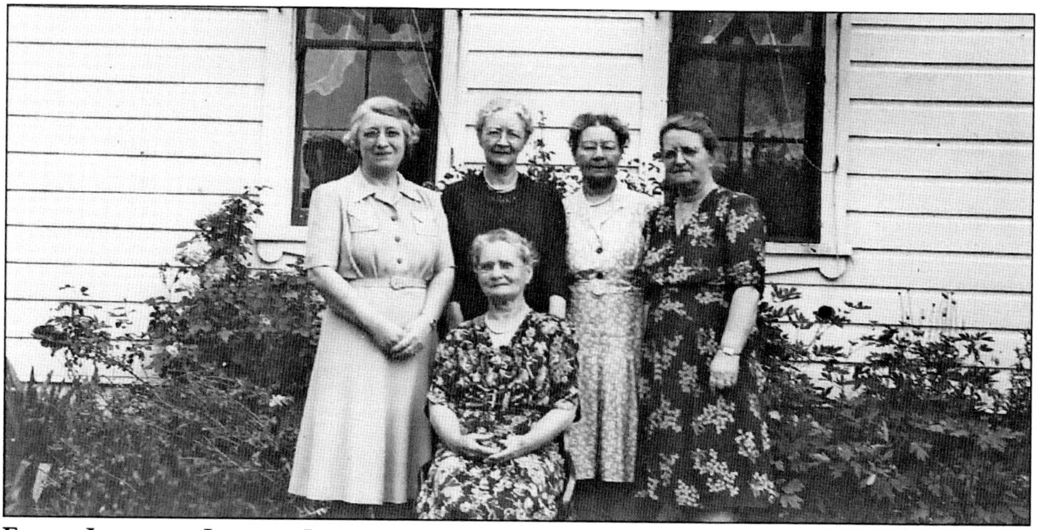

FIVE OF JAMES AND ISABELLA IMLAY'S CHILDREN AROUND 1953. From left to right are Margaret May "Maggie," Christina Ann "Chrissie," Agnes Elizabeth, and Grace Isabella. Mary Jane, seated in front, was born in 1873. The Imlay sons were James Wallace, Robert Alexander, George Morrison, and Charles Towers. (Kathleen Imlay Eames.)

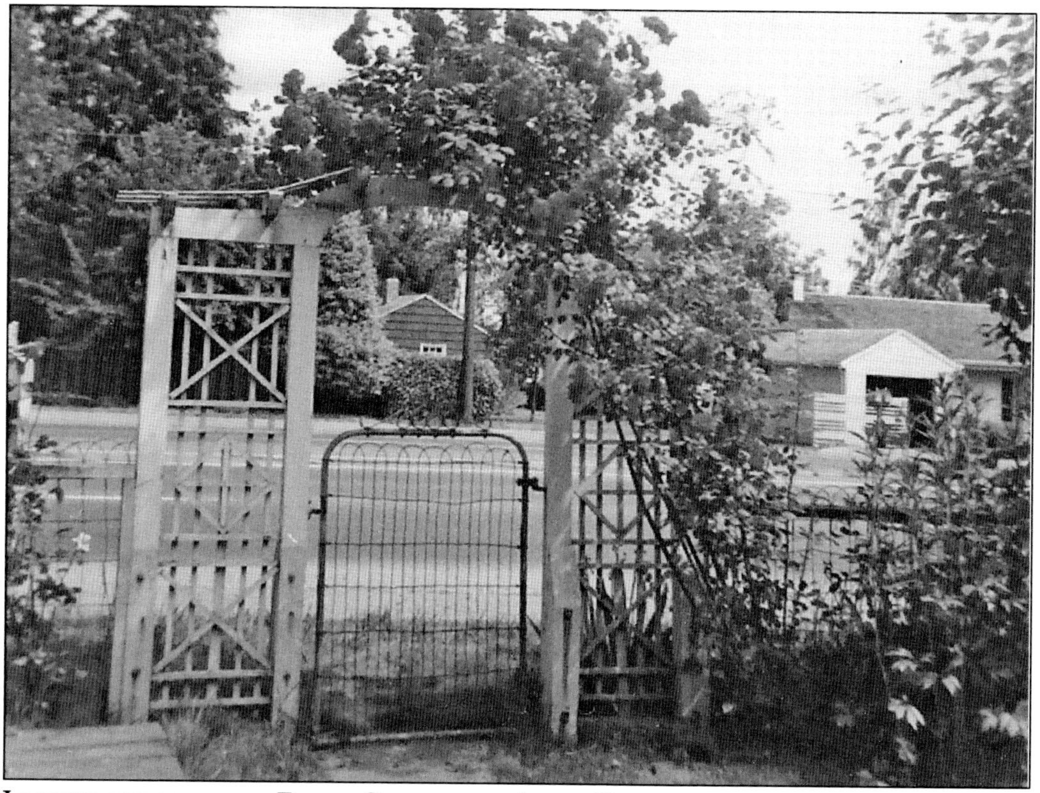

LOOKING THROUGH THE FRONT GATE OF THE IMLAY RESIDENCE TOWARD TUALATIN VALLEY HIGHWAY IN REEDVILLE. The house was located south of the railroad and east of the J.B. Imlay and Sons mill and feed store, which was operated by two generations of the Imlay family from 1891 until 1956. (Kathleen Imlay Eames.)

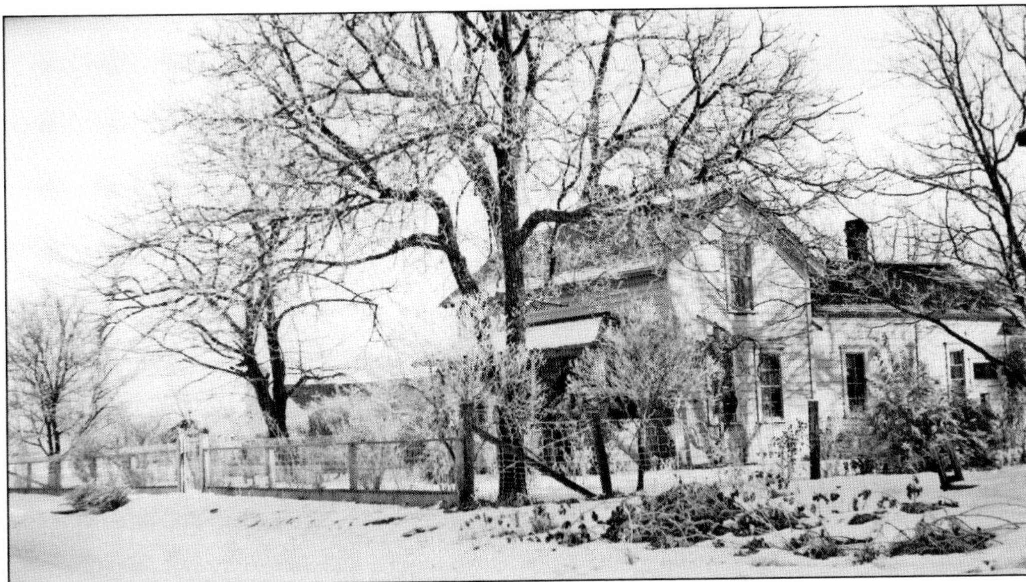

The Dant House in Reedville, 1946. Dant was born in Washington, DC, in 1852. He married the former Emma Allen, born in Reedville in 1860. Her parents were Reedville residents Issac and Asenath Allen. The Dant children were Eugene, Adrian, Ella, and Maud. (Washington County Museum.)

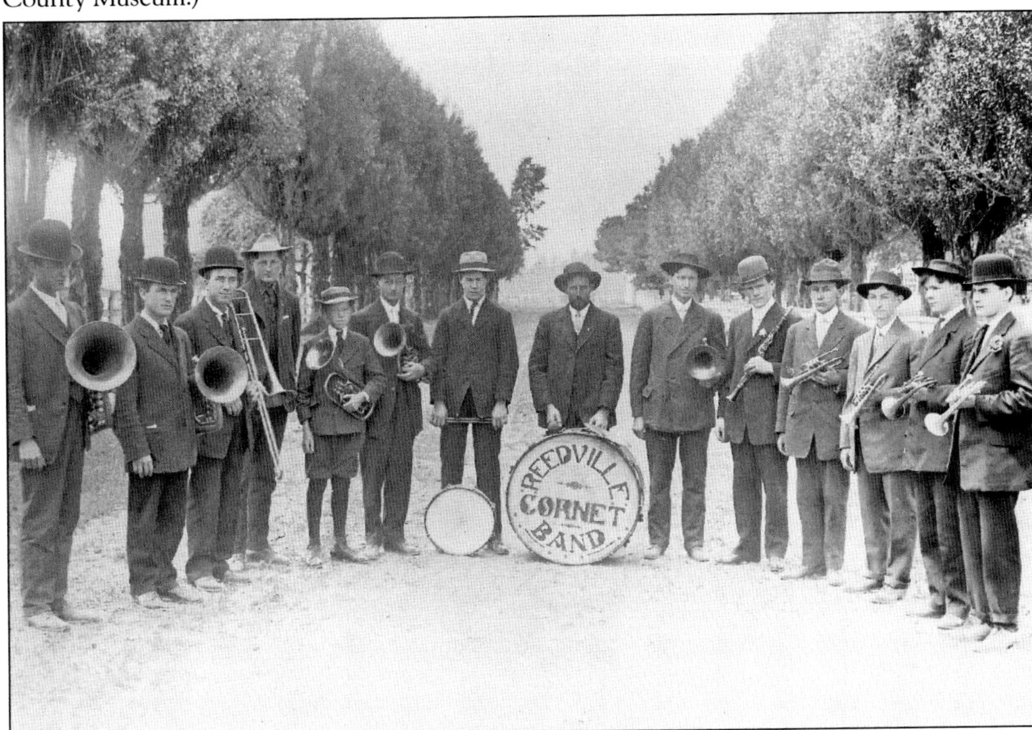

The Reedville Cornet Band, 1907–1908. Pictured from left to right on the drive to the Reed farm are O.E. Frank, Adrian Dant, Alwan Frank, Ernest Wolf, Tom Kirkwood, Jesse Hays, Charles Imlay Sr., Sherman Rhodes, Henry Frank, Claude Johnson, Charles Ross, Henry Hagg, George Imlay, and Will Millar. (Reedville Presbyterian Church.)

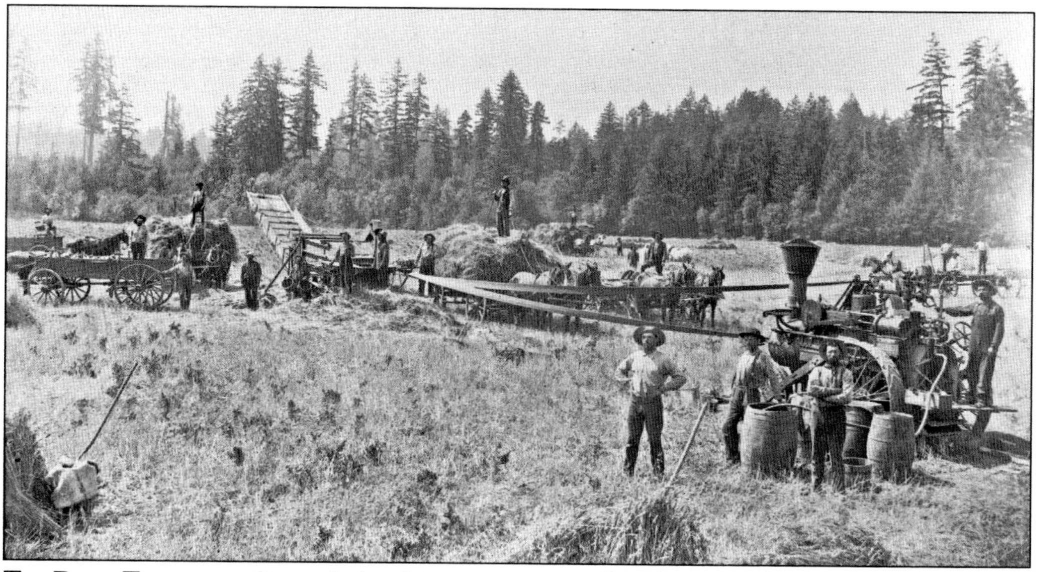

The Dant Threshing Crew. A threshing crew operated by Eugene and Adrian Dant is pictured (above) in 1886 on the Wheeler farm, near today's Aloha. The Dants' brother-in-laws Alexander "Ek" Allen and Julius Weisenback are also pictured, but not specifically identified. Weisenback was one of the managers of the Arthur H. Johnson farm. He was married to Emma Dant's sister, the former Ambersine Allen. After wheat was cut and stacked in bundles to dry, threshers gathered and fed them into steam-powered machines that separated grain from hay. The Dant crew is pictured (below) near the round barn on the Reed farm. (Both, Washington County Museum.)

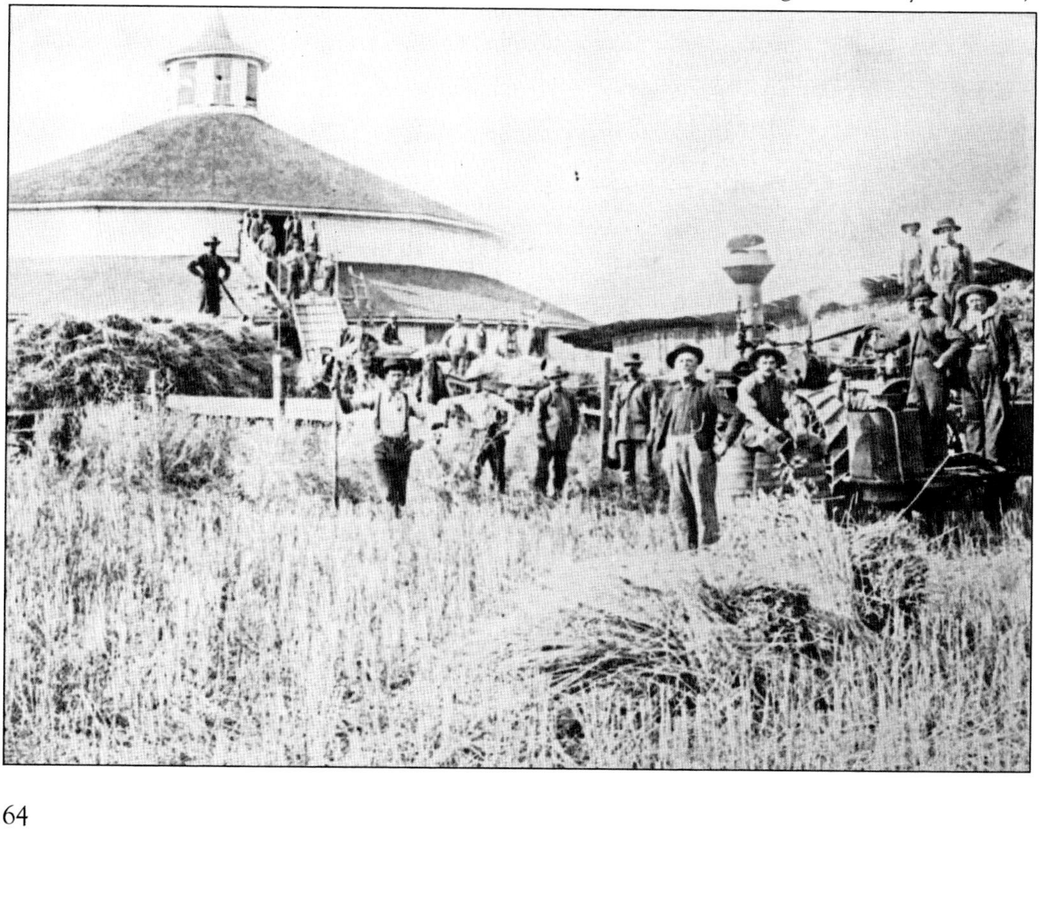

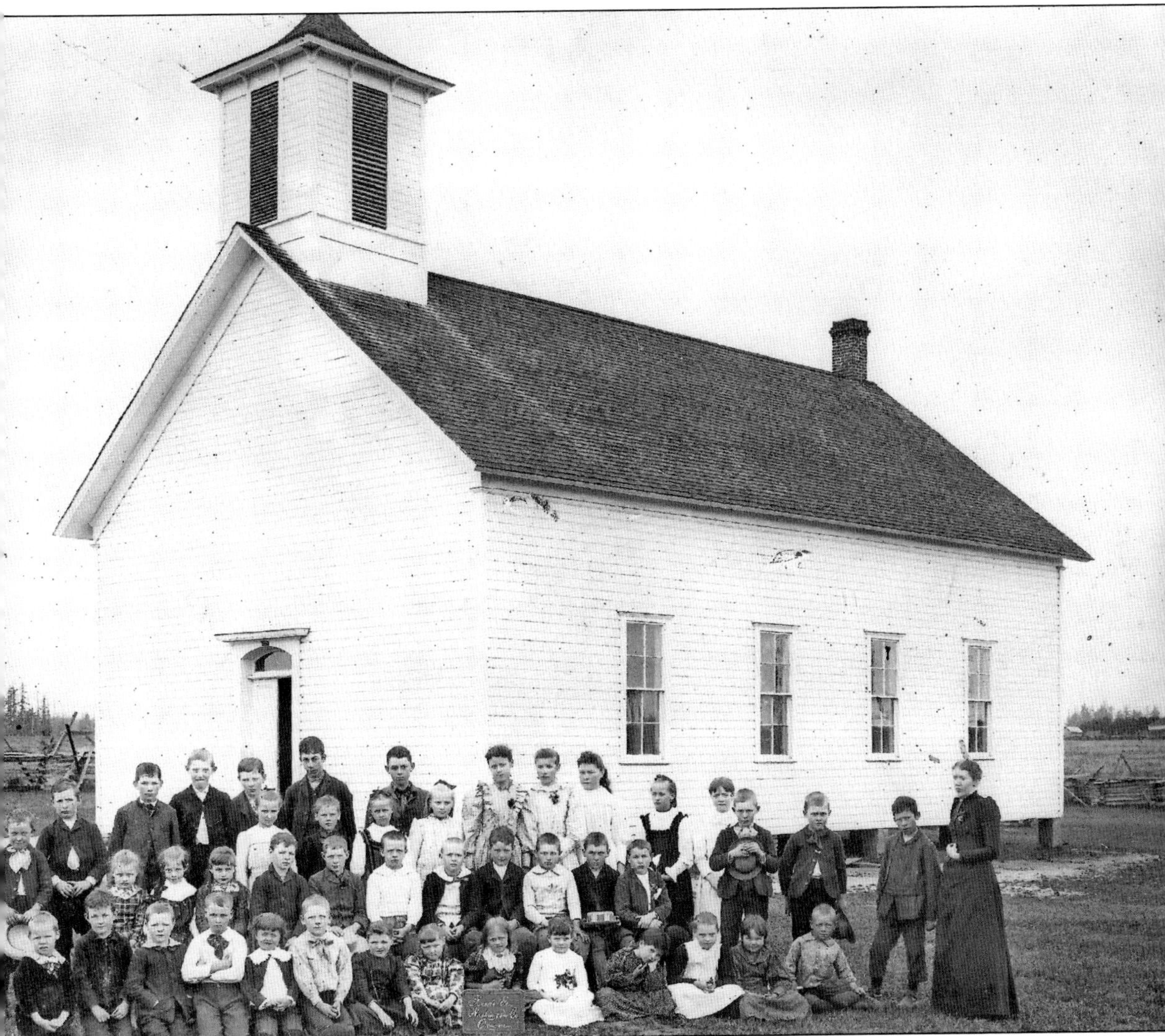

Reedville School in 1893. Teachers to the 44 students who were enrolled that year were Mrs. Woodward, Miss Harvey, Samuel Cazad, and Ward Swope. The deed required school directors Ed Barton and Noah Mull to build a structure within seven months to be "used for school and religious purposes as a place of worship or either of them." By 1865, Reedville School had 20 students. Enrollment reached 32 in 1873. In 1876, Reedville School District was formed by petition, and a two-room school was constructed on concrete footings in 1894–1895. The building was used as a classroom from Monday through Friday and for church meetings and Sunday school conducted by circuit rider ministers. (Oregon Historical Society No. bb009716.)

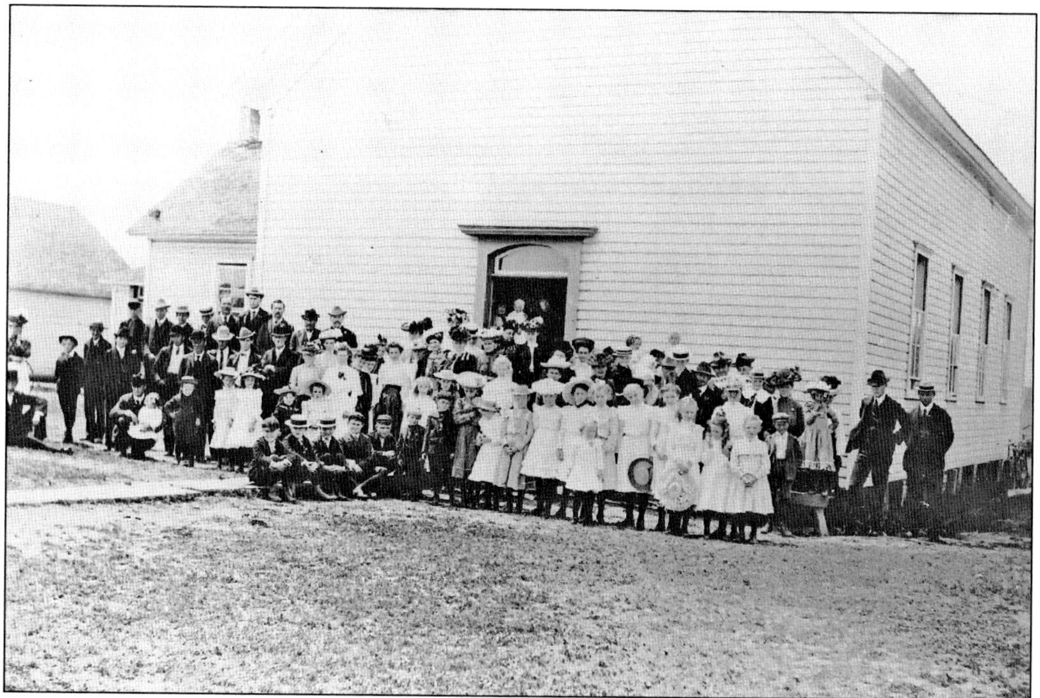

The Reedville Church Congregation, in Front of Reedville School (Above), at the Beginning of the 20th Century. For more than a decade, the school was used for church meetings and Sunday school. The first church (below) was dedicated by Rev. A. Robinson in 1907. The one-and-a-half-acre site was purchased in 1892 by Tualatin Plains Presbyterian Church from the Ladd and Reed Farm Company. After the first church building was constructed for the Reedville congregation, the Reedville Presbyterian Church purchased the deed from the Tualatin Plains church for $1. The building included a sanctuary that seated 75 to 100 people and two rooms for Sunday school. (Both, Reedville Presbyterian Church.)

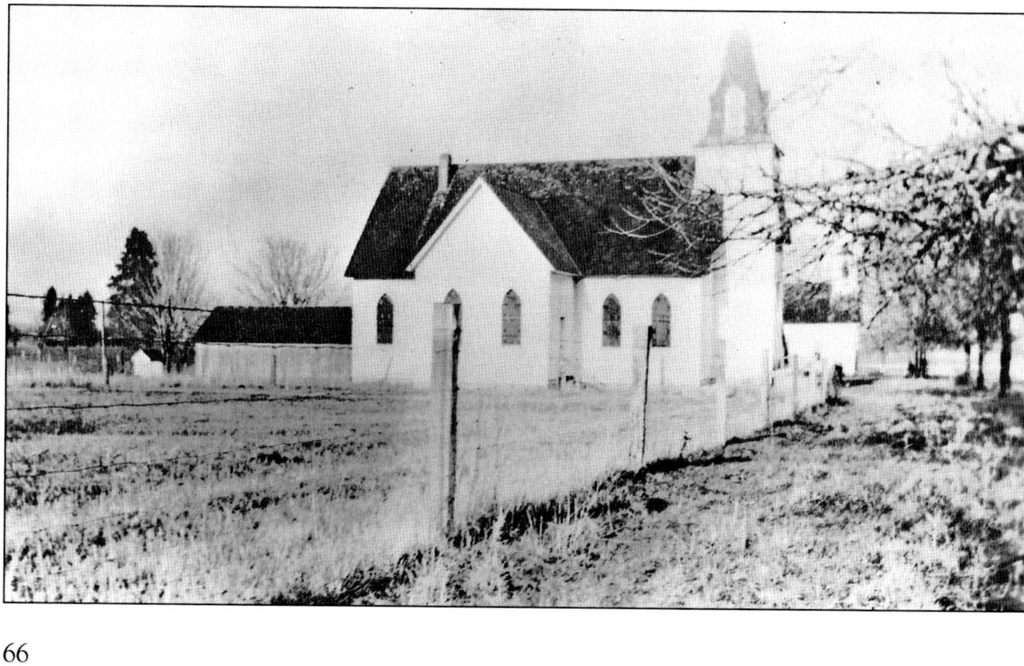

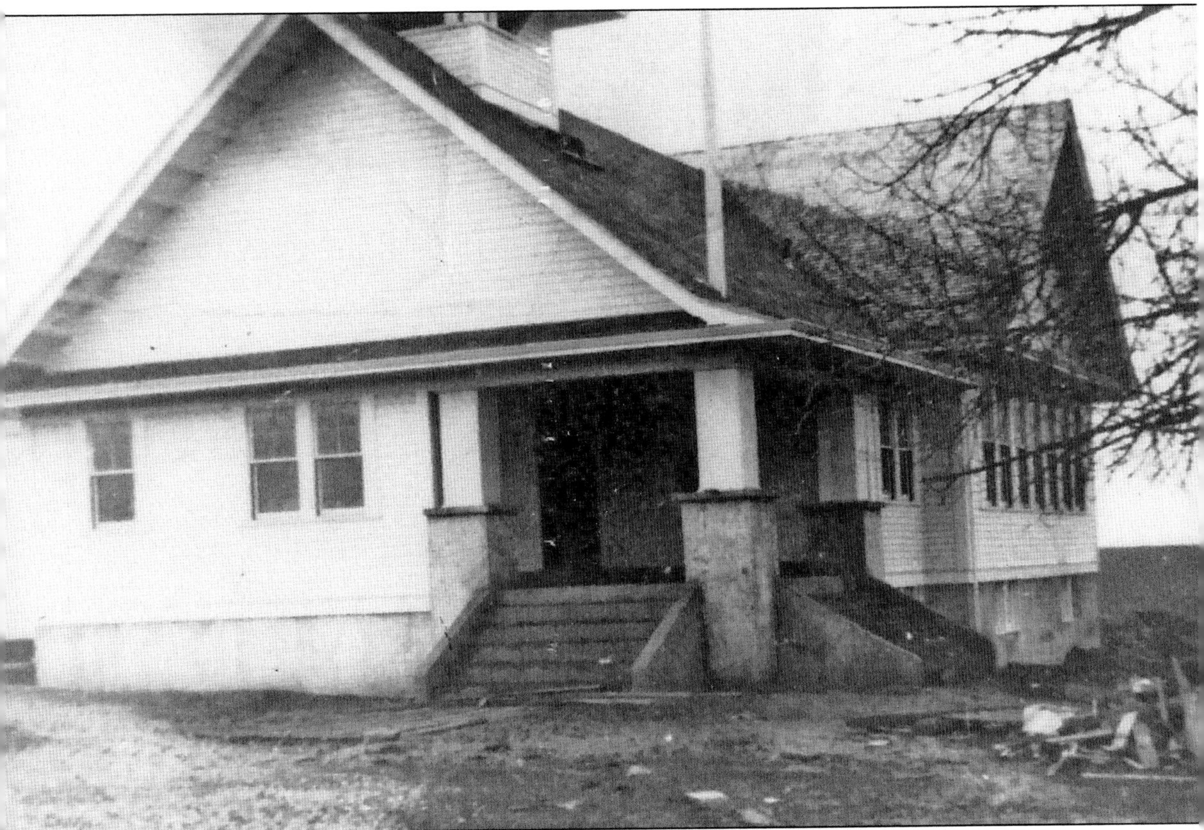

THE REEDVILLE SCHOOL. In 1920, the old two-room school building was sold, and a new three-room school with a basement was constructed (above). The new school cost $8,000. Local residents provided materials and services. J.B. Imlay was paid for shingles, John Kirkwood for hauling lumber and tiles, and John York for typing and blueprint services. C.L. Kinnaman excavated the basement. The Reedville Parent Teacher Association was organized in 1922. Ella Brown was the president. Dues were 10¢ per month. During the winter, students' mothers took turns preparing and serving hot meals, which sold for 2¢. Teachers Oleva Berger and Mary Doran received $125 as a monthly salary. W.J. Wilcox, a Reedville School Board member and father of Reedville School clerk Marion Graf, designed the building. John "J.A." York was another board member in 1920. Anna Lingman held the position of Reedville School clerk for 25 years. (Kathleen Imlay Eames.)

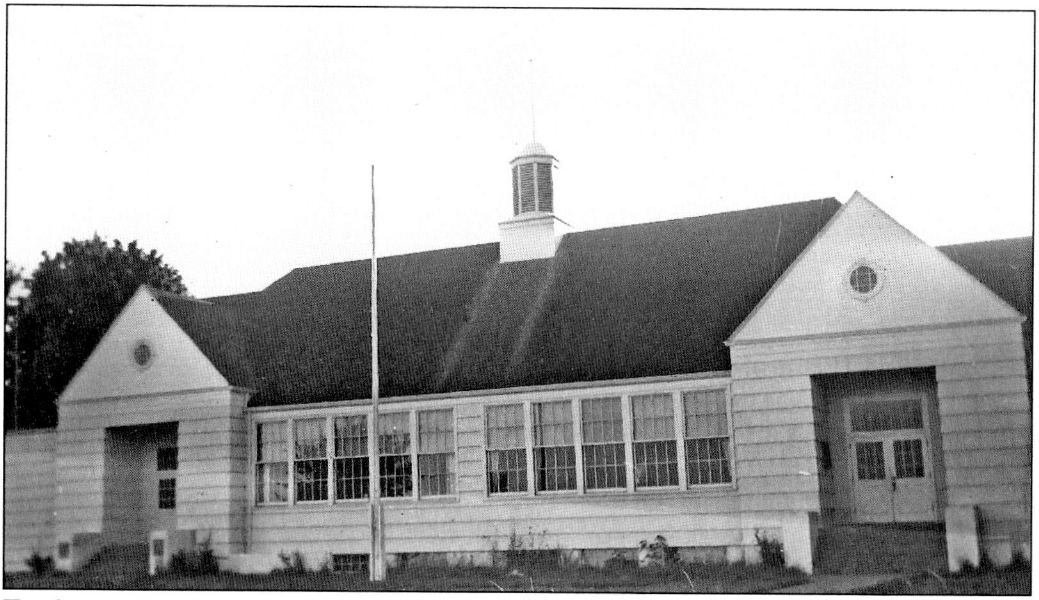

The School Remodeled. In 1938, the Works Progress Administration (WPA) remodeled Reedville School (above), adding four classrooms, a music room, and a gymnasium. School board members included Henry Hagg and Charles Imlay. The PTA helped raise $150 to complete the gymnasium's ceiling and walls just in time for the dedication ceremony. (Kathleen Imlay Eames.)

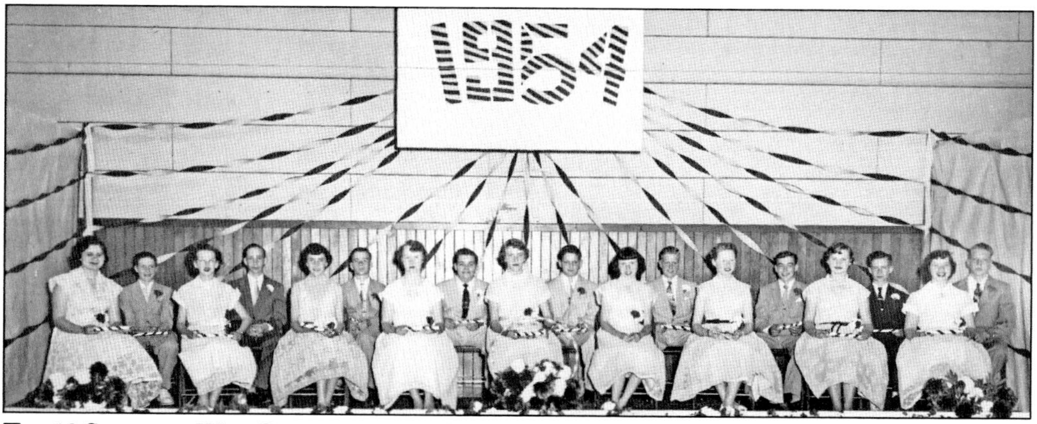

The 18 Students Who Graduated from Reedville School on May 19, 1954. Their class motto was "Believe that you can." Class colors were red and white, and the class flower was the carnation. That year, spring vacation was two days long, March 18 and 19. (Washington County Museum.)

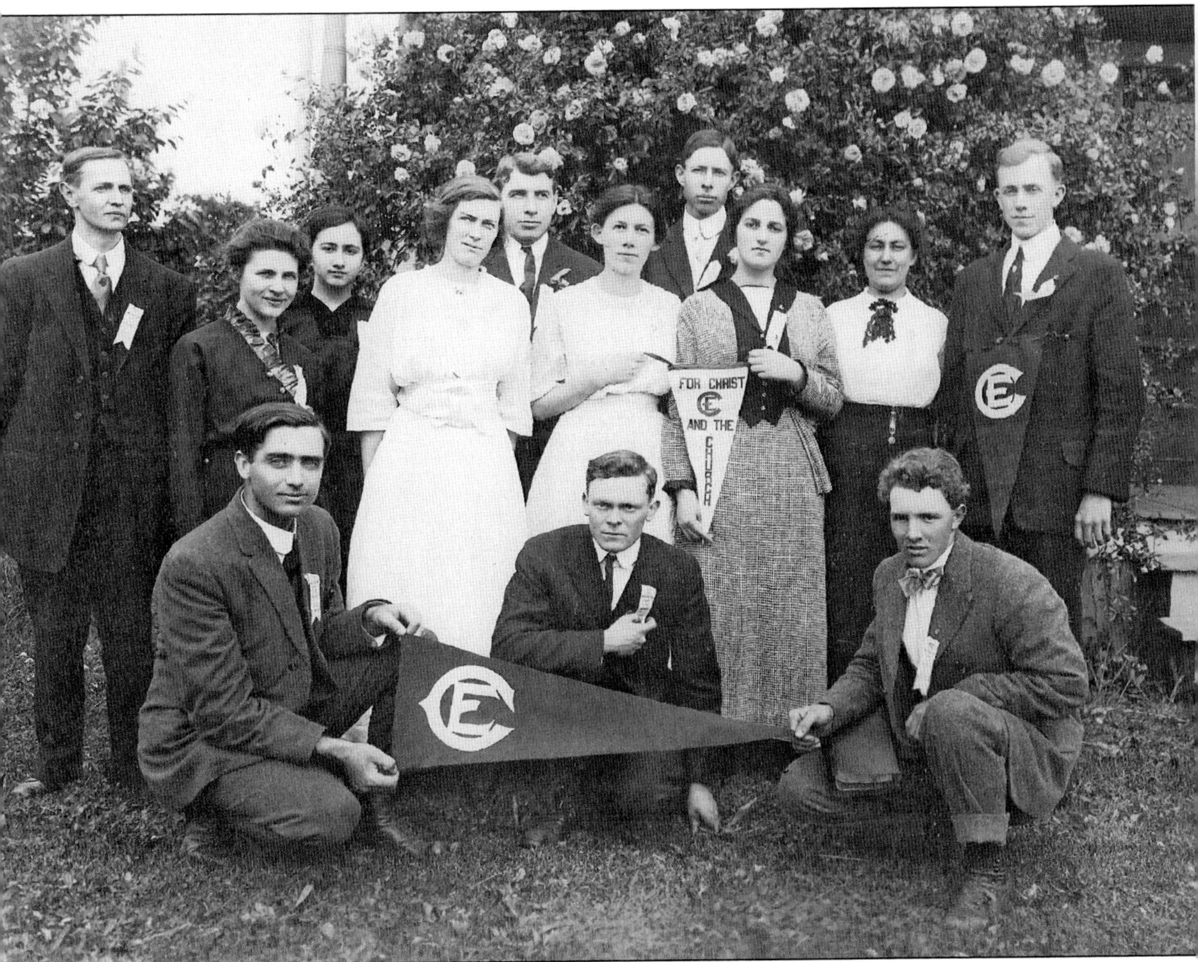

The Executive Committee of the Christian Endeavor Union (CEU), 1914. The CEU met regularly while a church in Reedville was being organized, sometimes sharing a building with the Reedville School. From left to right are (first row) Claude Hutchens, K.J. Dixon, and Rex Dallas; (second row) Liola House, Norma Dixon, Elcy Walker, and Edith Gerrirus; (third row) Mr. Simpson, Edith Robb, Clause Bryant, Annabe Taylor, and Alva Patten. A Washington County Christian Endeavor Union was chartered for Reedville Presbyterian Church in 1895. Although a church building was not constructed for another 12 years, the group was a part of a larger organization of seven local communities. It participated in conventions held in Portland and surrounding communities that culminated in parades featuring elaborate floats. A CEU group met at Reedville Presbyterian Church until the mid-1960s. (Reedville Presbyterian Church.)

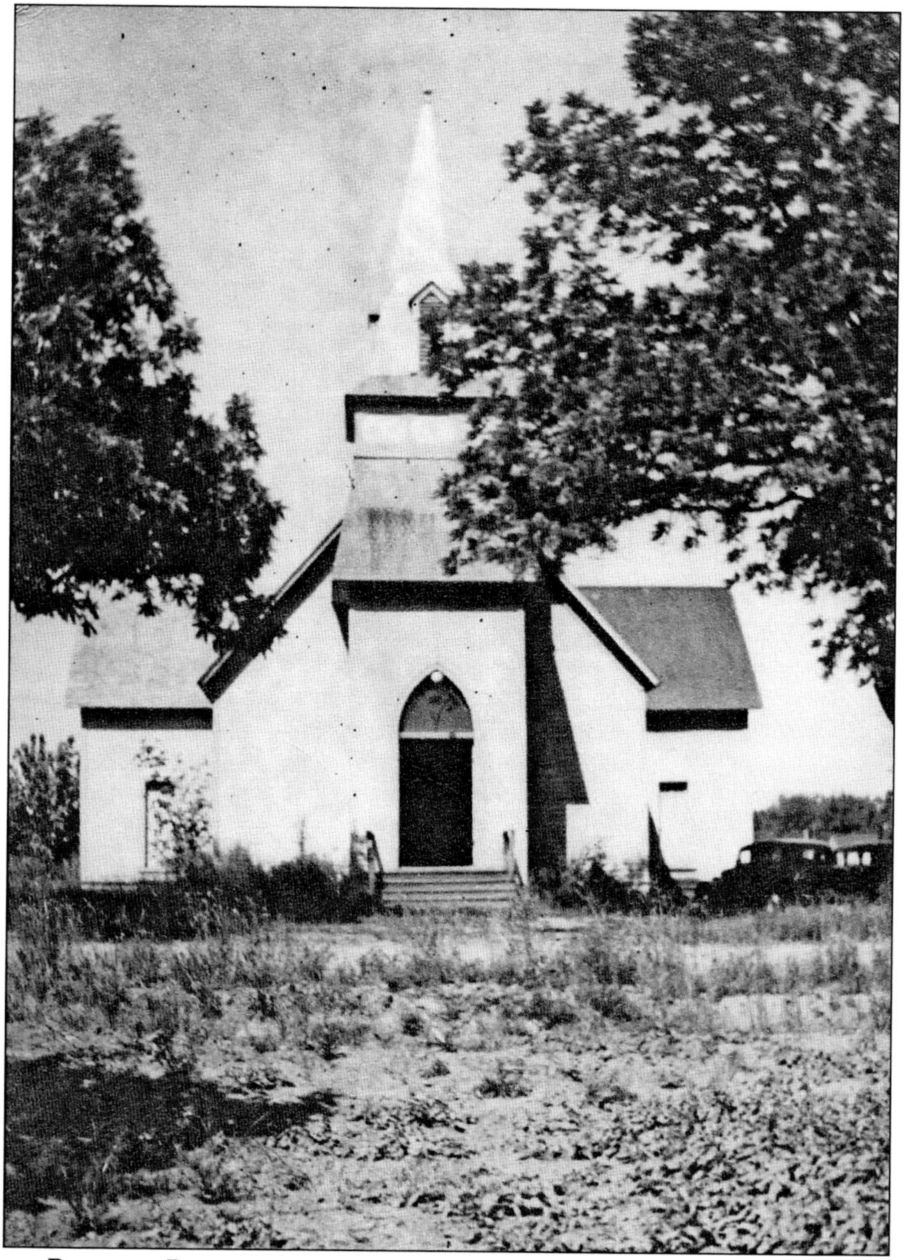

The First Reedville Presbyterian Church in 1940, Before It Was Destroyed by Fire. On Sunday, November 26, 1944, a fire of unknown origin ignited in the woodshed. It was discovered in the west end of the building by a sailor who was driving by. Community members rushed to remove the piano, pulpit, communion table, and pews before the building was completely engulfed in flames. The American, Christian, and service flags, Sunday school records, and photographs of church members serving in the military during World War II were saved. The fire was prevented from spreading to the nearby Reedville School by the Beaverton Rural Fire Protection Department. The loss was only partially covered by insurance. A second church building was constructed by volunteers and dedicated in 1947. A grand piano, salvaged from the fire, is still in use today. (Reedville Presbyterian Church.)

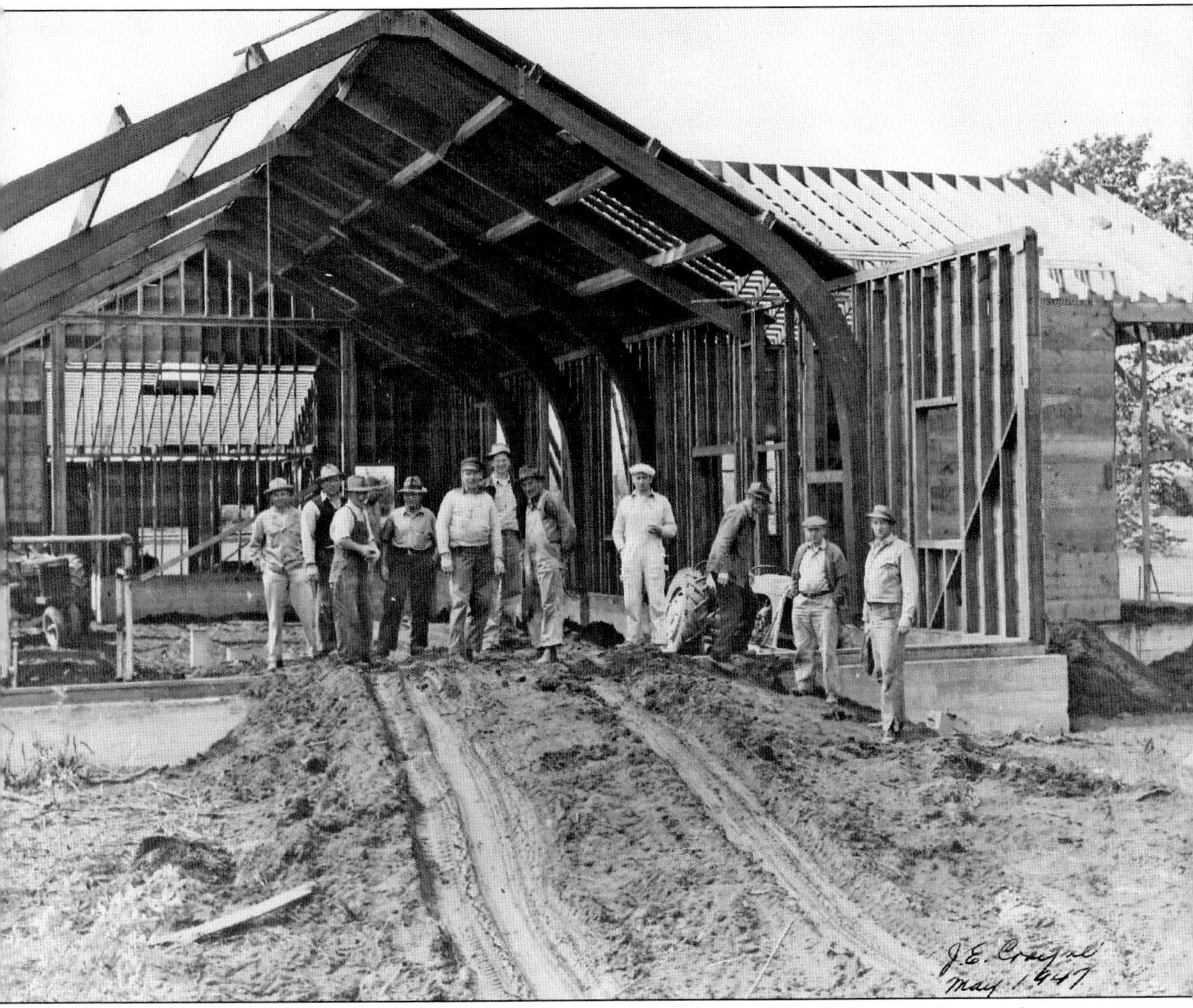

VOLUNTEERS REBUILDING REEDVILLE PRESBYTERIAN CHURCH IN 1947. From left to right are Bob Millar, Fred Lambert, Oscar Hagg, Melvin Vandermost, Archie Brownlee, Gordon Diehl, Allan Larrance, Tom Miller, Vic Perry, Elmer LaRue, and Al Schappert. The original church building was destroyed in a fire in 1944, during World War II. In 1947, when the war was over, the congregation bid on, and was awarded, a decommissioned US Army chapel from Camp Adair, north of Corvallis, Oregon. It was one of 36 buildings, including 12 chapels, that were salvaged as surplus and distributed throughout the state of Oregon. Church volunteers traveled to Camp Adair, disassembled the building, then loaded and transported the materials in 18 truckloads to Reedville within a two-week period. The building was reassembled on site. The chapel was converted into a sanctuary that is still in use today. (Reedville Presbyterian Church.)

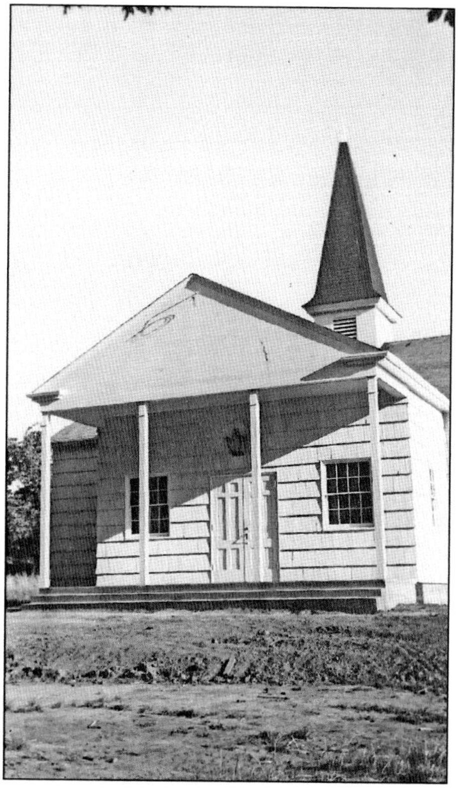

The Reconstructed Reedville Presbyterian Church, Dedicated on June 29, 1947. The congregation waited three years before bidding on and being awarded a decommissioned US Army chapel. It was used as a sanctuary in the new church. The original church was destroyed by fire in 1944. (Reedville Presbyterian Church.)

Reedville Presbyterian Church, Established in 1907, as It Appears Today, Viewed from Southwest 209th Avenue. The site is adjacent to the 1938 Reedville School. They were built on land originally deeded by Nathan and Mary Robinson. (Reedville Presbyterian Church.)

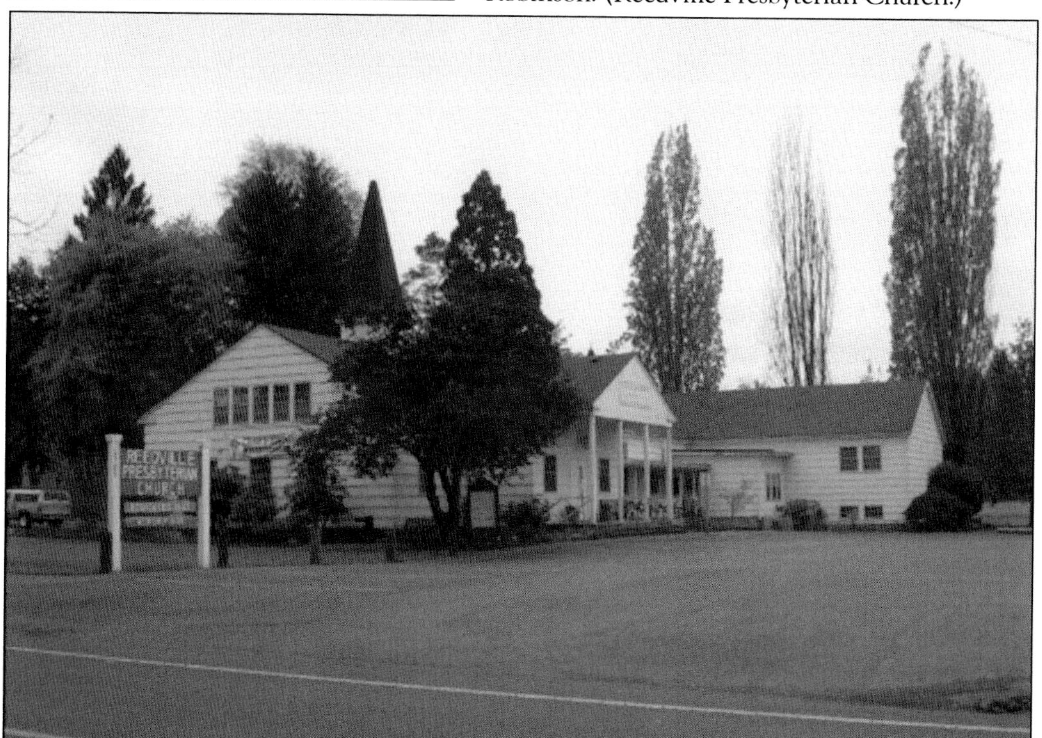

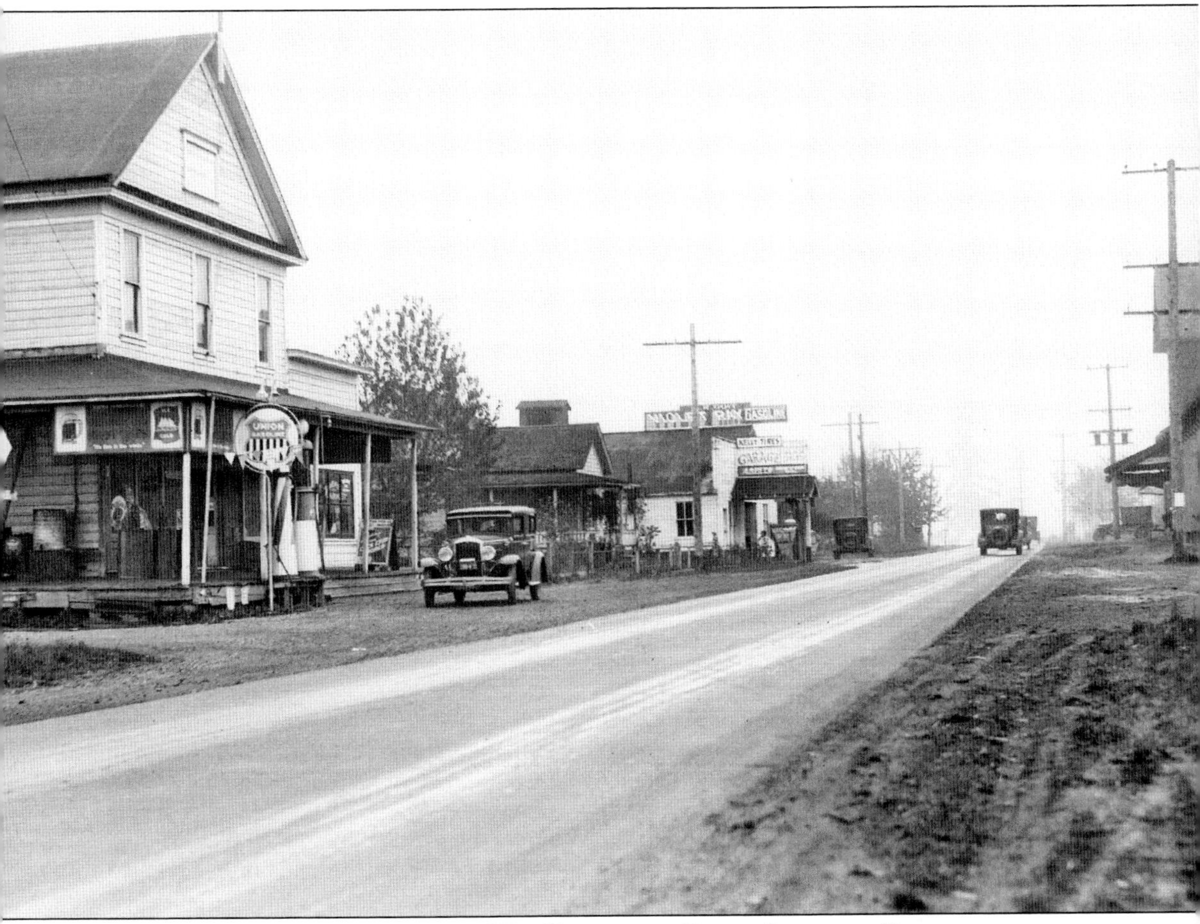

Looking toward Aloha from What Was Platted as Front Street in Reedville around 1929. Later, Front Street was incorporated into Tualatin Valley Highway. The historic Reedville store (left) was located on the northwest corner of today's Southwest 214th Avenue. Lafayette Goit's residence was next door. They were located across the highway from the J.B. Imlay & Sons mill, feed, and seed store. Built around 1890, the Imlay buildings are still in operation today as Harvey Marine. Tualatin Valley Highway, a two-lane road built for automobiles, became part of the Oregon State Highway System in 1918. It was widened and resurfaced in 1933. In 1925–1926, the population of Reedville was 105. In addition to the Imlay mill and Reedville church, there was a mercantile, four dairies, two poultry breeders, and four automotive-related businesses. (9904-G16 © Historic Photo Archive.)

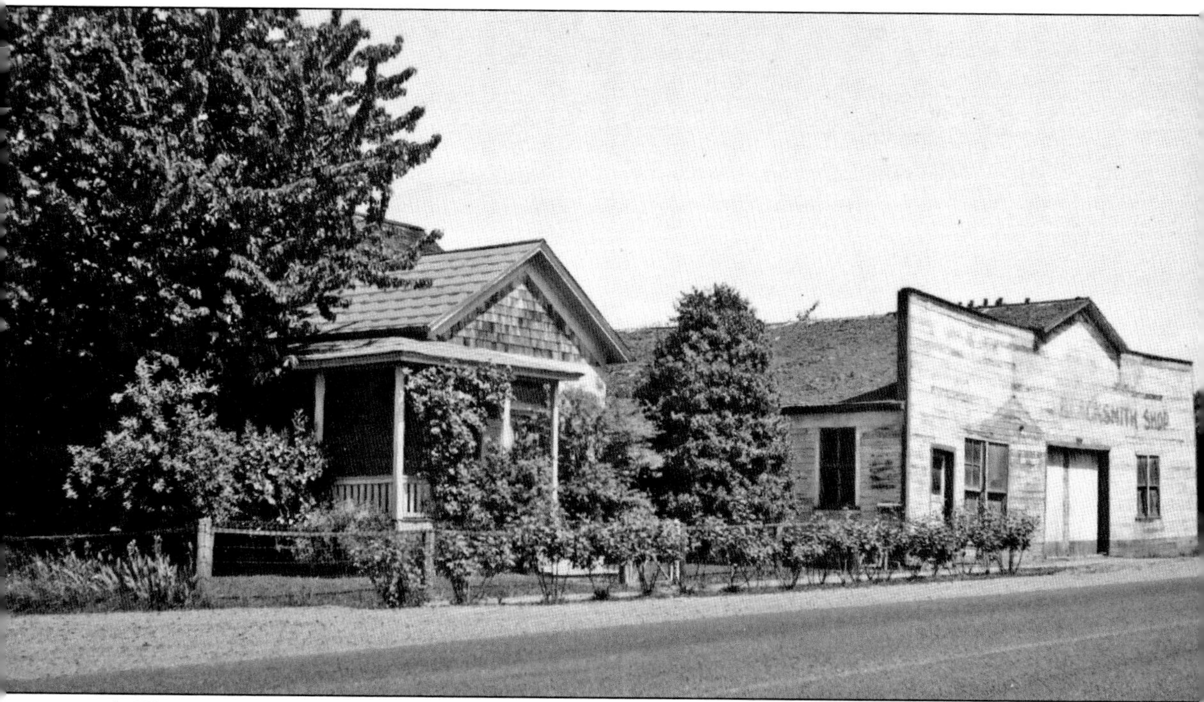

A House and What Was Once a Blacksmith Shop and Motor Garage Belonging to Lafayette "Laffy" Ransford Goit in Reedville around 1947. They were located on the north side of Tualatin Valley Highway, east of the old Reedville store on today's Southwest 214th Avenue. Goit was a blacksmith specializing in wagon wheels and plowshares. After the beginning of the 20th century, hand-forged smithing skills were becoming obsolete due to the popularity of the internal combustion engine. By 1929, Goit operated the L.R. Goit Garage and Black Smith shop, selling Violet Ray gasoline, Kelly tires, and Aristo motor oil. Goit was born in Tuscola, Michigan, in 1866. He married Ann Kirby in Dawson, Nebraska, in 1890. There were two children, George Robert and Sarah Ann. Later, in 1912, Goit married Anna M. Goeddertz in Portland. They moved to Reedville in 1916. (Washington County Museum.)

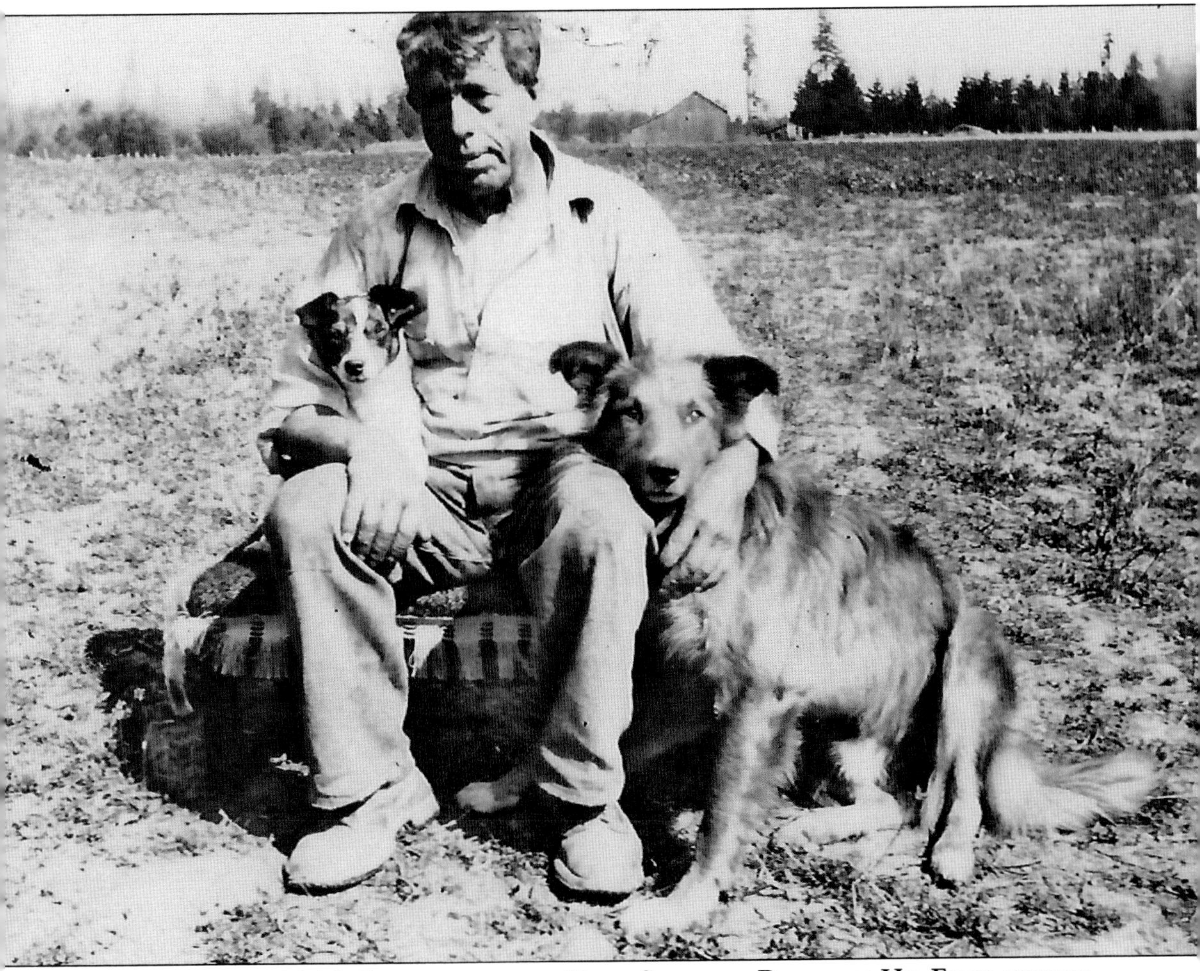

James Marshall "J.M." Churchley with Dogs Snip and Bubbs on His Farm outside Reedville. The son of Job David Churchley, a tailor, and Mercy Ann Howill, J.M. Churchley was born in 1876 in England. Churchley immigrated to the United States and married Josie Bonge in Portland in 1895. They purchased acreage near Reedville in 1912. Initially, the land was heavily forested. The Churchleys felled and chopped trees into cordwood for fuel and transported it by horse and wagon to the rail depot in Reedville, destined for the Churchley Brothers Wood Yard in Portland. Churchley held the office of secretary-treasurer in the business he operated with his brothers. In the 1920s, the Churchleys operated a dairy with a small herd of Jersey cows. The family cultivated corn, potatoes, onions, and wheat on the farm. (Susanna Schappert Keith.)

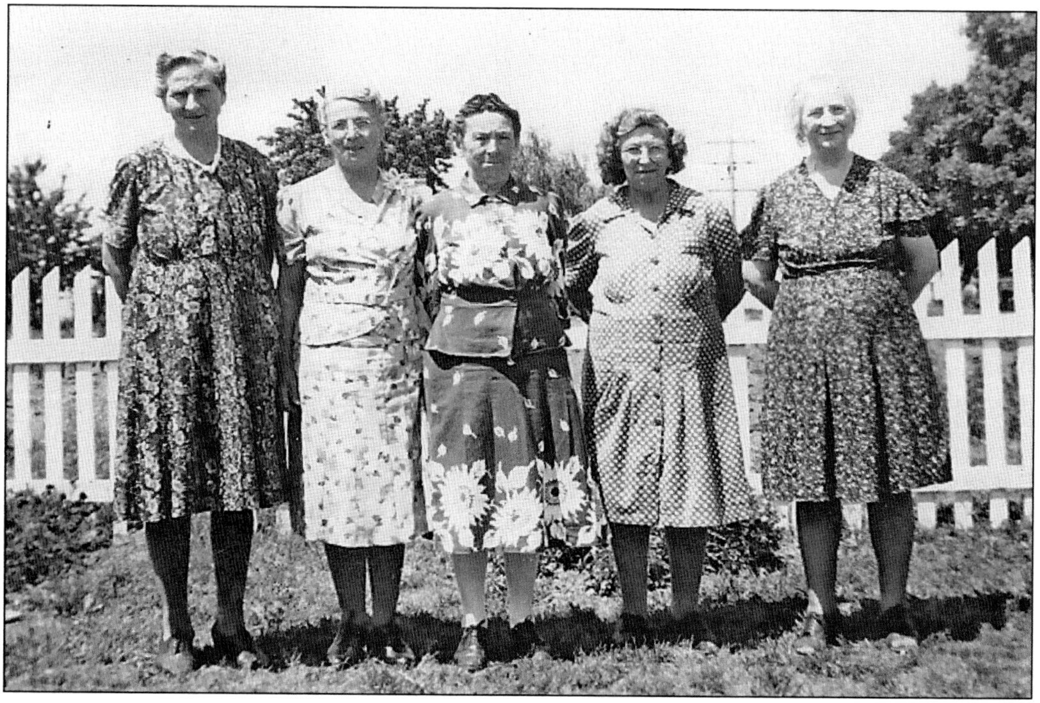

JOSIE CHURCHLEY AND HER SISTERS AROUND 1950. Born in Nebraska in 1879, Josie (above center) moved to Cedar Mill and, in 1895, married J.M. Churchley in Portland. Their children were Howard, James, Clarence, Jesse, Gertrude, and Homer "Scotty." They attended Jacktown and Rosedale Schools. Howard and Clarence also owned property on Front Street in Reedville. Below is the residence of J.M. and Josie Churchley on their farm near Southwest Rosedale Road. The Churchleys settled on a farm near Reedville in 1912. Their house faced what was Churchley Road. (Both, Susanna Schappert Keith.)

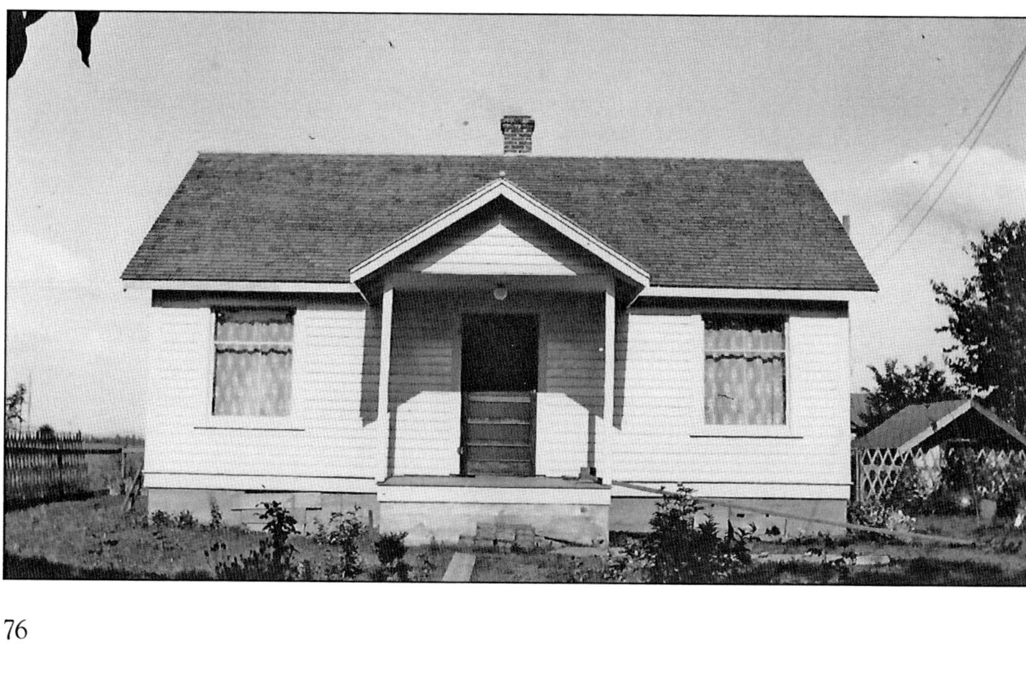

J.M. and Josie Churchley's Daughter Gertrude and Her Husband, Ralph Schappert, 1930s. She was born and grew up on the family farm near what was once Churchley Road, today's Southwest 229th Avenue. Each of the Churchley children received 10 acres of land from their father. (Susanna Schappert Keith.)

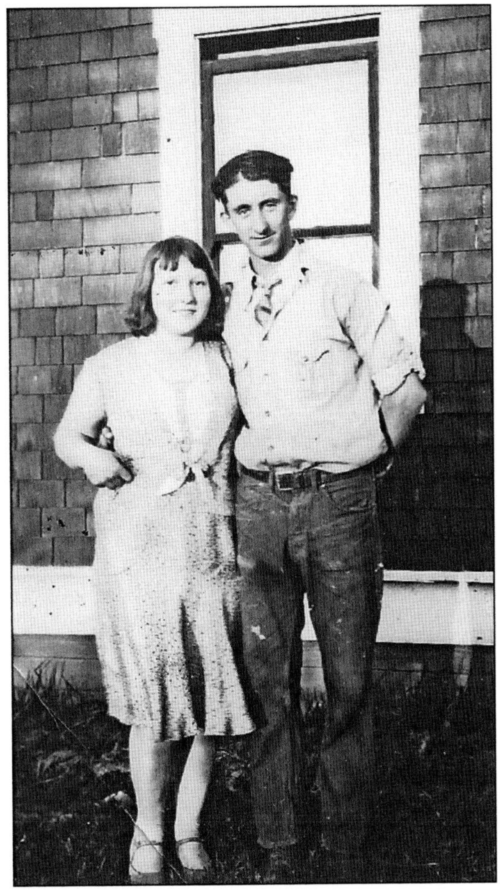

Ralph Schappert Plowing a Field with a Team of Horses. During the Great Depression, tractors were scarce, so farmers used draft horses to pull plows, discs, and other implements for cultivating the soil and for planting and harvesting crops. The Schapperts grew potatoes, corn, and wheat on their farm. (Susanna Schappert Keith.)

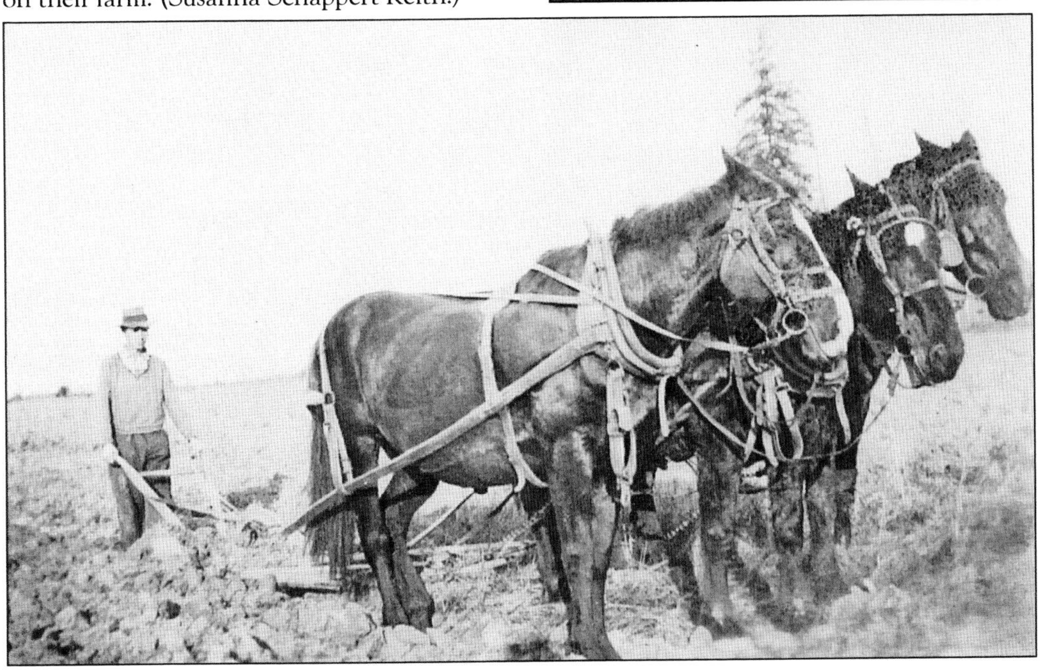

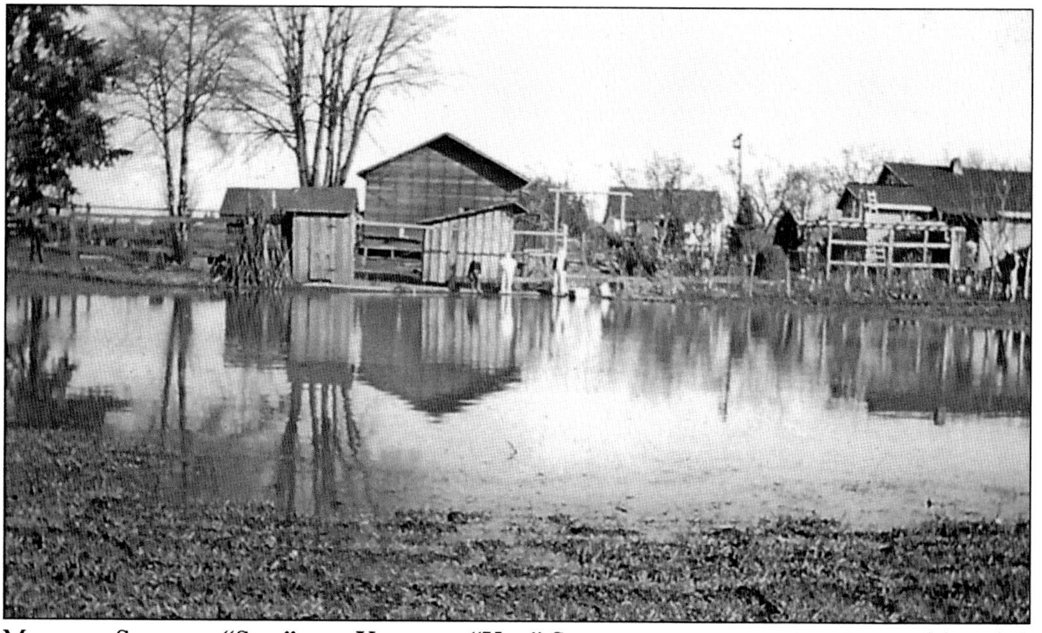

Michael, Susanna "Sue," and Kenneth "Ken" Schappert in the 1940s. Pictured from left to right in the distance, they are overlooking a field on the family farm that flooded every winter. For decades, the Schapperts cut and felled timber and removed tree stumps to clear their land for cultivation and grazing. (Susanna Schappert Keith.)

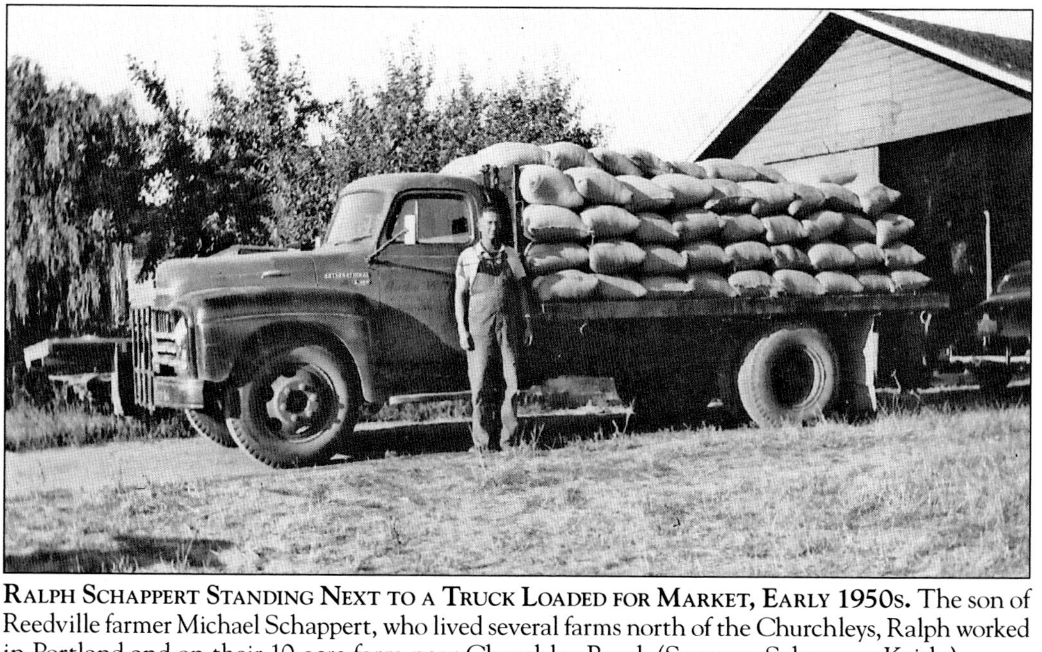

Ralph Schappert Standing Next to a Truck Loaded for Market, Early 1950s. The son of Reedville farmer Michael Schappert, who lived several farms north of the Churchleys, Ralph worked in Portland and on their 10-acre farm near Churchley Road. (Susanna Schappert Keith.)

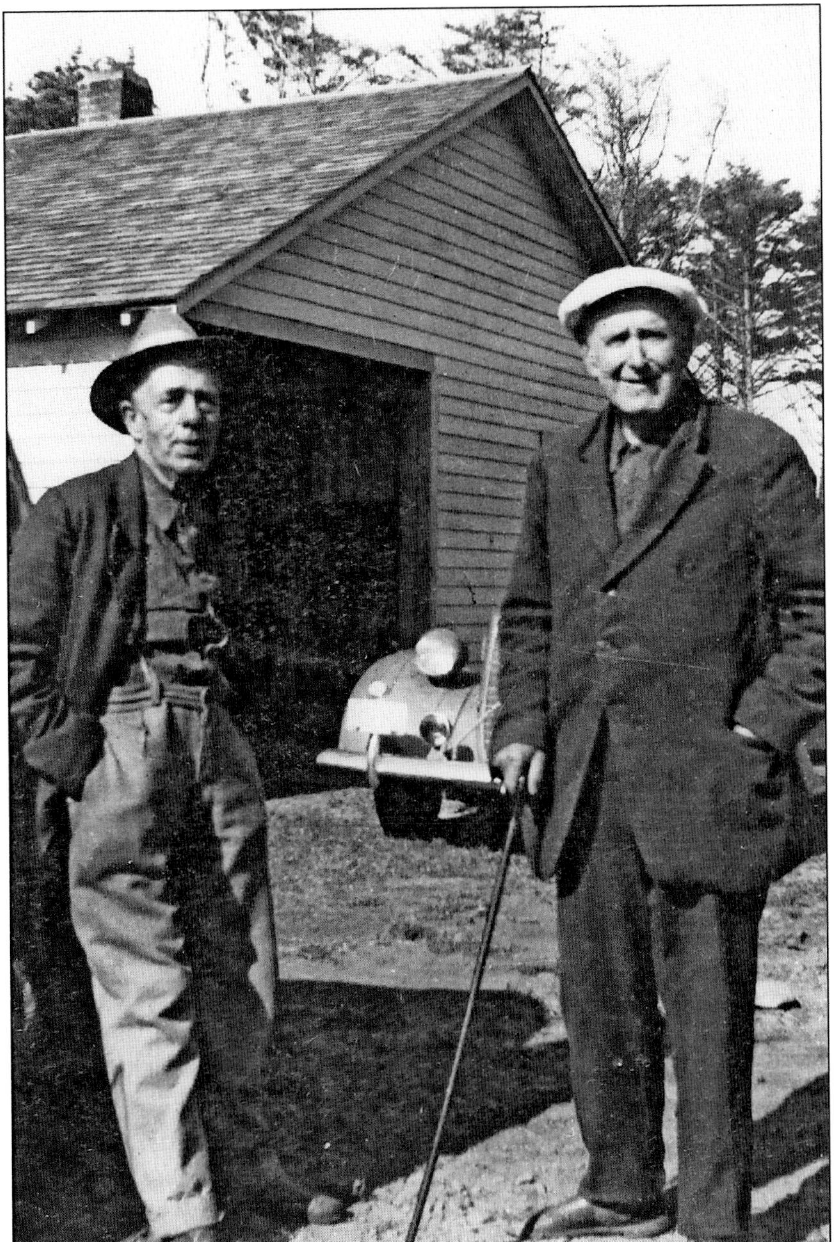

Reedville Farmers and Neighbors J.M. Churchley and David Hagg, 1930s. Both were European immigrants who settled in Washington County at the turn of the 20th century. Hagg, originally from Sweden, arrived in Portland in 1883 from New Britain, Connecticut. In 1887, he married Augusta Stenstrom. They purchased 160 acres of land south of the Reed farm in 1890. For three years, Hagg walked to and from his job in Portland; then he lived, farmed, and operated a dairy in Reedville for 62 years. Churchley, originally from England, purchased acreage in 1910 near today's Southwest Rosedale Road and 229th Avenue. In the late 1800s, railroads published and distributed promotional brochures to recruit European immigrants to the western United States. In Oregon, the population nearly doubled every decade between 1860 and 1890, when it grew at a rate of 1,000 per week. (Susanna Schappert Keith.)

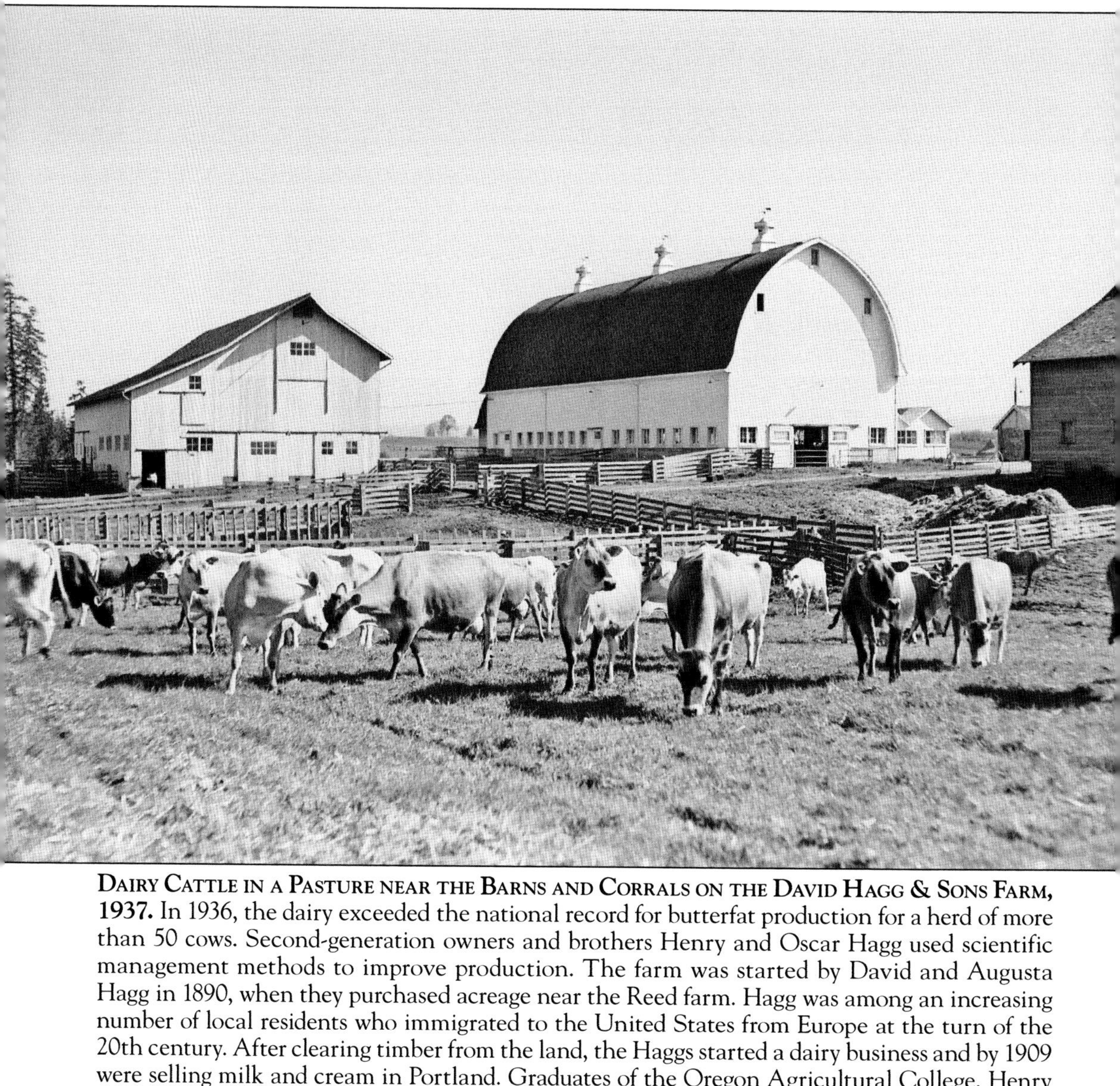

DAIRY CATTLE IN A PASTURE NEAR THE BARNS AND CORRALS ON THE DAVID HAGG & SONS FARM, 1937. In 1936, the dairy exceeded the national record for butterfat production for a herd of more than 50 cows. Second-generation owners and brothers Henry and Oscar Hagg used scientific management methods to improve production. The farm was started by David and Augusta Hagg in 1890, when they purchased acreage near the Reed farm. Hagg was among an increasing number of local residents who immigrated to the United States from Europe at the turn of the 20th century. After clearing timber from the land, the Haggs started a dairy business and by 1909 were selling milk and cream in Portland. Graduates of the Oregon Agricultural College, Henry and Oscar Hagg were dairy industry leaders and founding members of the Aloha Grange. Henry championed agricultural education and research. Oscar was president of the Oregon Dairymen's Association and director of the Oregon Dairy Council. (9969-2961 Alfred A. Monner © Historic Photo Archive.)

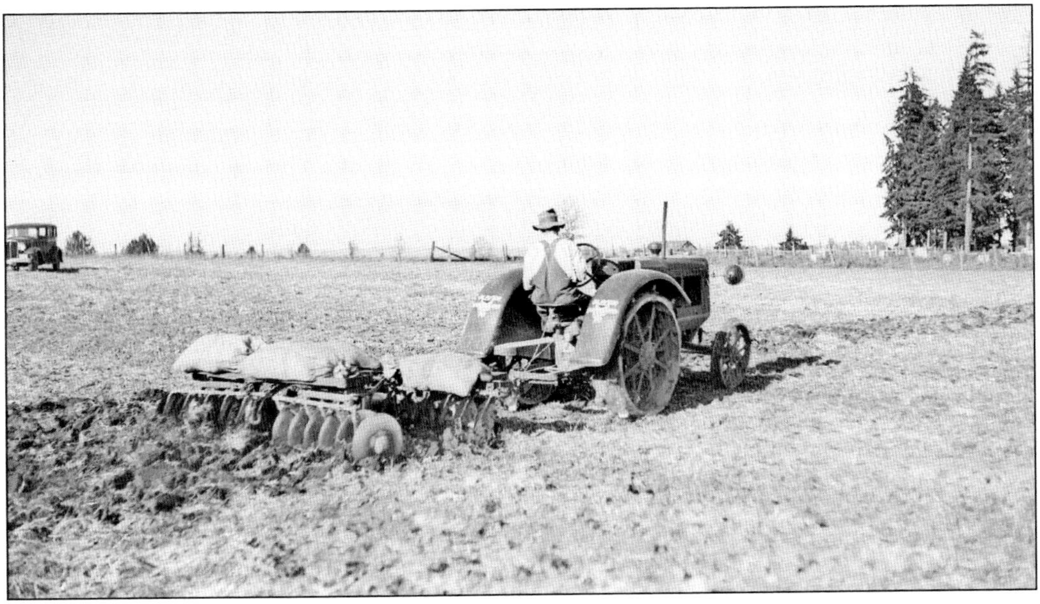

Preparing the Soil for Planting on the David Hagg & Sons Farm in Reedville. On April 30, 1937, a disc harrow pulled by a tractor prepared the seedbed in one of the fields (above). The next day (below), a team of horses drag a spring-tooth harrow across the soil. In 1937, the farm had a herd of 100 cows and heifers, of which 15 were pure-bred Jerseys. The dairy started with a small, mixed herd of cows, then introduced pedigreed stock which they found to be no guarantee of high milk and butterfat production. (Above, 9969-2958; below, 9969-2963, Alfred A. Monner © Historic Photo Archive.)

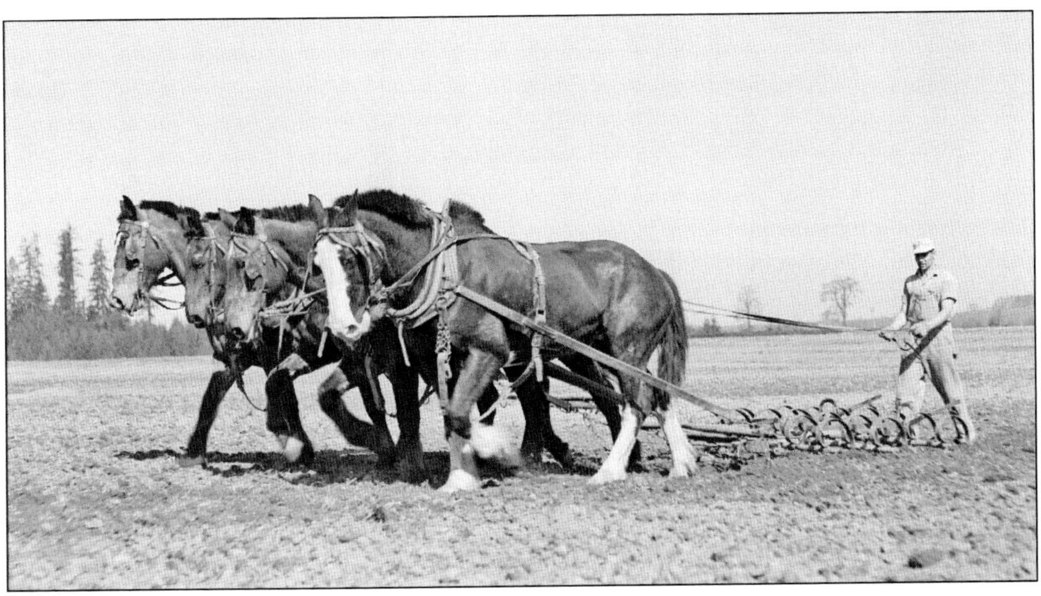

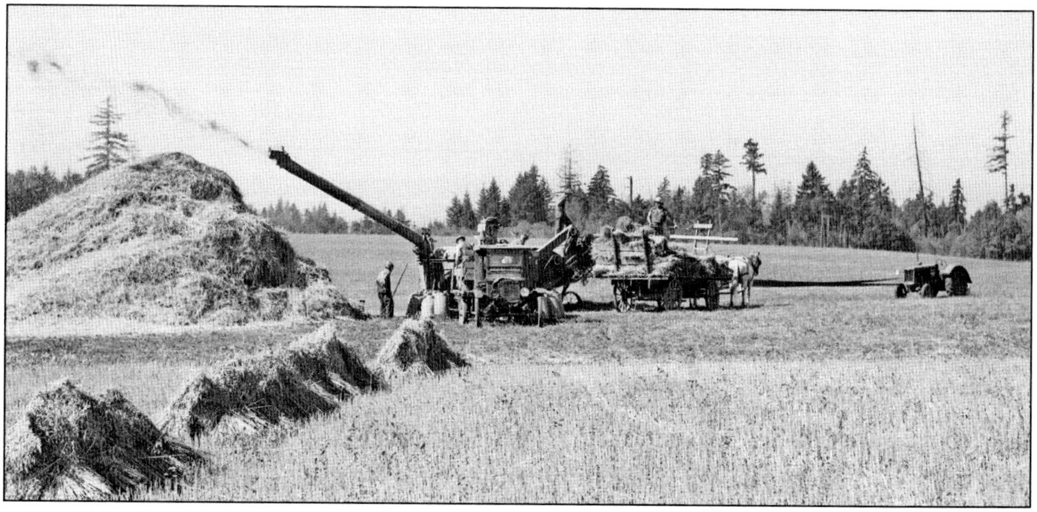

Harvesting Oats on the David Hagg & Sons Farm near Reedville, September 1937. Oat stalks in the foreground (above) were cut, bundled, and stacked in windrows. After drying, they were loaded onto a horse-drawn wagon or bundle rack and fed into a threshing machine that separated stalks from grain, then transported by elevator into burlap bags and loaded into a wagon (below). The sacks were transported to the railroad depot or the J.B. Imlay & Sons mill in Reedville. Hay was blown out the back of the machine into a stack. (Above, 9969-3273; below, 9969-3277, Alfred A. Monner © Historic Photo Archive.)

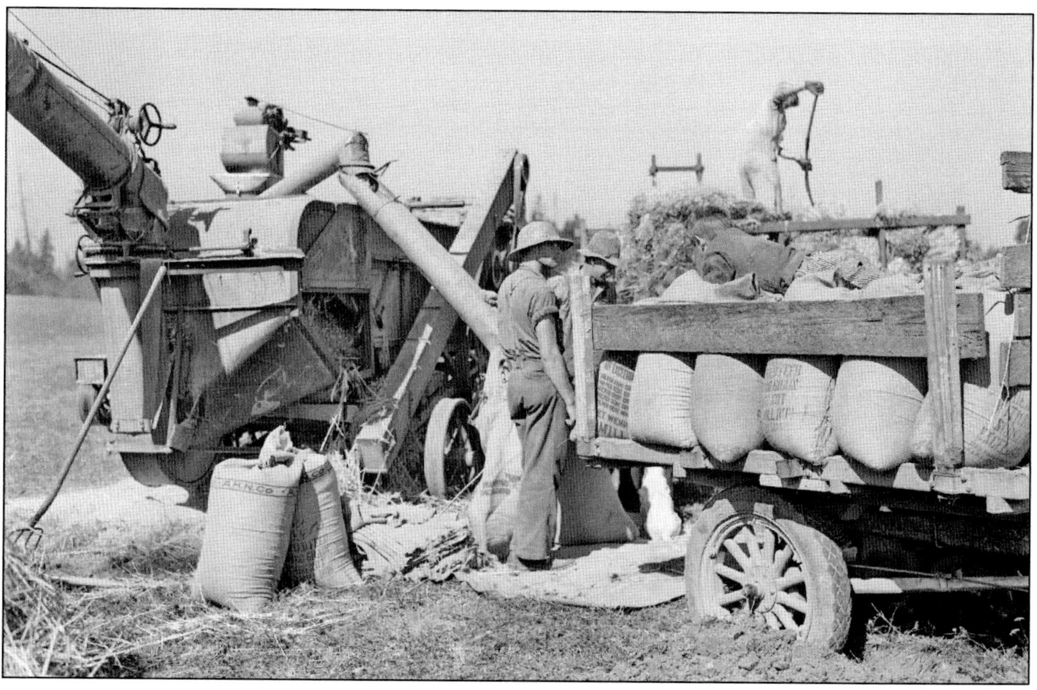

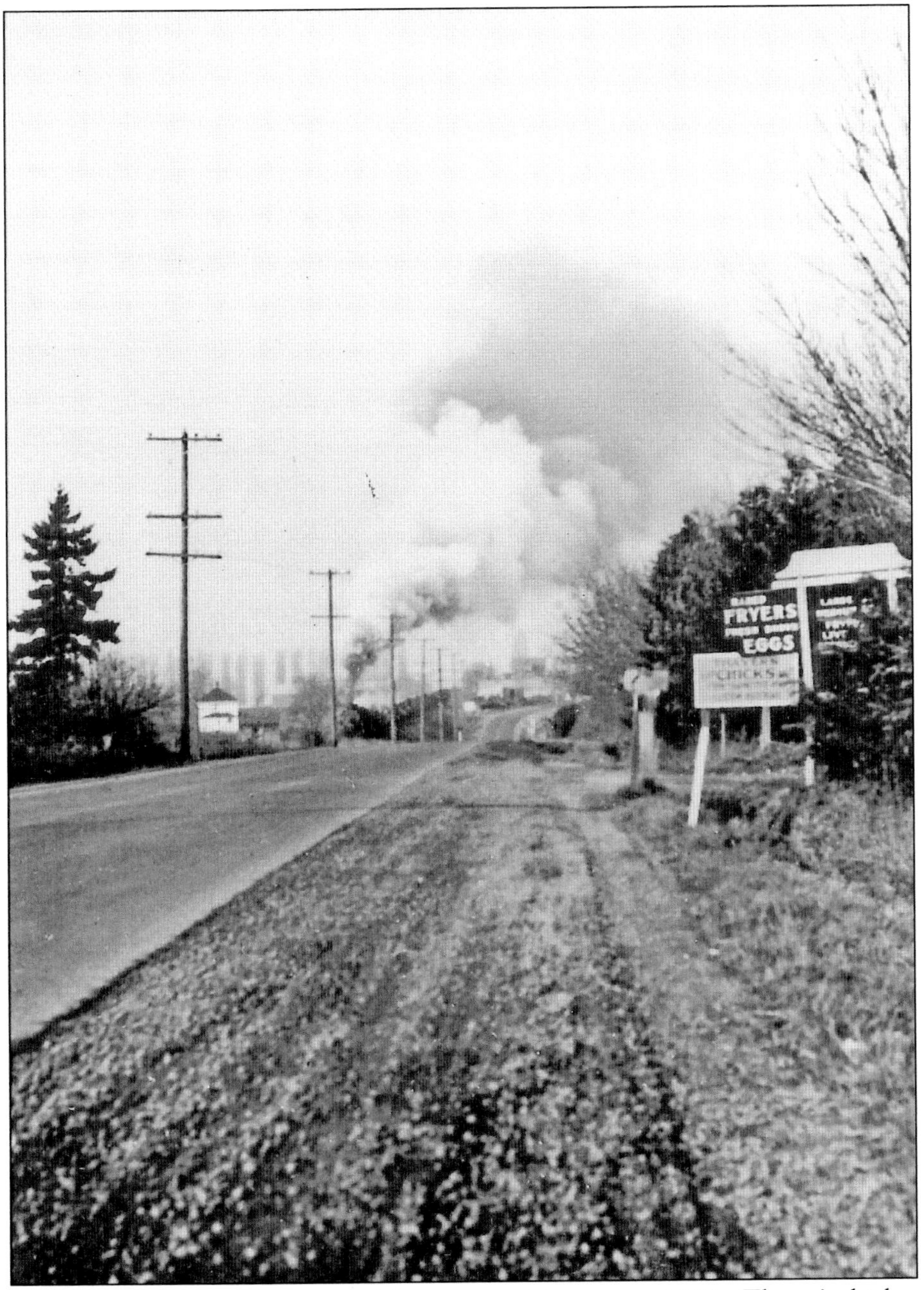

Tualatin Valley Highway Looking West toward Reedville, 1940s. Thayer's chicken farm (right) was located on the north side of the road. In the distance at left, a steam locomotive is traveling east toward Beaverton. Beyond is the A.M. Jannsen Well Drilling Company machine shop (left). The double row of poplar trees is located on what was then the Kelly farm. The 10-acre Thayer's chicken farm, which specialized in Rhode Island Reds, included a hatchery, range houses, a retail store, and several residences. Every Friday, company employees set out in a green panel truck on their regular route, traveling west on Highway 26 to Tillamook, up Highway 101 as far as Gearhart, and back to the Reedville farm, selling chickens and eggs along the way. Thayer's chicken farm operated from 1931 until the early 1960s. (Carolyn Thayer Guinther.)

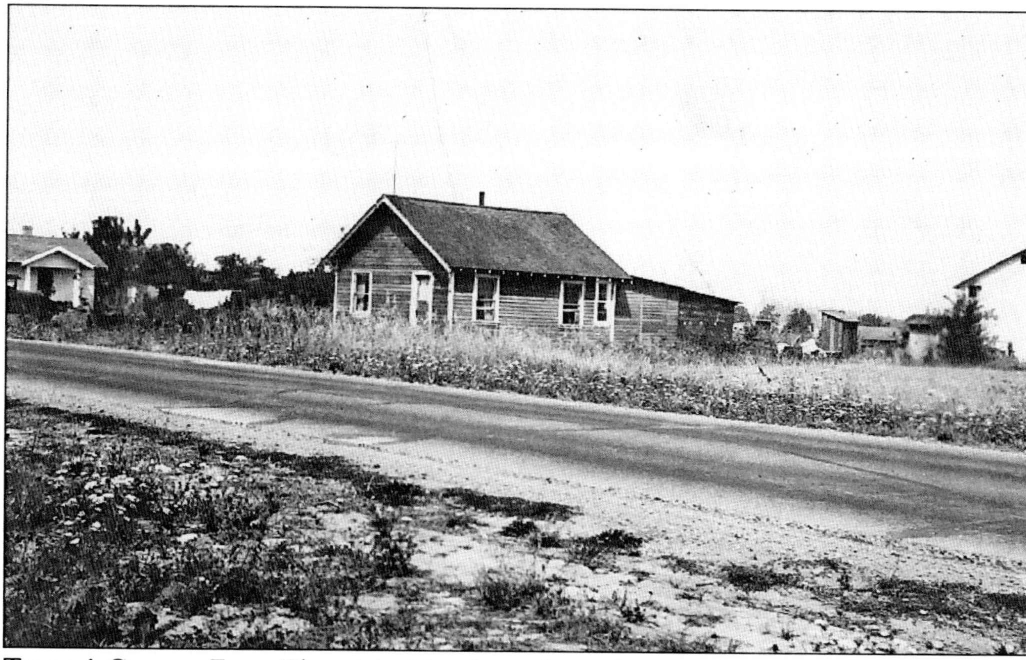

THAYER'S CHICKEN FARM. The original farmhouse (center) was on the property when the Thayer family purchased 10 acres in 1931. Located north of Tualatin Valley Highway, it was between today's Southwest 198th and 209th Avenues on land that was once part of the Masters' Donation Land Claim. (Carolyn Thayer Guinther.)

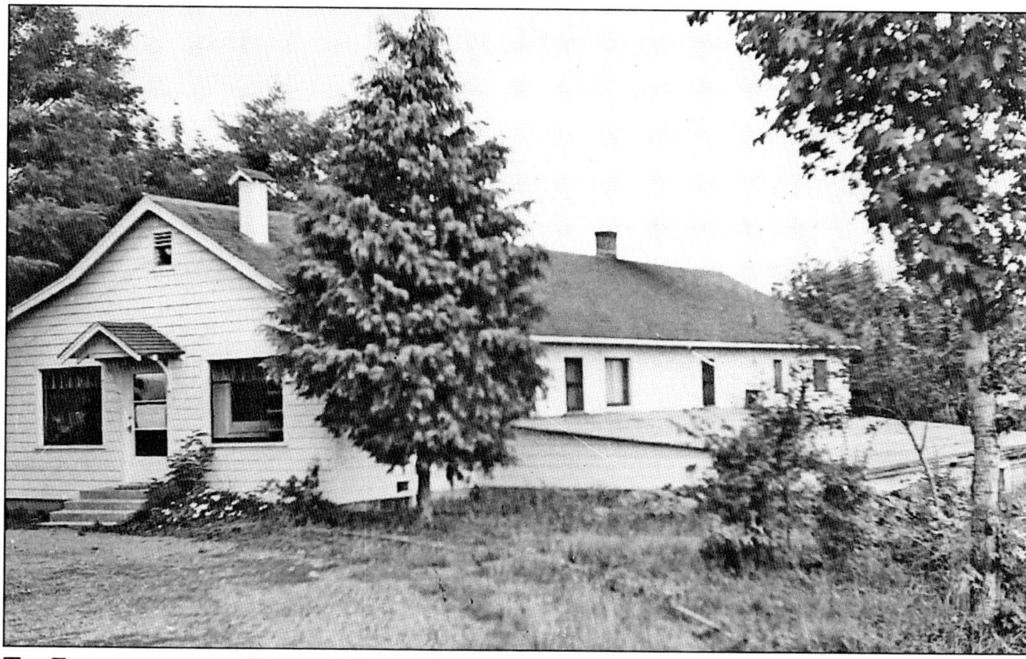

THE ENTRANCE TO THE THAYER'S RETAIL STORE. In addition to owning and managing the business, Helen Thayer and her daughter Carolyn lived behind the store. A building extending to the right contained one of three incubators used to hatch chicks. Helen Thayer's mother, Zeviah Porter Allen, also lived on the farm. (Carolyn Thayer Guinther.)

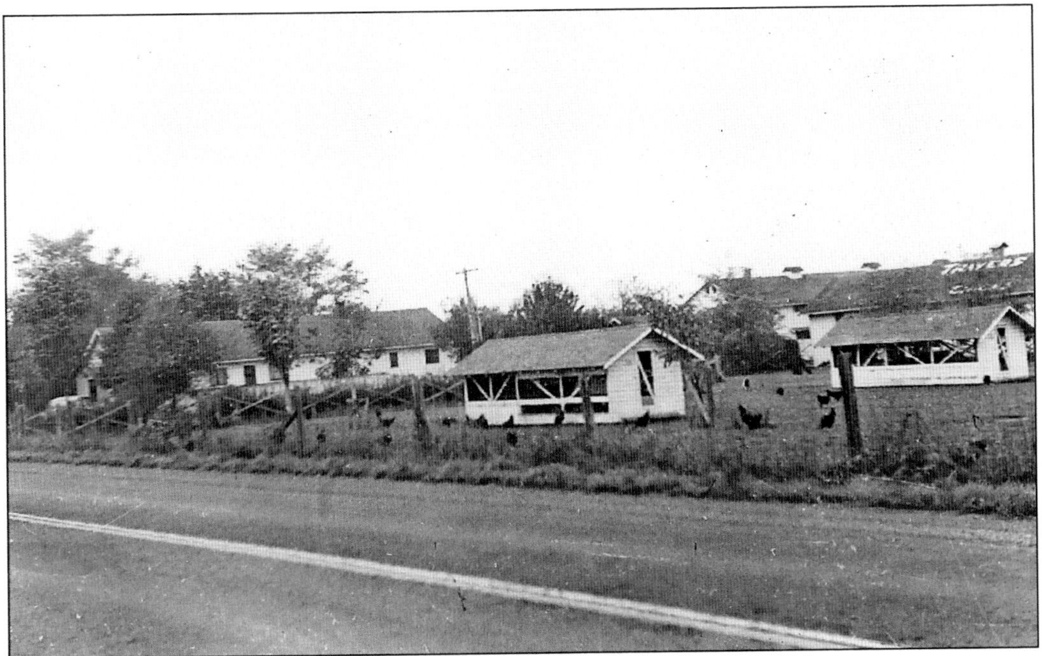

The Thayer's Retail Store, Residence, and Hatchery Building (left) in Relationship to the Range Houses (Center and Right). Rhode Island Reds free ranged on the 10-acre farm. On either side of the residence and retail store were old walnut orchards. Thayer's chicken farm was located about halfway between today's Southwest 198th and 209th Avenues. What is now Alexander Street would have been the farm's northern property boundary. The farm faced the two-lane Tualatin Valley Highway (below) looking in toward Aloha in July 1941. Thayer's hired employees who lived nearby and also provided housing on site. (Both, Carolyn Thayer Guinther.)

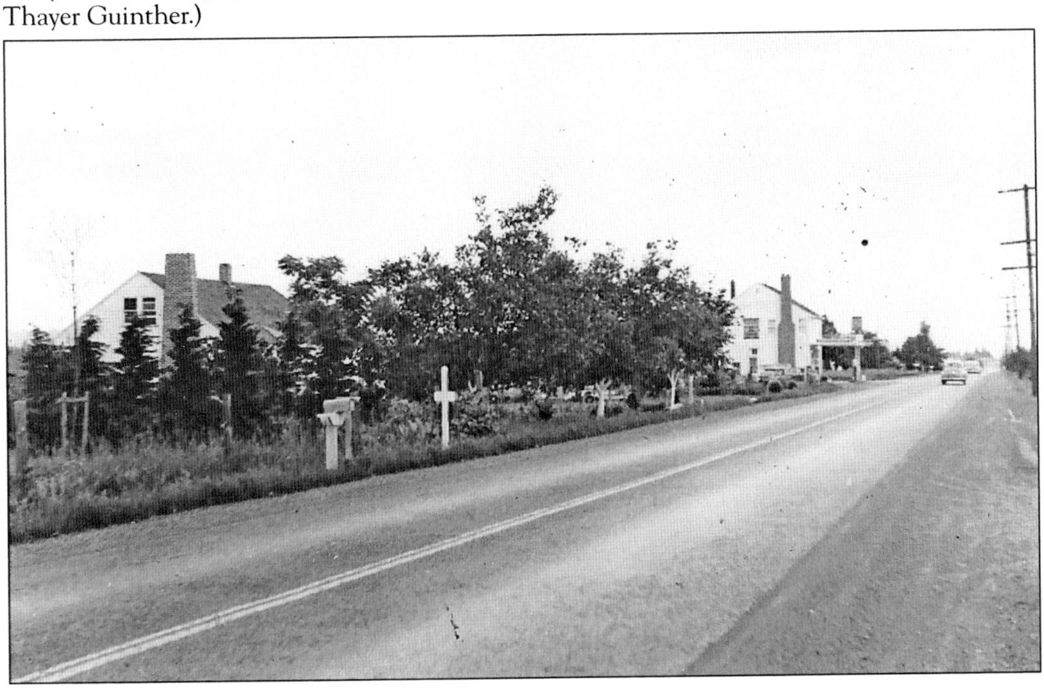

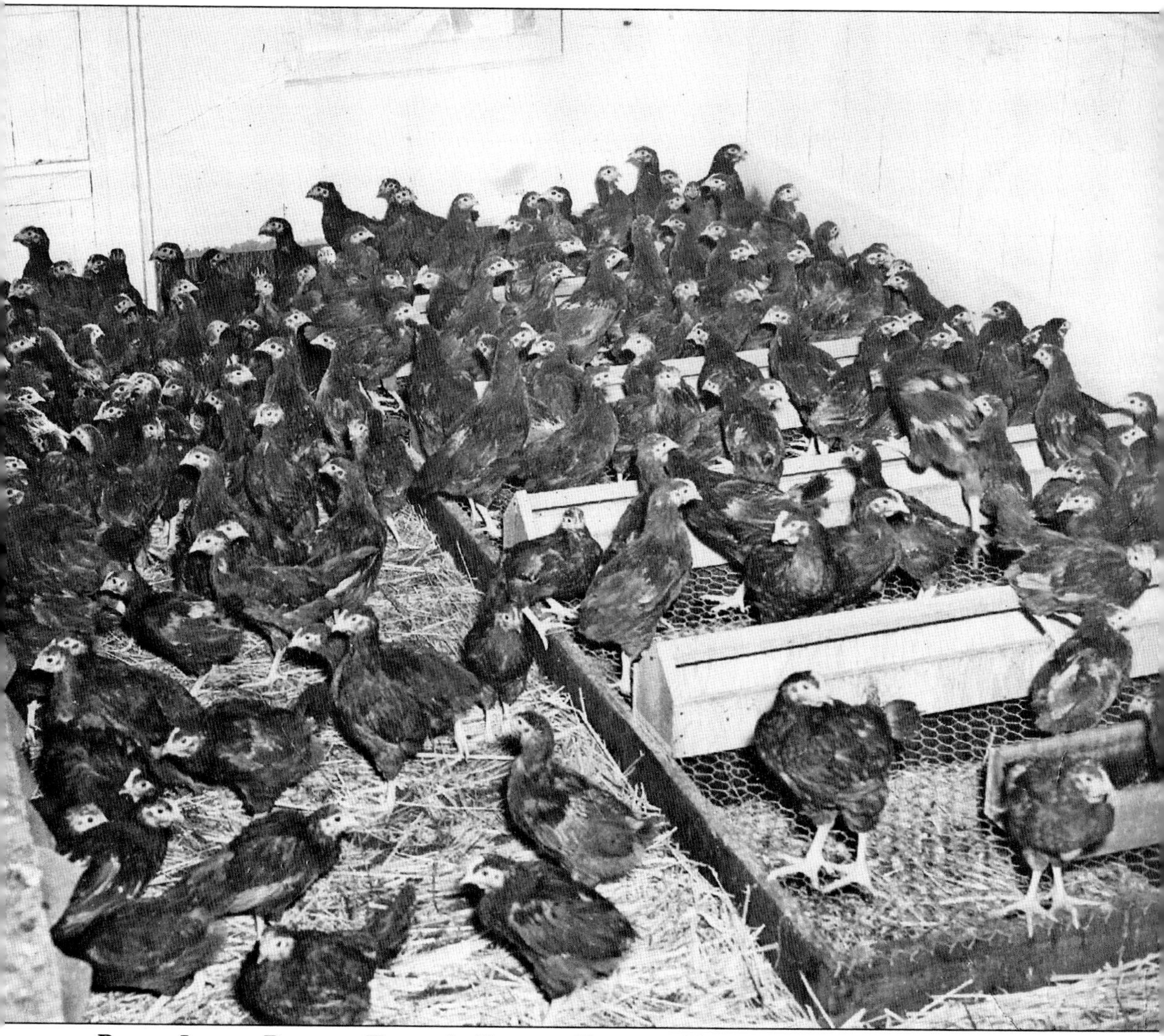

Rhode Island Reds on Thayer's Chicken Farm on Tualatin Valley Highway. Thayer's specialized in Rhode Island Reds, a breed of chickens developed in Little Compton, Rhode Island, about 1830. A blend of many breeds, Golden Buff or Golden Red chickens, as the breed was originally named, were first exhibited about 1879. A dual-purpose chicken, not a show bird, they are widely considered to be the most successful dual-purpose breed in North America. Rhode Island Reds, the official bird of the state of Rhode Island, produce in the range of 200–250 eggs per year. Hardy birds, they are adaptable to all sorts of conditions or feed. While Rhode Island Red roosters are aggressive, hens from the egg-laying strains are usually non-broody and quiet in disposition. One of the most successful and widespread farm flocks, the original, single-combed Rhode Island Red species is now endangered. (Carolyn Thayer Guinther.)

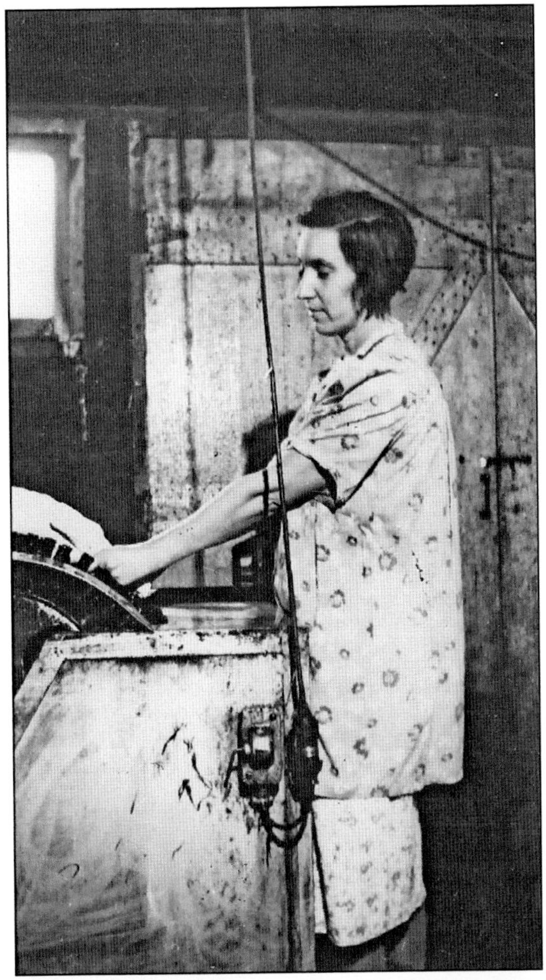

Thayer Employee Gertrude "Gertie" Stout Fackler Operating an Automatic Chicken-Plucking Machine. The machine was invented in the 1940s by Kent Tomlinson and Andrew Toti, who also invented the inflatable lifejacket nicknamed the "Mae West." In the 1940s, Tomlinson designed the C-25 poultry plucker finger, unique its elliptical, tapered shape. The Kent Company is the oldest plucker finger manufacturer in the world. From left to right below, Thayer company employees Gertie Fackler, Winnie Selves, and an employee identified as Fern process chickens on the Thayer farm in the 1940s. Founded in 1931, the farm was in operation for more than 30 years. (Both, Carolyn Thayer Guinther.)

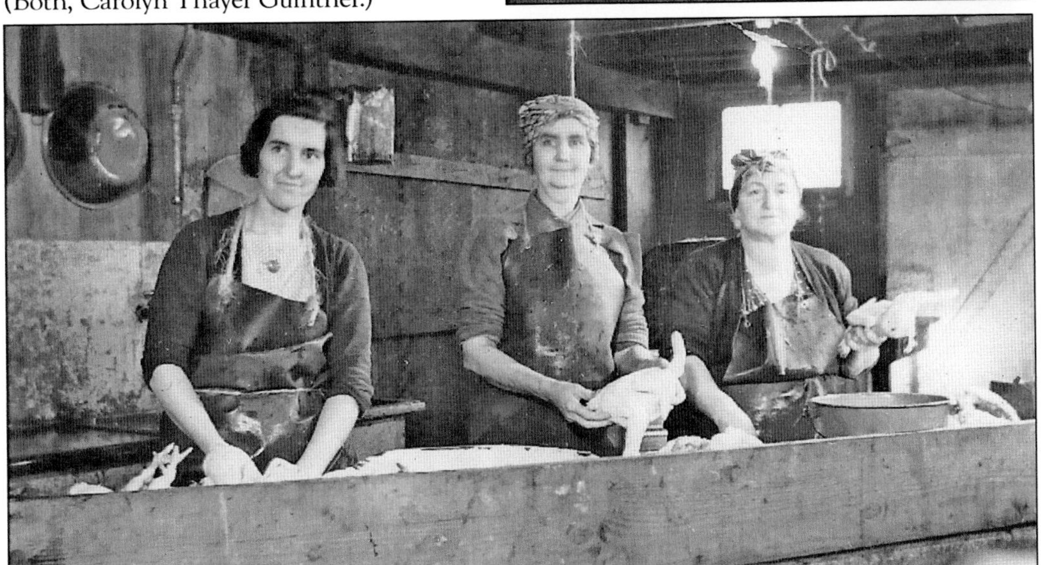

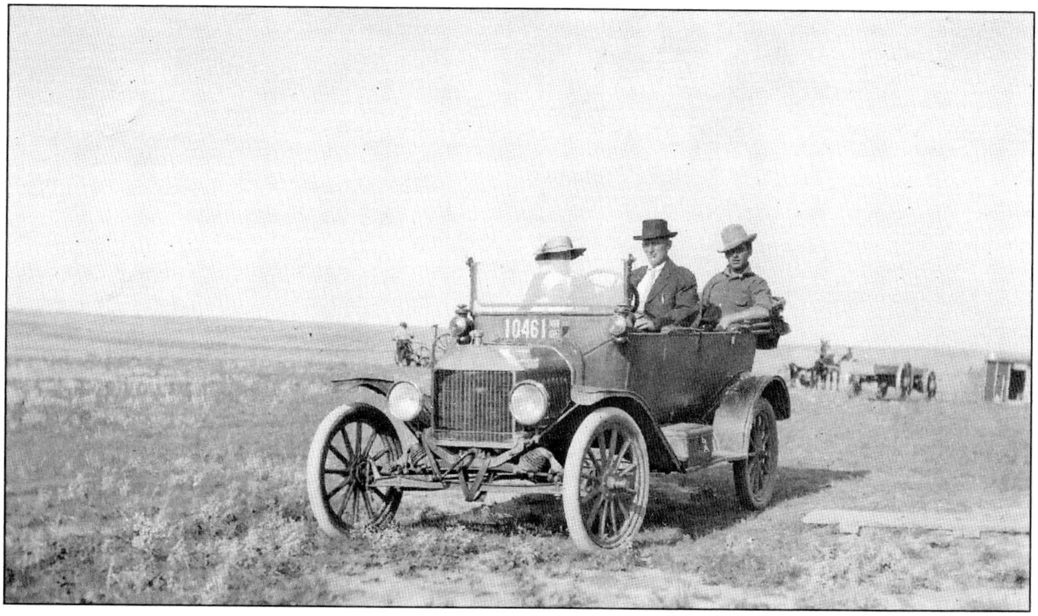

The Jannsens. From left to right are Ruby Jannsen, her husband, Alfred M. "Al" Jannsen, and her brother-in-law Gus Jannsen. Al was the founder and president of A.M. Jannsen Drilling Company. Born in Clinton, Iowa, in 1885, he lived in South Dakota, North Dakota, Washington, and Montana before moving to Reedville around 1921. His father was a farmer who drilled wells as a sideline. Al was one of five brothers operating a drilling service in Montana at the beginning of the 20th century. They used stream-powered drilling rigs (below) transported by horse-drawn wagons. In 1909, he started the A.M. Jannsen Drilling Company in Portland. (Both, Jannsen Well Drilling Company.)

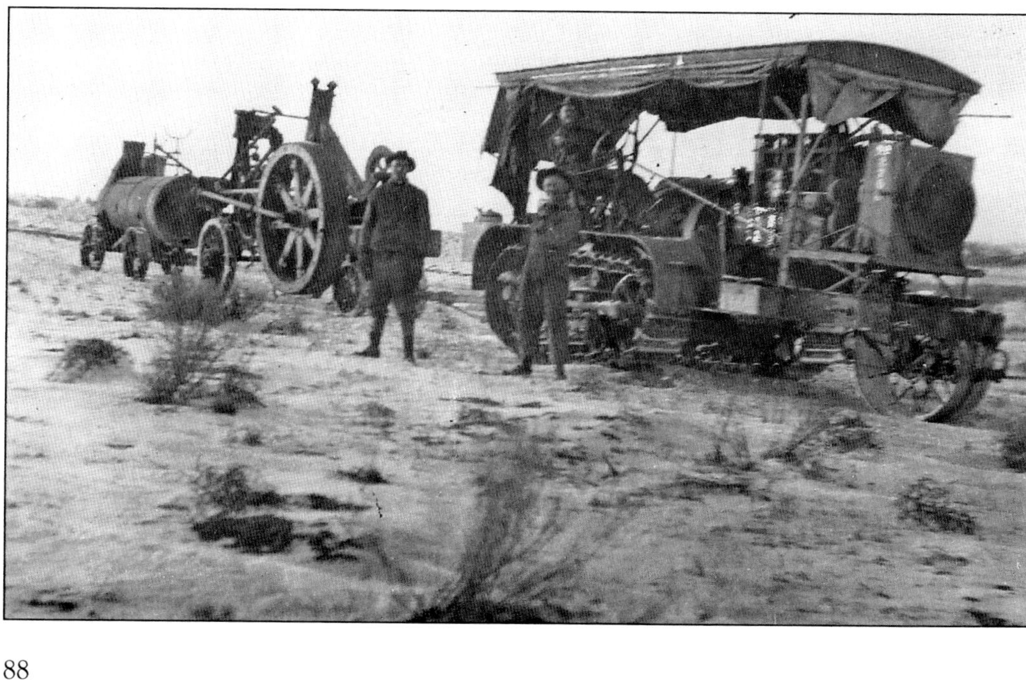

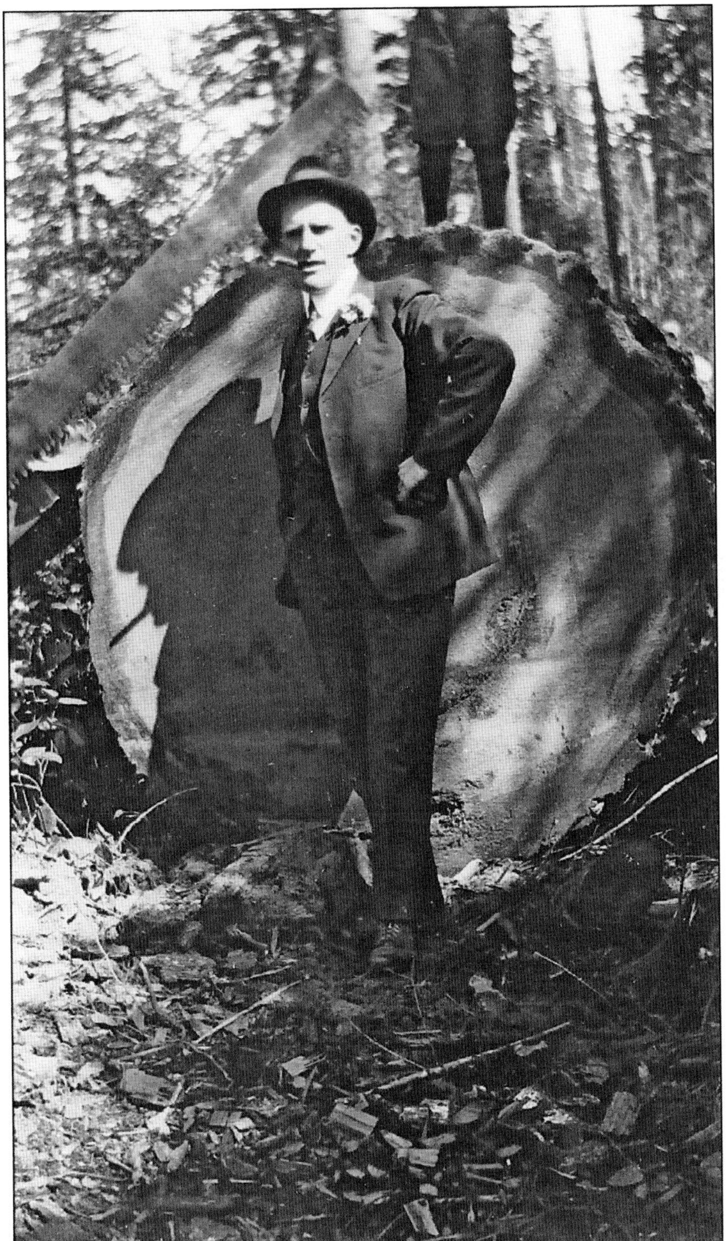

A.M. Jannsen, 1909. Jannsen Well Drilling Company is one of the oldest water-well drilling companies in the Pacific Northwest. In 1921, the Jannsen family moved to Reedville. They purchased land on the corner of Tualatin Valley Highway on what was then Kinneswood Avenue, today's Southwest 209th. The Jannsens built a machine shop that operated in that location for three decades. In 1950, the company built its headquarters on the north side of Tualatin Valley Highway. Three generations have guided the company's varied projects, drilling for gas, oil, water, or earth samples. The company has contributed to major projects including the East Bank Freeway in Portland, the Fort Clatsop restoration, and Bonneville Dam. The Jannsens drilled test holes for all Willamette River bridges in Portland and Cascade Locks as well as an experimental well for Oregon State University. (Jannsen Well Drilling Company.)

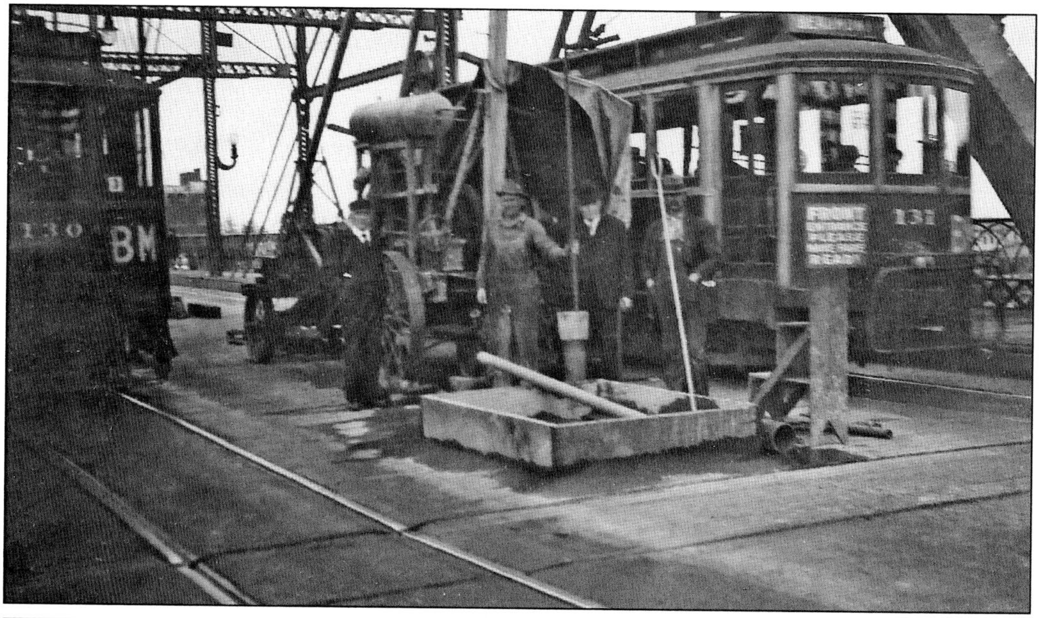

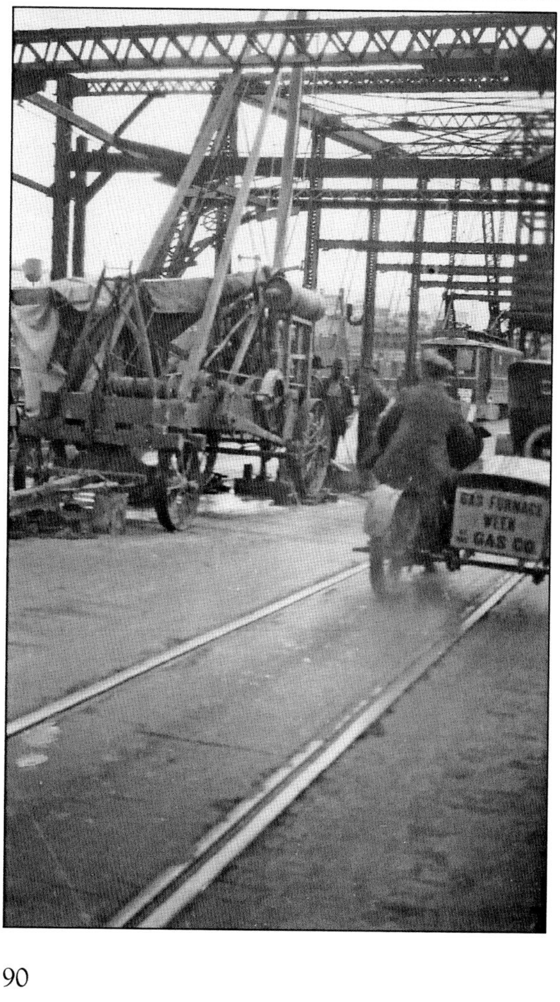

PORTLAND'S OLD BURNSIDE BRIDGE. Company president and founder A.M. Jannsen (above center) holds a cable attached to a drill in the 1920s on the east end of the old Burnside Bridge in Portland (above and left). The cable tool method, where a heavy bit is repeatedly raised and dropped to create a hole, was used to test the ground. Although it is time-consuming, an experienced driller can use the cable tool method through any formation. In the 1970s, the company drilled an average of 75 to 100 wells a year and operated 15 mobile drilling rigs. (Both, Jannsen Well Drilling Company.)

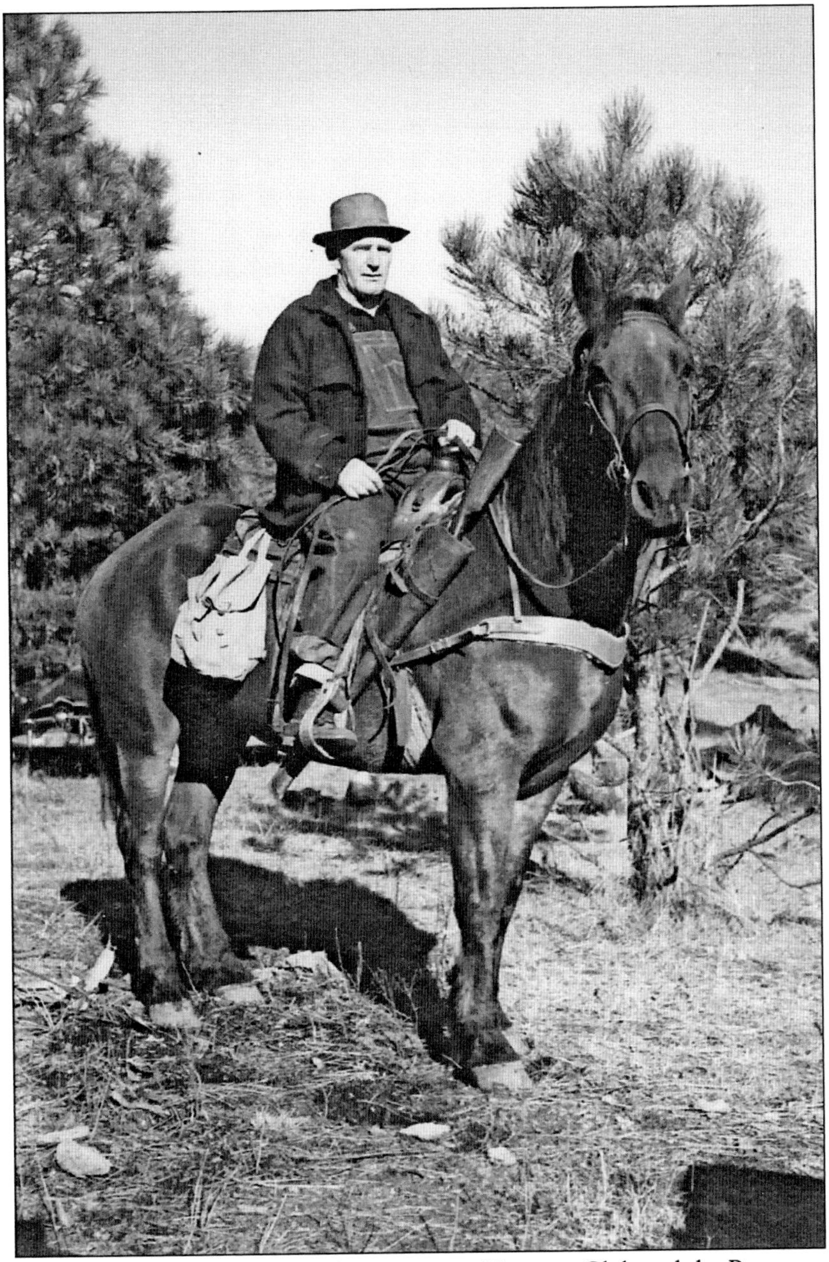

Al Jannsen, 1949. He was member of the Beaverton Kiwanas Club and the Beaverton Masonic Lodge and both a Republican and Democratic candidate for the Oregon State Legislature. He served on the Reedville School Board for nine years and was chairman of the nonunion high school board of Washington County for six years. Al was president of the Oregon Well Drilling Association and a charter member of the Washington County Rod and Gun Club. Today, the company Jannsen founded in the early 1900s still operates as a family-owned business. It has been located in Reedville for nearly 100 years. The Jannsen family moved to Reedville in 1921. Their first company building was constructed in 1924. It was relocated in 1963 when the company expanded operations and again in 1980. Many of the wells the company drilled 60 to 70 years ago are still in service. (Jannsen Well Drilling Company.)

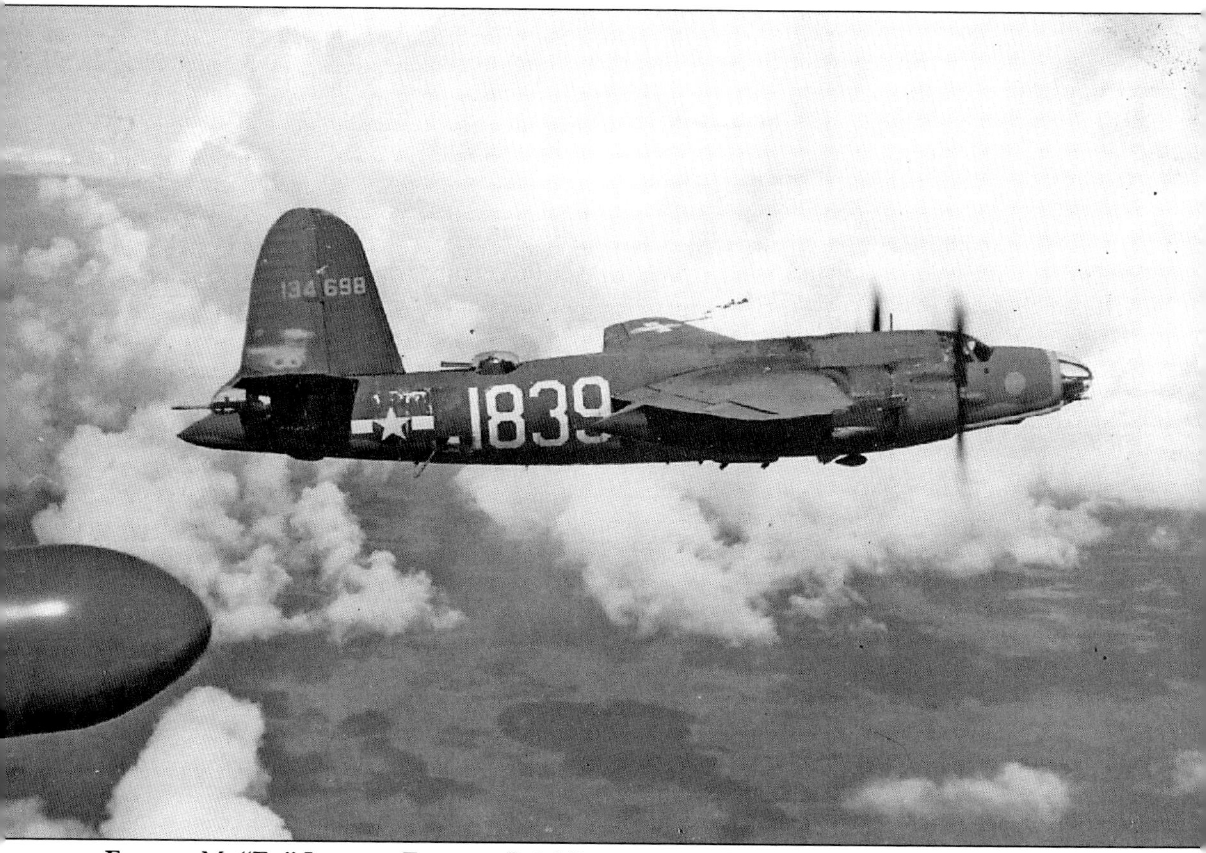

EDWARD M. "ED" JANNSEN FLYING A B-26 BOMBER OVER FRANCE DURING WORLD WAR II. The son of A.M. and Ruby Jannsen, Ed attended Reedville Elementary School, Beaverton High School, and graduated with an engineering degree from Oregon State College. He joined the US Army Air Corps in 1940, and saw combat action both during the D-Day Invasion and the Battle of the Bulge. By the end of the war, Ed completed 65 missions. The average was about 20. His brother, Wilbur Jannsen, was a P-47 fighter pilot. Ed left the service in 1945 and joined the A.M. Jannsen Drilling Company in Reedville. His first job, at about age 10 or 11, was scraping and painting pipe to make it last longer. When he was 14, Ed started driving a truck for the family business. (Jannsen Well Drilling Company.)

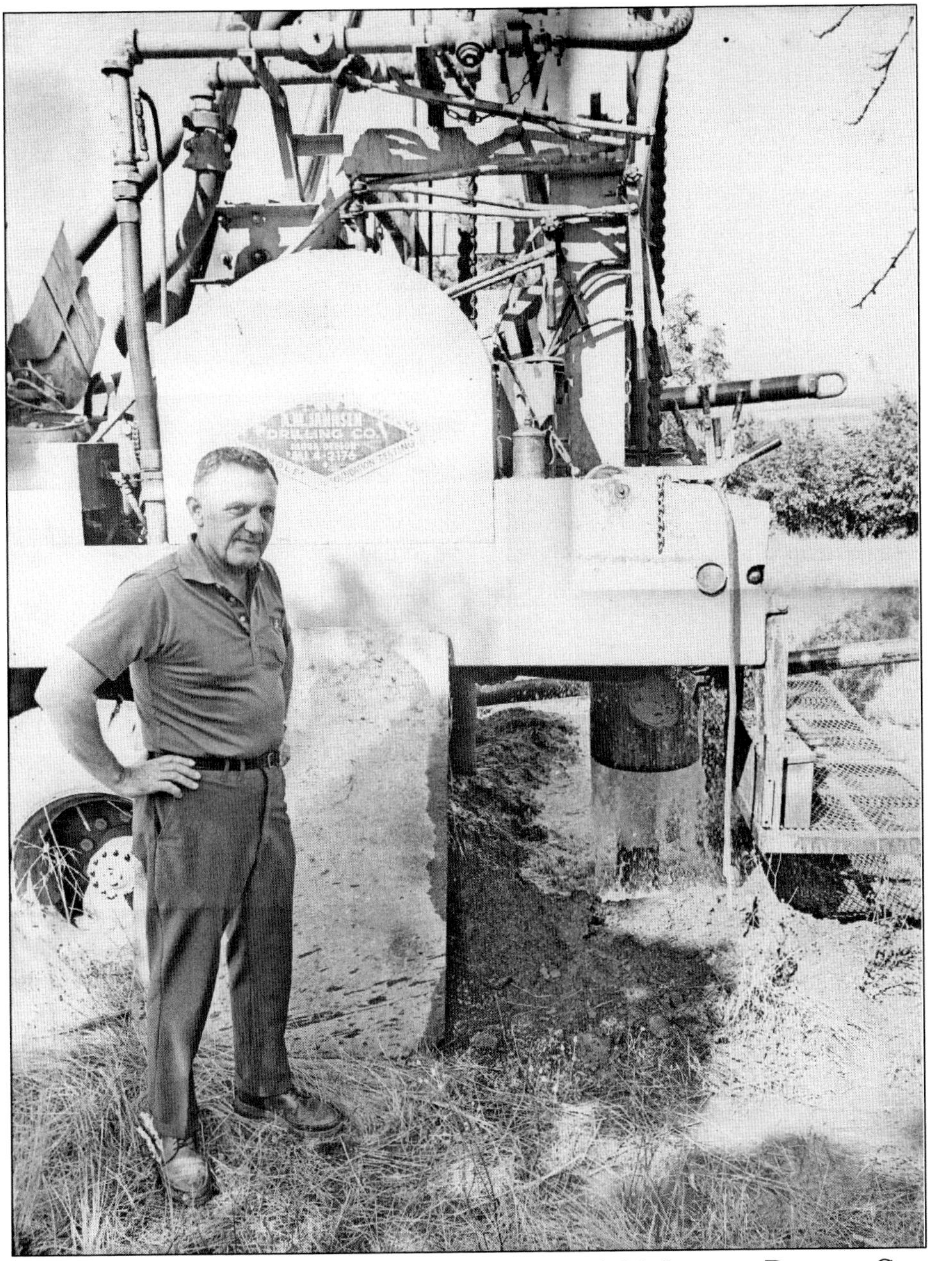

Ed Jannsen, the Second Generation to Operate the A.M. Jannsen Drilling Company. In 1950, he joined his father and brother, Wilbur, in the family business, assuming the role of president. Ed's sons also joined the company—Preston in 1965 and Roy in 1970. The Jannsens became charter members of the Ground Water Association/Oregon Drilling Association in 1948. They are currently active members of the Oregon and National Ground Water Associations. Ed worked with Oregon governor Paul Patterson in 1955 on the Water Resources Commission. The company has brought in water for municipal, irrigation, and industrial projects, including two wells on Cooper Mountain for the Aloha-Huber Water District. In the early 1900s, they used steam-powered drill rigs hauled by horse-drawn wagons. That method was replaced by cable tool and churn technology, then high-speed air rotary drills. (Jannsen Well Drilling Company.)

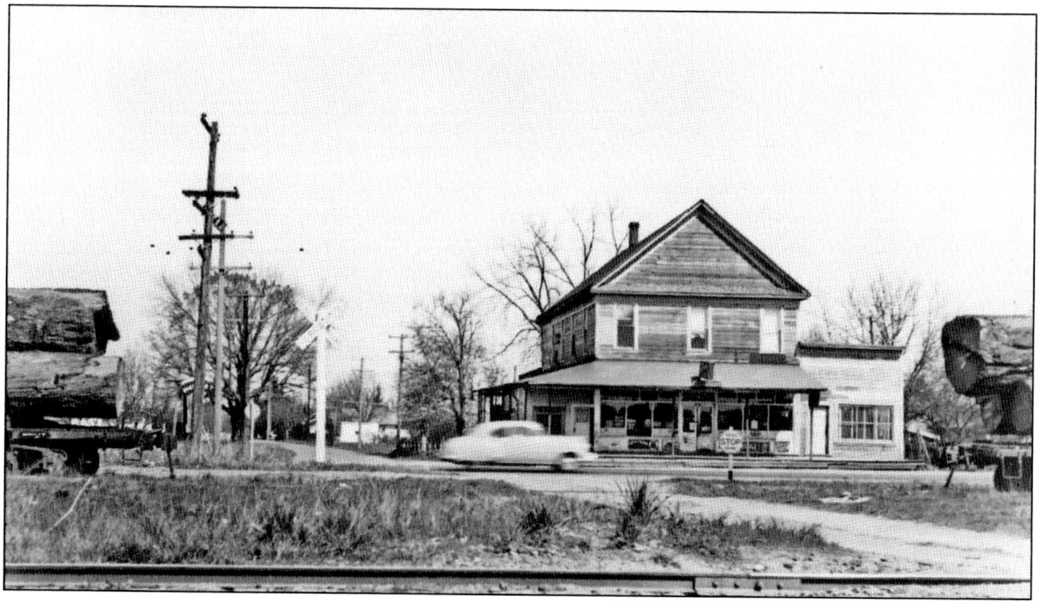

The Reedville Store before (Above) and after (Below) Tualatin Valley Highway Expansion in the Mid-1950s. North of the store on today's Southwest 214th Avenue was a white house where Eugene W. Dant and his family lived (left). For decades, railroad cars transported timber that had been burned in a series of forest fires and salvaged by more than 200 logging companies. In the 1950s, the Garfields operated the market. The Reedville Post Office was located inside the store. It opened in 1887 and ceased operations on December 31, 1954. (Both, Washington County Museum.)

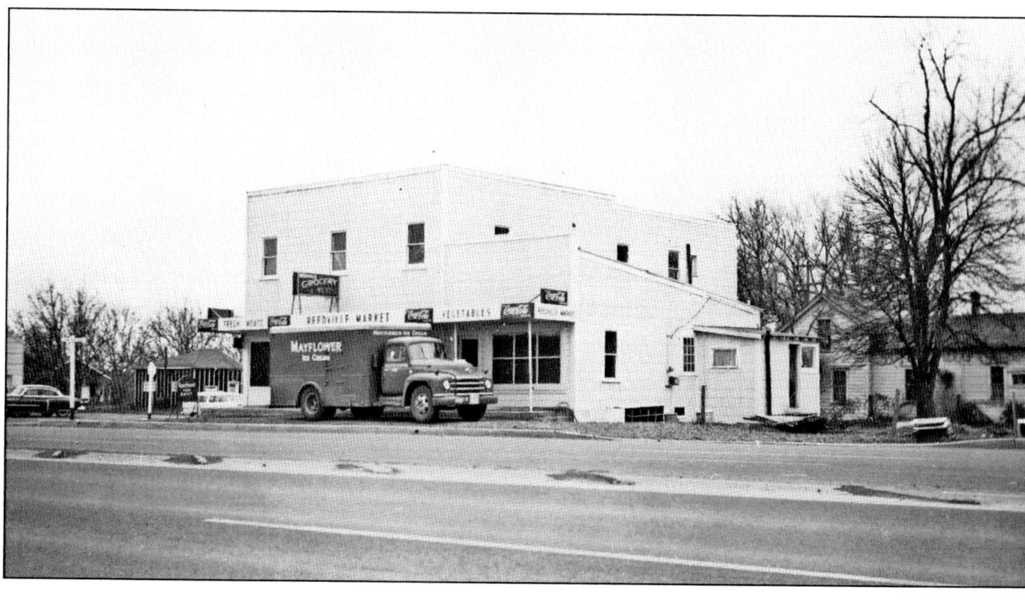

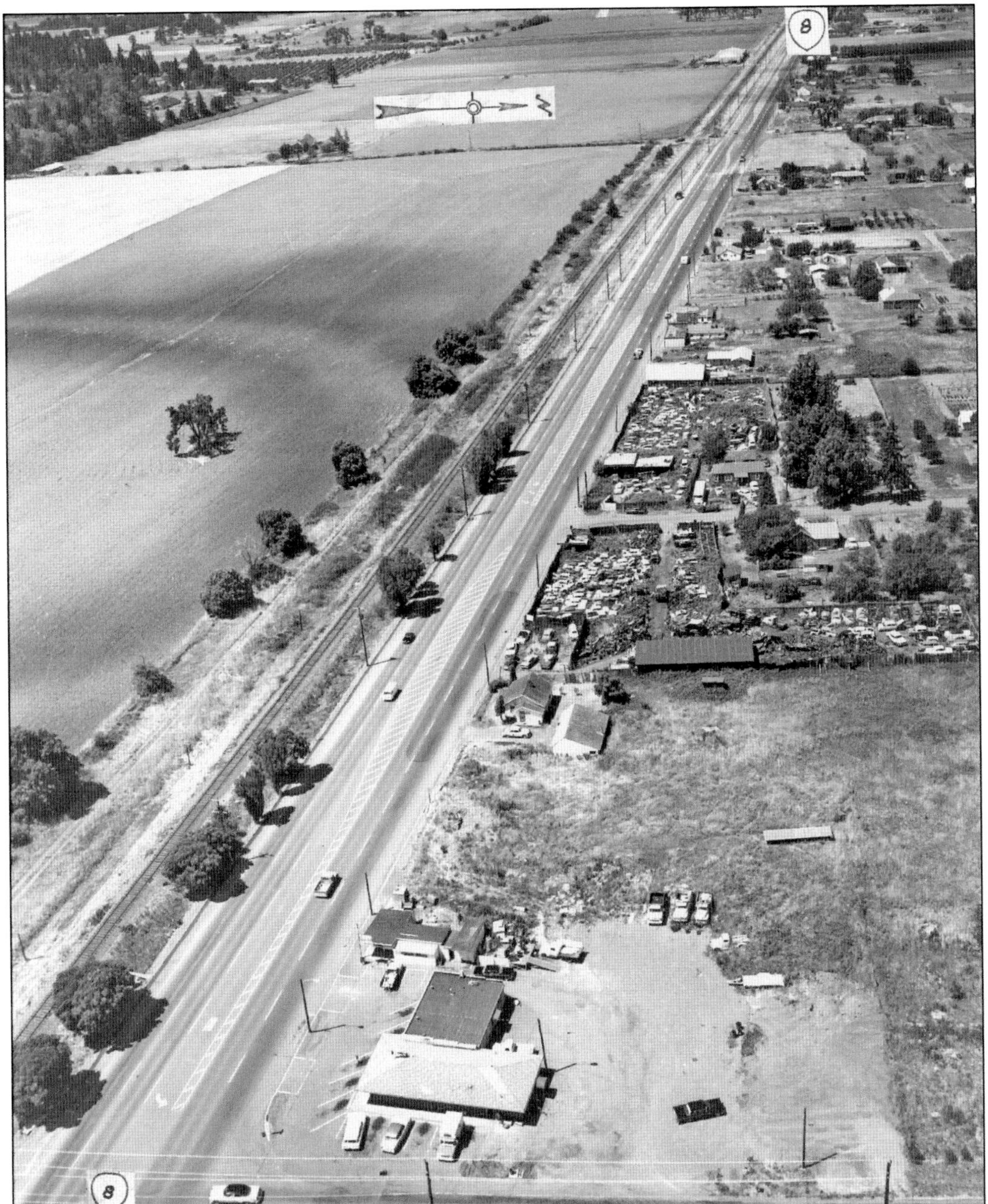

Tualatin Valley Highway Looking Southwest from What Was Once Market Street (Today's Cornelius Pass Road), 1965. On the northwest corner of the intersection, today's Reedville Café is located in a field next to Reedville Auto Wrecking. The former Churchley Road (top left) is now Southwest 229th Avenue. West of Beaverton, the highway parallels the rail, built in 1871. The original Tualatin Valley Highway, a two-lane road dating to 1918, was installed north of the railroad. From 1912 to 1929 Red Electric streetcars ran between Forest Grove and Portland with a passenger stop in Reedville. In the mid-1950s, the throughway, also known as Route 8, was expanded to a four-lane road by the Oregon State Highway Commission. (Business Services History Center, Oregon Department of Transportation.)

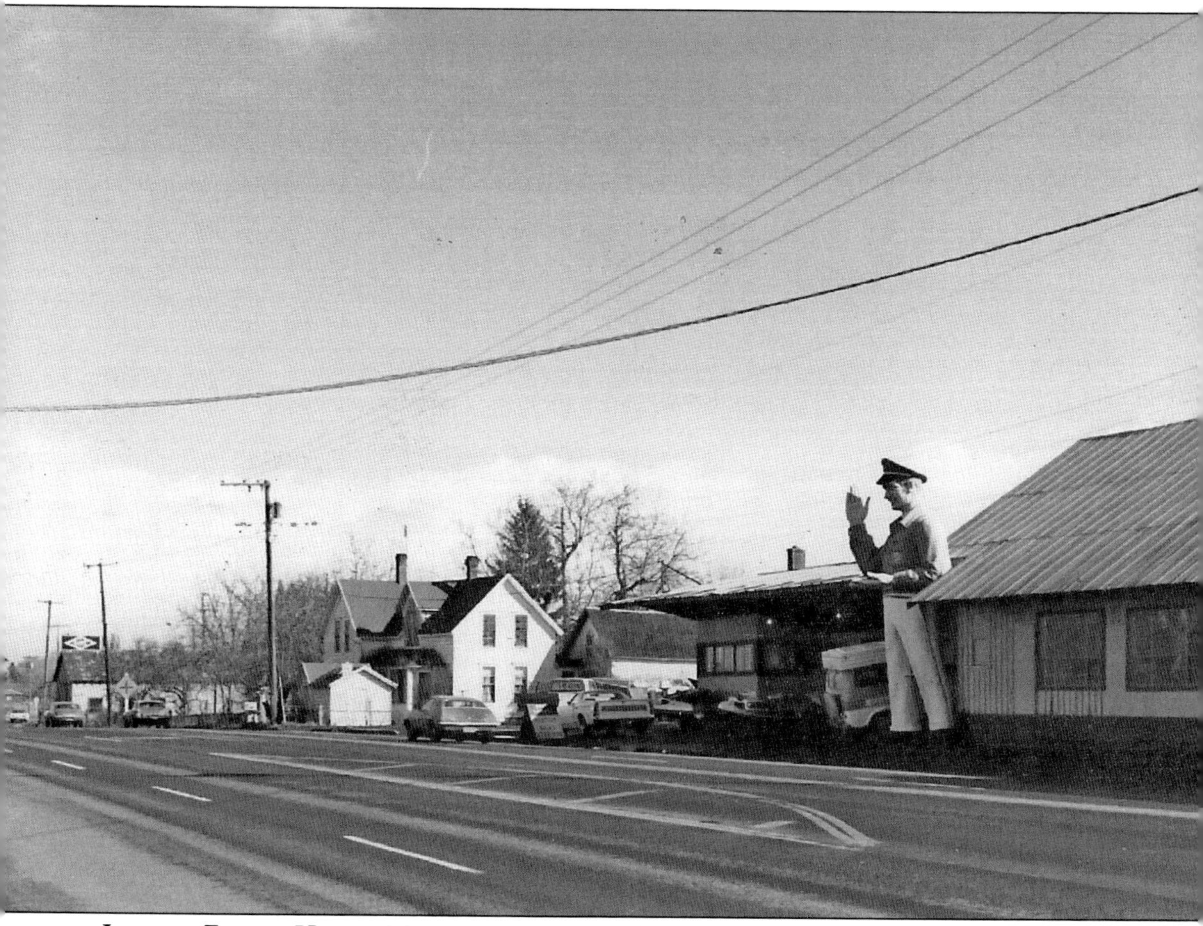

LOOKING EAST AT HARVEY MARINE ON TUALATIN VALLEY HIGHWAY, 1960s. The former J.B. Imlay & Sons warehouse and mill was purchased Edgar "Ed" Harvey for his boat-building business. Years earlier, while attending Lewis and Clark College in Portland in the early 1950s, Harvey worked part-time for George Yates. He operated Yates Boat Works in Beaverton, building lapstrake wooden boats and airplanes. After serving in the US military during the Korean War, Harvey funneled his discharge pay into a boat-building business and hired his former boss Yates as an employee. From 1960 to 1975, Harvey also owned the Harvey Marina in Lake Oswego and Ski Dock, the largest private moorage on the Columbia River. In 1974, Harvey Marine installed the former *Big Friends* statue in the front of its retail store. (Harvey Marine.)

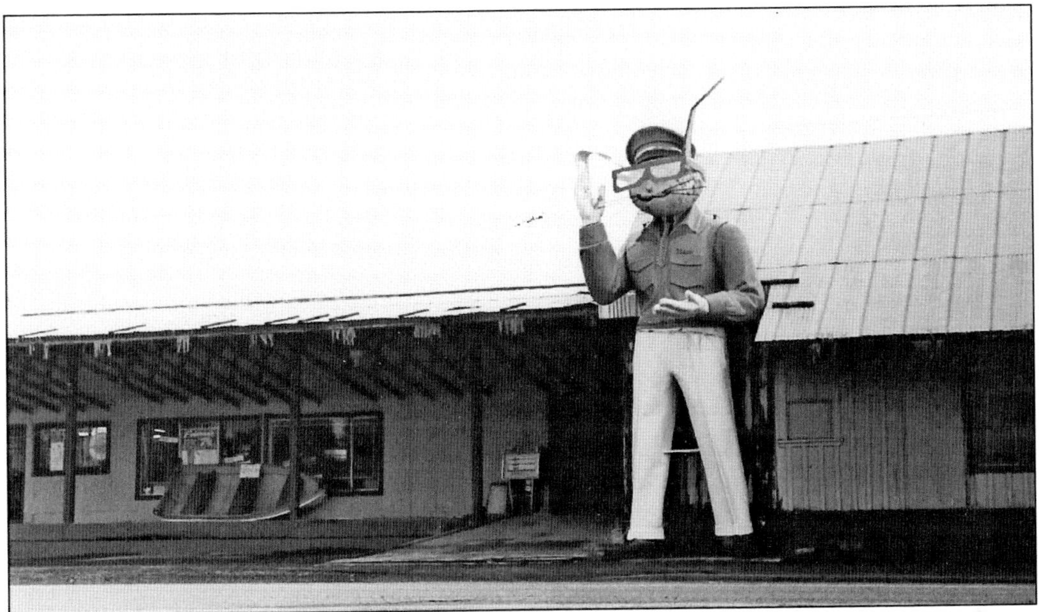

The Original *Harvey the Rabbit* Sculpture in Front of Harvey Marine on Tualatin Valley Highway (Above). In the early 1960s, film character *Harvey*, a six-foot, three-and-one-half-inch tall invisible rabbit, became the symbol of Harvey Marine. In 1969, Edgar Harvey acquired a former Big Friends sculpture, created by artist Sasha Schnittman, for the Texaco "The Man Who Wears the Star" advertising campaign. Several hundred were manufactured by International Fiberglass for Texaco service stations. In 1974, the statue was altered by replacing the human head with a Harvey-inspired rabbit head constructed by Harvey Marine employees (below). (Both, Harvey Marine.)

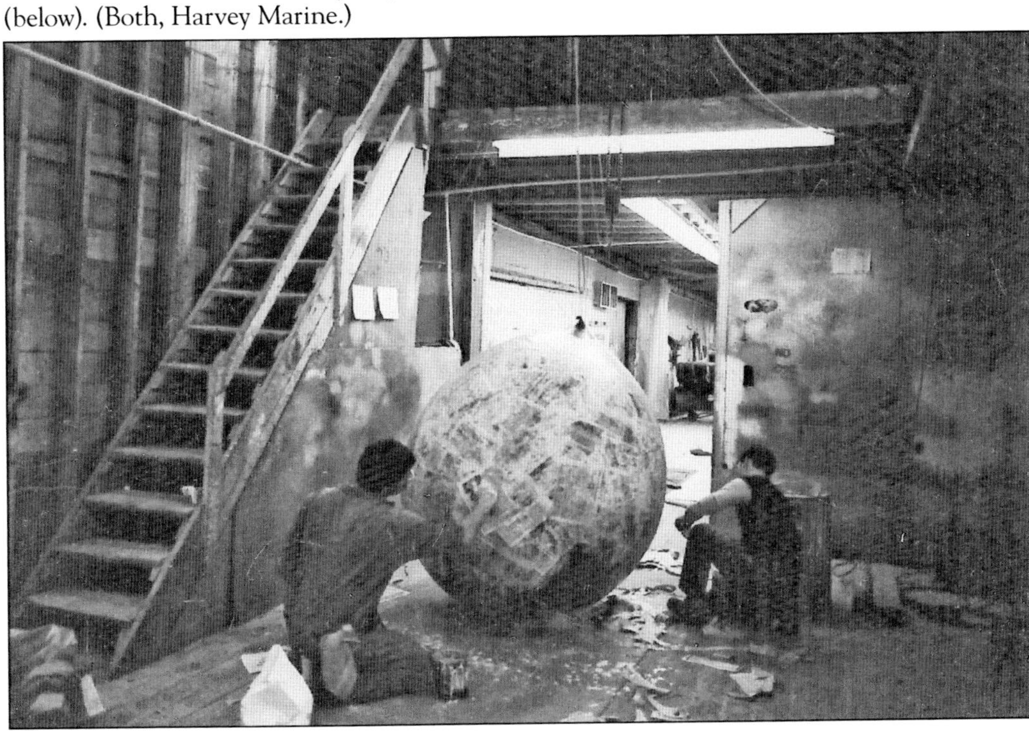

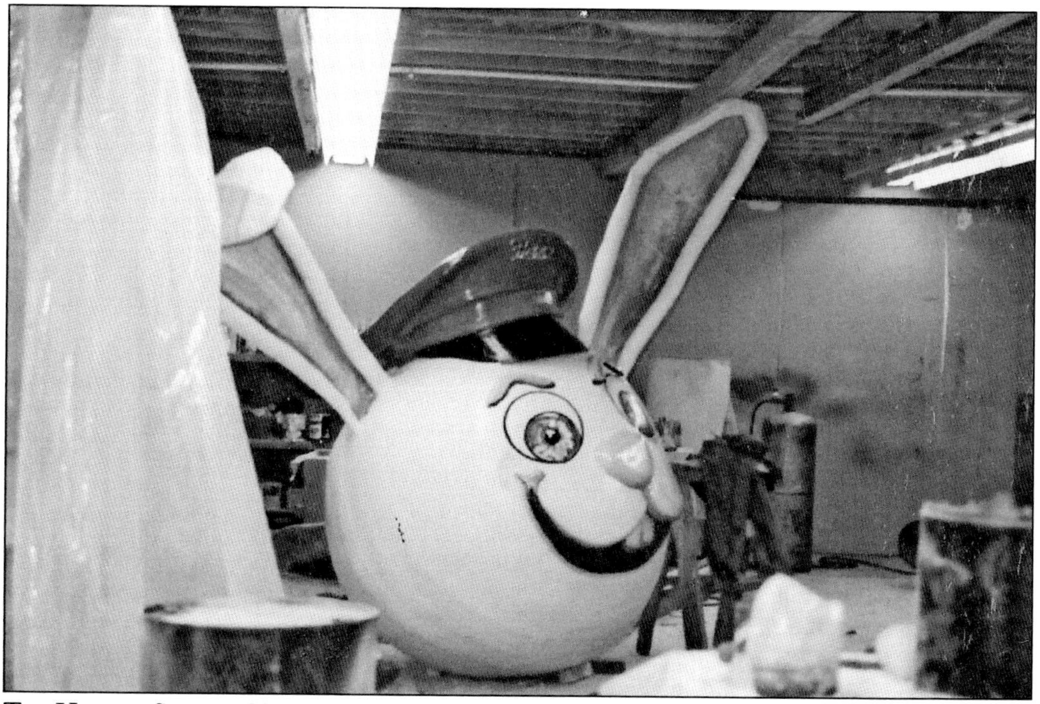

The Harvey Statue. Harvey's current rabbit head (above) was built on-site at Harvey Marine and constructed of fiberglass. During early attempts to form a sphere as a base for Harvey's head, workmen used a weather balloon for a base. Eventually, foam and papier-mâché formed Harvey's head. It was hoisted by crane (below) to the top of the former *Big Friends* sculpture. (Both, Harvey Marine.)

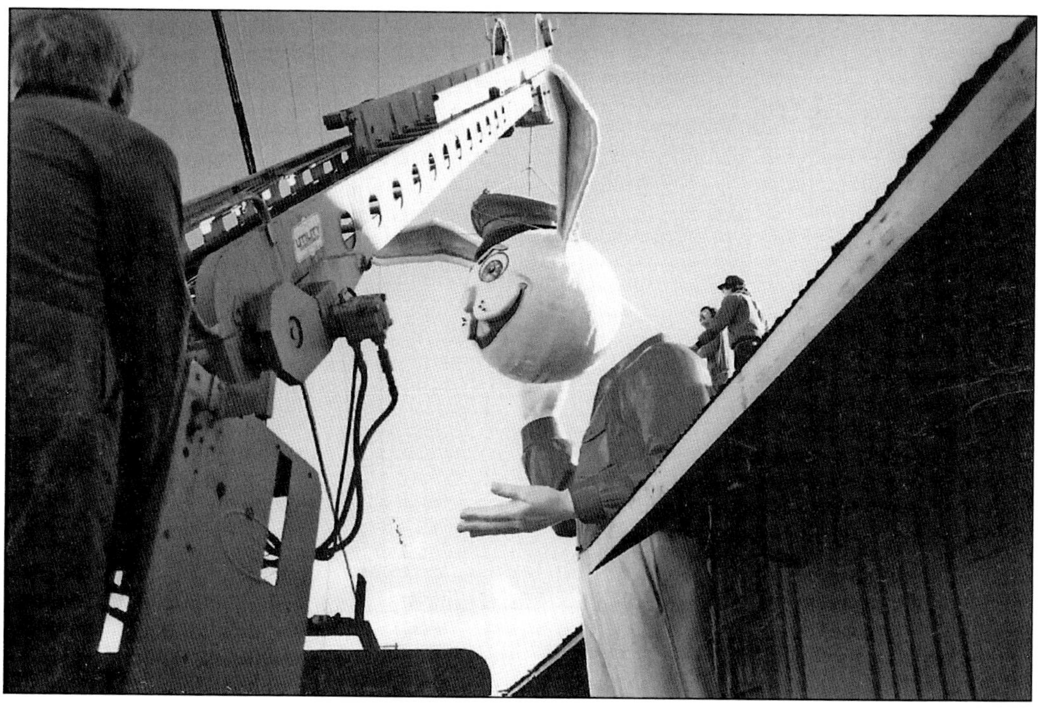

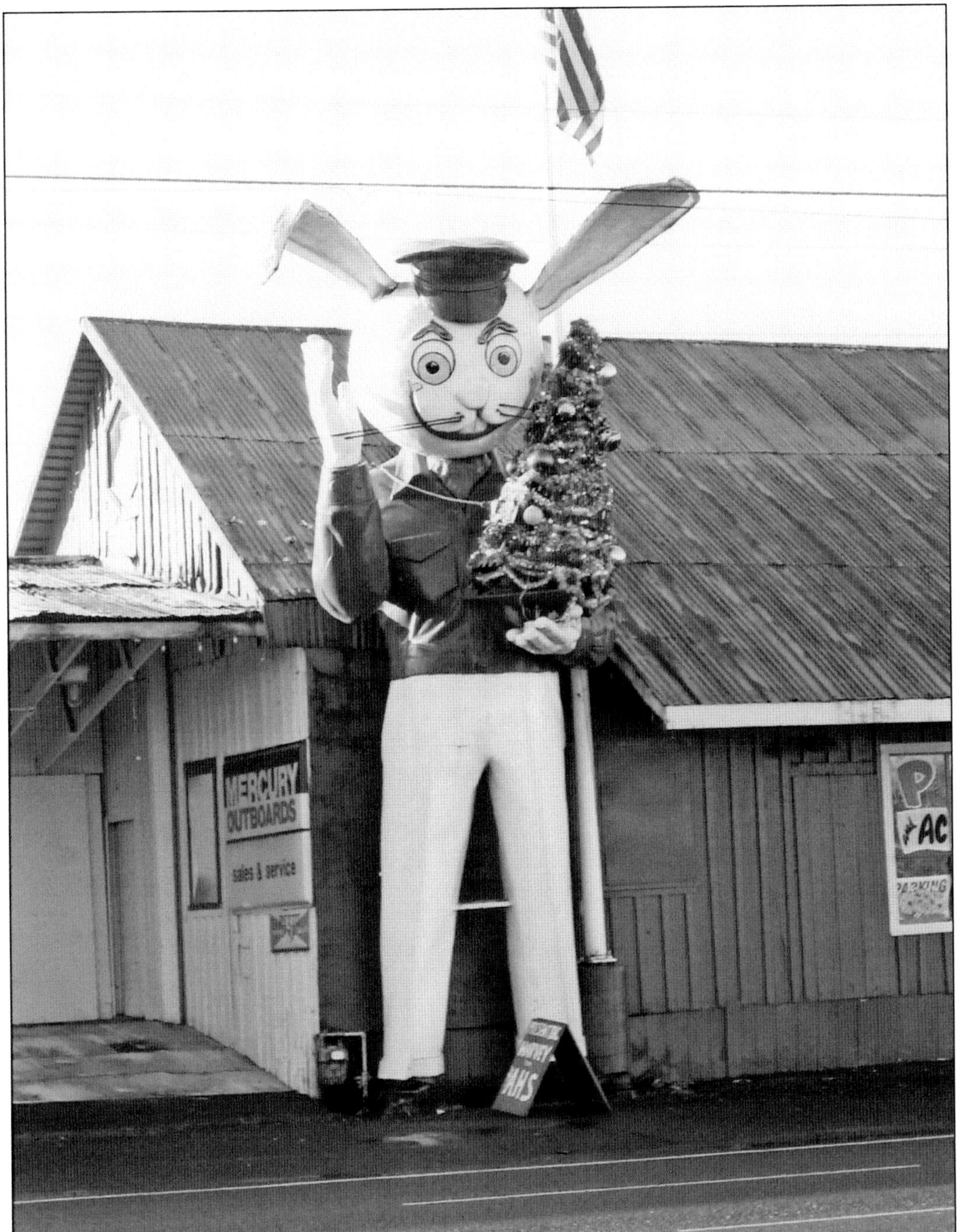

Harvey the Rabbit (Right) Has a Cult Following. Of the estimated 50,000 cars that pass by daily, one driver out of 20 either honks or yells greetings to Harvey. His fans also write letters when they're sad or to tell him how happy he's made their drive. (Photograph by the author.)

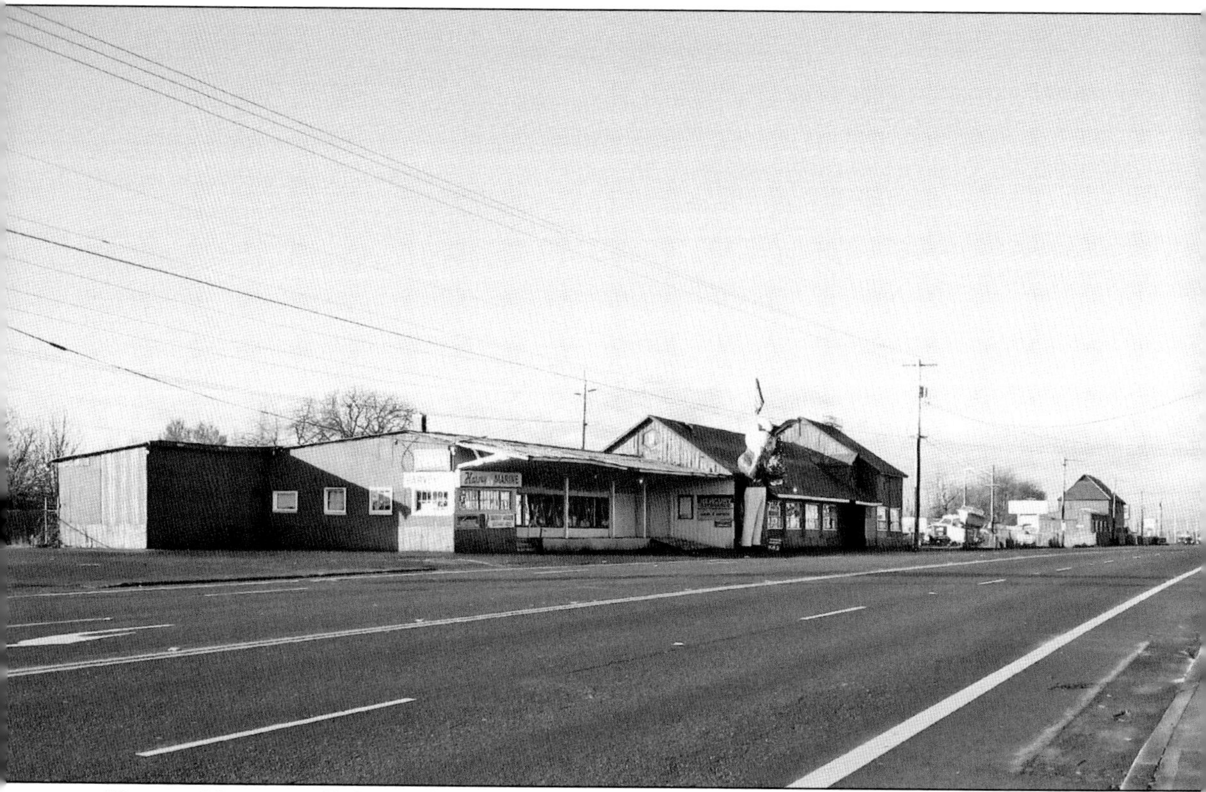

Harvey Marine as It Looks Today on Tualatin Valley Highway in Reedville. The former J.B. Imlay & Sons mill was built in the early 1890s and purchased by Edgar Harvey in 1960 for his boat-building business. The *Harvey the Rabbit* sculpture was added in 1974. (Photograph by the author.)

Six

HUBER

The historic village of Huber, once known as Perkins Crossing, was located on what was then the Southern Pacific Railroad. It was near the eastern boundary of the ranch owned by Richard Perkins. In 1901, the Perkins property sold at auction to the Shaw-Fear Company.

Near present-day Southwest 170th Avenue, Jacob Huber, who owned a farm near Perkins Corner, cleared a road from the intersection of the Plains-Falls and Harris Ferry Roads to the railroad. Known as Huber Road, it connected to the F.W. Livermore Building Materials store, where lumber from the third Livermore mill at Perkins Corner was sold.

In 1901, the Perkins farm sold to the Shaw-Fear Company. They subdivided and sold lots in their Beaverton Reedville Acreage development. Southern Pacific converted their branch steam railroad to electricity in 1910 and leased the line to the Red Electric interurban railway. A passenger depot opened on what was then known as Huber Road.

The Shaw-Fear company donated a site for the Aloha-Huber school in 1911 which was built on Willow Avenue. Early school board members included Frank Livermore, Dan Shaw, Julius Weisenback, and John York. Shaw-Fear employee M.E. Blanton installed sidewalks and a street to the school. Today's Southwest Blanton Street was the first road to connect the villages of Aloha and Huber. Blanton built a house in 1912, at the intersection of Huber Road and what is now Blanton Street. It was listed on the National Register of Historic Places in 1989.

Tualatin Valley Highway, a two-lane road for automobiles, was built adjacent to the railroad in 1918. The Red Electric line discontinued service in 1929. From 1956 to 1958, the Oregon State Highway Commission expanded 4.69 miles of Tualatin Valley Highway to a four-lane thruway.

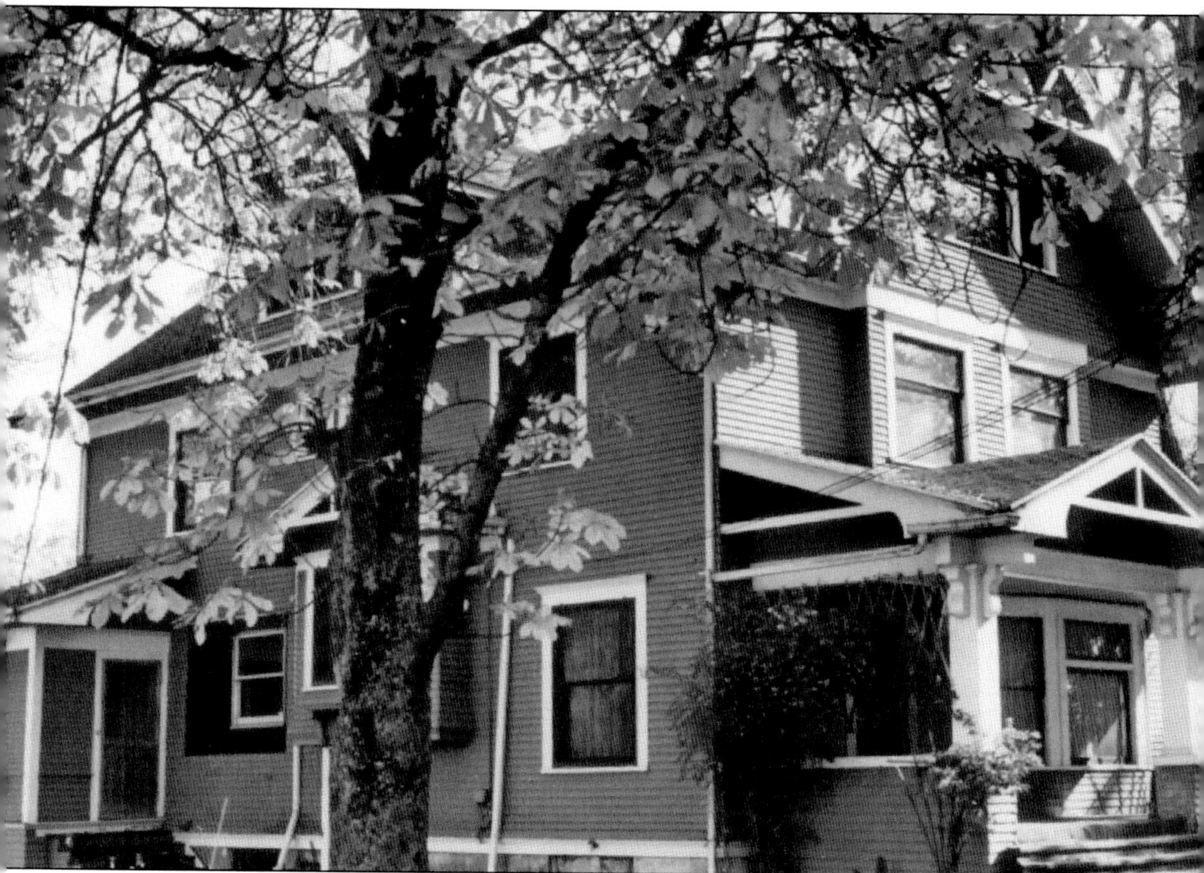

M.E. Blanton House. The M.E. Blanton house was built in 1912 facing what was once Huber Road, today's Southwest 170th Avenue. Blanton was an employee of the Shaw-Fear Company, the developer of the Beaverton Reedville Acreage. After the company deeded acreage for the first Aloha-Huber School, Blanton graded the roads and sidewalks to the site, which was located on what later became known as Blanton Street. He owned the house until 1920. The 3,000-square-foot structure, still standing today, is a significant and well-preserved example of one the earliest phases of suburban architecture in the United States. The two-and-one-half-story building with boxed eaves and a gabled roof and dormers is typical of the Craftsman style introduced by Gustav Stickley. The Blanton house was listed in the National Register of Historic Places in 1989. (National Register of Historic Places nomination for the M.E. Blanton House.)

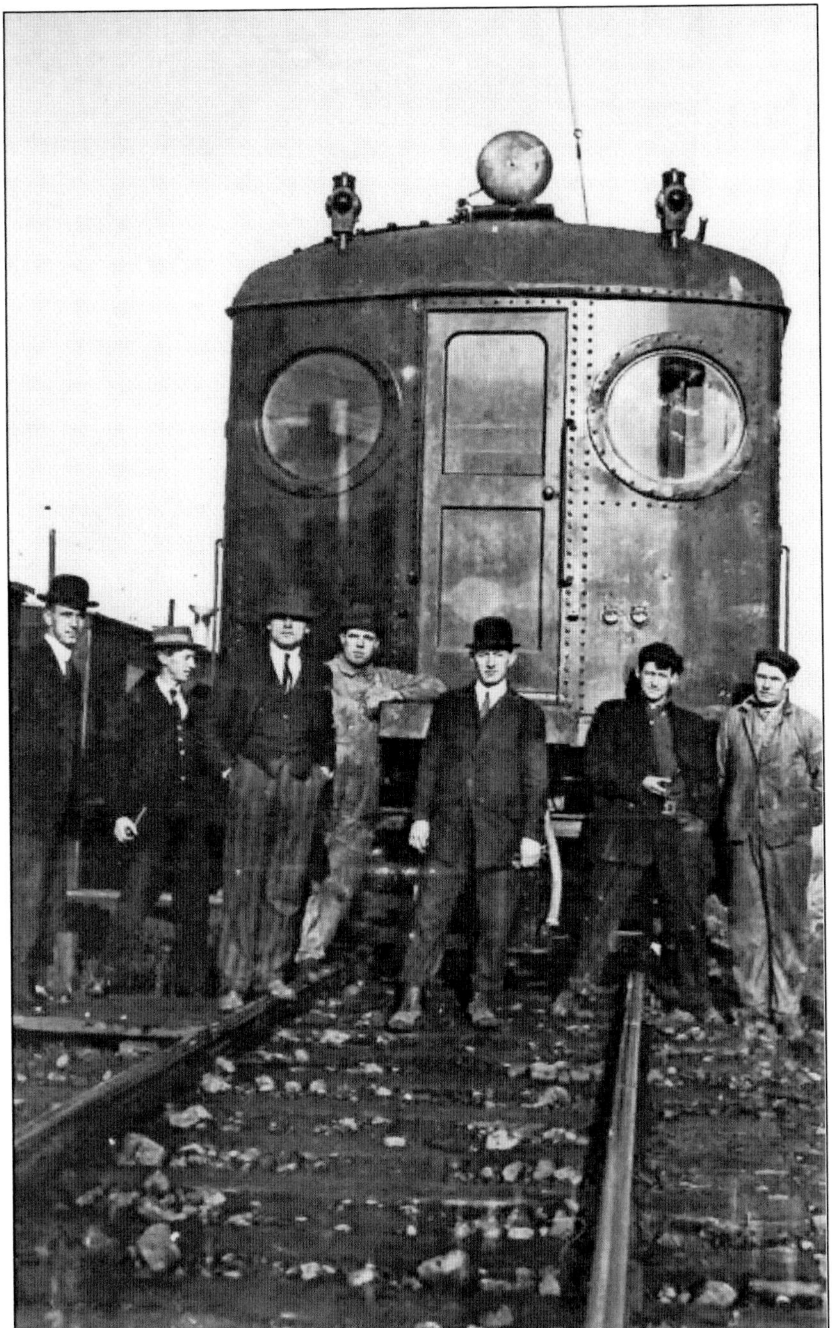

A Red Electric Streetcar, Early 1900s. The line operated on the Southern Pacific Railroad that connected Portland's Union Station and Forest Grove. In 1905, the Willamette Valley Traction Company was organized to develop an electric railroad in the Portland metropolitan area. The Southern Pacific Railroad, one of the largest in the West, was one of the first in the nation to convert its branch steam railway to electricity. Service began in 1907. In 1909, a stop was added at Wheeler Station, today's Aloha. There were other passenger stations at St. Mary's, Huber, Tobias, Reedville, and Witch Hazel. (Beaverton Historical Society.)

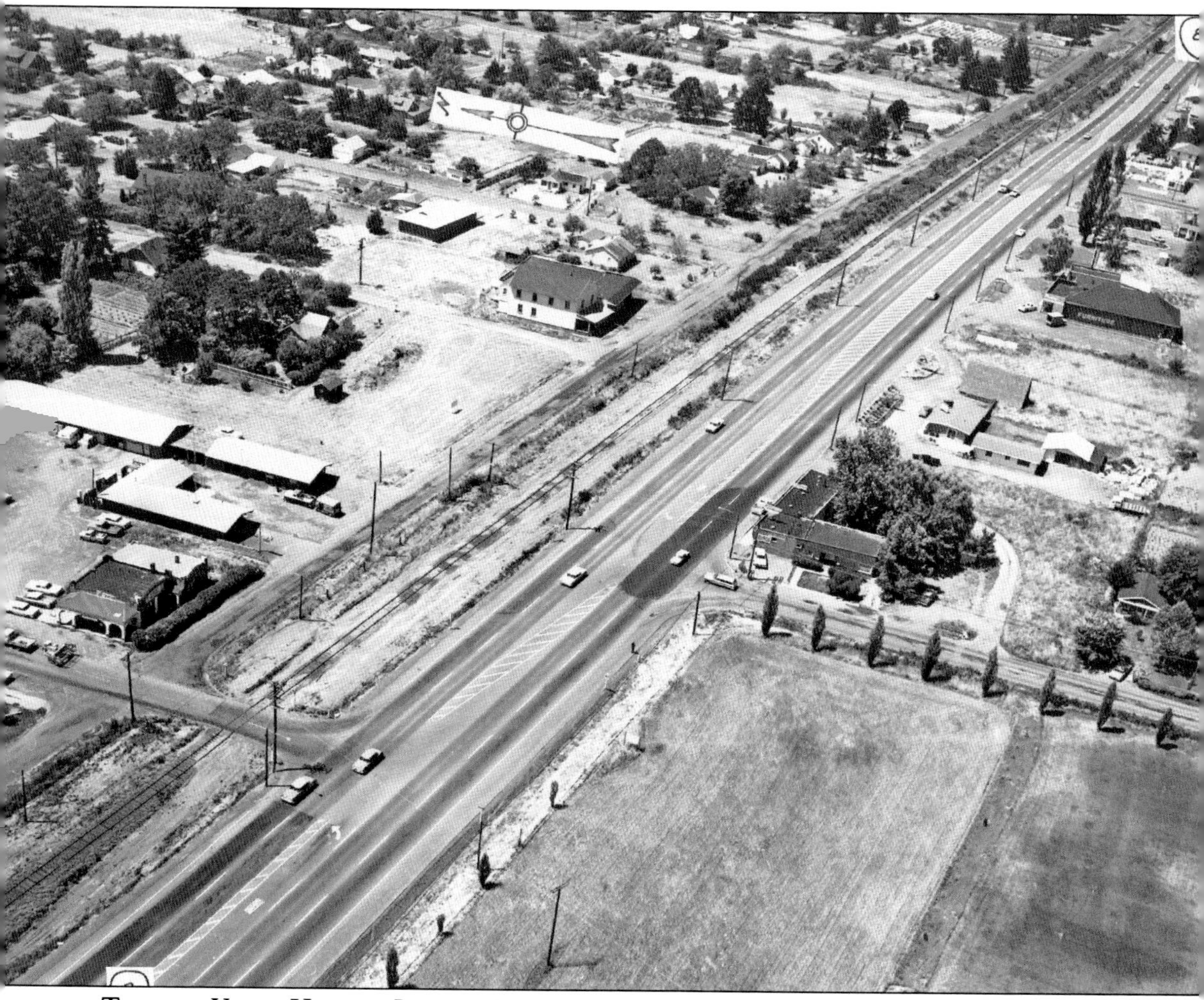

TUALATIN VALLEY HIGHWAY LOOKING WEST AT THE HUBER COMMUNITY NEAR TODAY'S SOUTHWEST 170TH AVENUE (LEFT), 1965. The Livermore building materials store (left) operated next to the railroad in the early 1900s. Still standing today, the structure has housed a variety of businesses, including a nut processing plant, the Old Nut Loft Art Center and Nonna Emilia Ristorante Italiano. The Huber Grange was located on the north side of Tualatin Valley Highway, which was constructed in 1918 as a two-lane highway for motor vehicles. In 1933, the road was improved with funding from the National Recovery Administration. In the mid-1950s, the Oregon State Highway Commission expanded Tualatin Valley Highway to four lanes of traffic between Beaverton and Reedville, a distance of 4.69 miles (Business Services History Center, Oregon Department of Transportation.)

Seven

Aloha

Today's unincorporated Aloha community first developed on the site of what was once Richard Torney's territorial land claim, established in the 1840s. It sold to James H. McMillen in 1850. After he was brought to trial and found not guilty of mortally wounding neighbor A.J. Masters, the property sold again to Jacob and Jemima Wheeler and British cattlemen Richard S. Perkins and Arthur H. Johnson in 1856–1857. A founder of the Washington County Agricultural Society, Perkins built a five-bedroom house near present-day Southwest Rosa Road.

In 1901, the Perkins property sold at to the Shaw-Fear company. They subdivided the land and sold lots in their Beaverton-Reedville Acreage development, the Pasadena of Old Oregon. In 1907, Jacob and Jemima Wheeler's farm was subdivided, and David Wheeler helped Silas, Hawley, and Julius Buck build S.N. Buck & Sons Market in 1908, on what was then Wheeler Avenue, today's Southwest 185th.

Shaw-Fear donated land for the Aloha-Huber school. Built in 1911 on Southwest Blanton Street, it was the first road to connect the villages of Aloha and Huber.

In 1912, the Buck brothers, who operated a village post office in their store, submitted an application to the US Postal Service for an Aloah branch. The name was suggested by their sister, Dora Buck Wade, in honor of a favorite resort near her home on Wisconson's Lake Winnebago. The application, when returned, was approved with the name Aloha, a clerical error. The first postmaster was Julius Buck.

The Aloha Grange No. 773 was built by volunteers in 1932, at the height of the Great Depression. Founding members included Henry and Oscar Hagg, dairy industry leaders and co-owners of the David Hagg and Sons farm in Reedville.

By the mid-1900s, businesses in Aloha's commercial district developed along Southwest 185th and Tualatin Valley Highway. They included Aloha Feed, Imlay's Home Town Hardware, Earl Fultz's shoe repair, Aloha Pharmacy, Ivan Bernard's Barbershop, Nancy Carol's coffee shop, and Stubbs Market.

Aloha High School was constructed from 1966 to 1972, on the site of the former Kinnaman dairy.

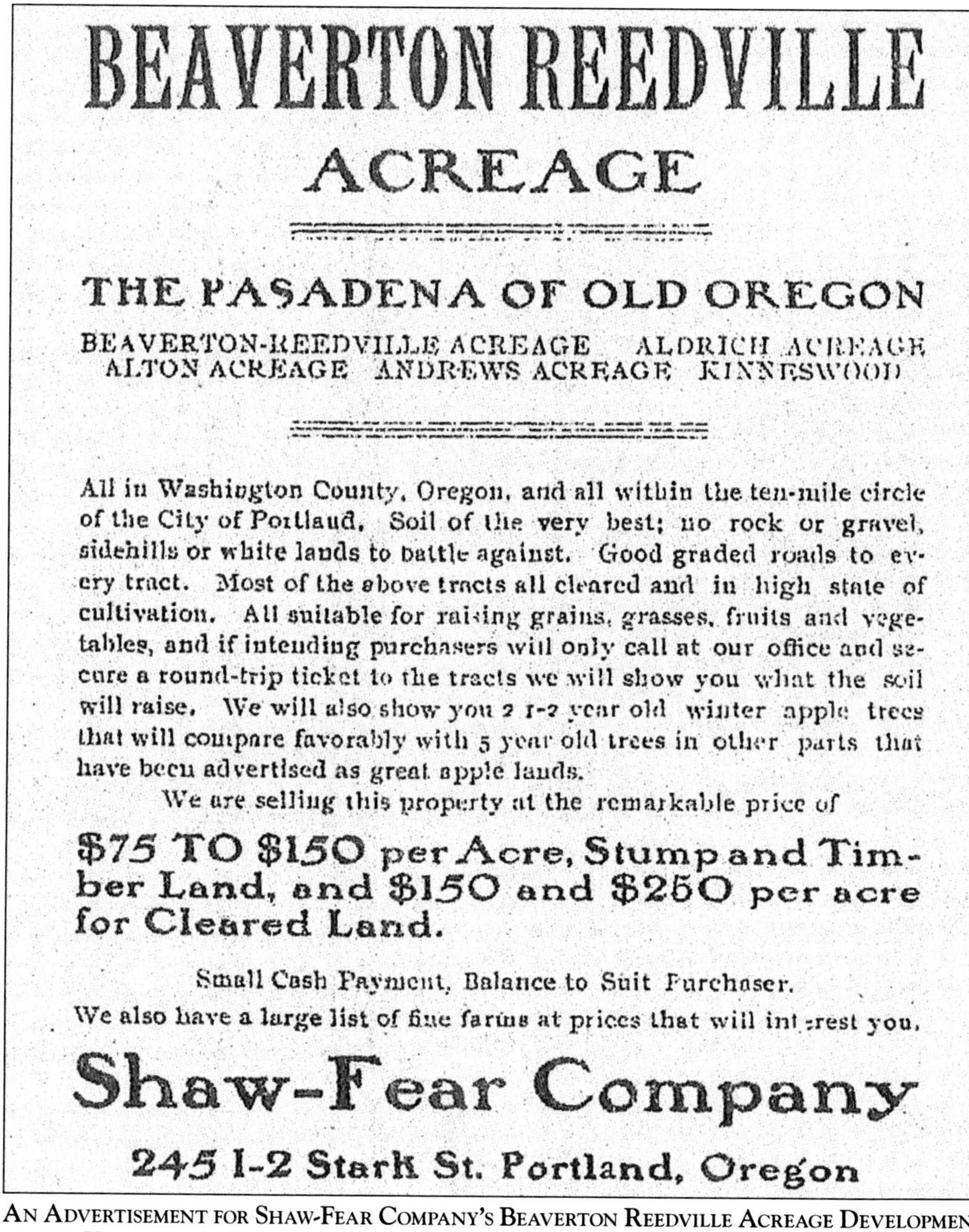

AN ADVERTISEMENT FOR SHAW-FEAR COMPANY'S BEAVERTON REEDVILLE ACREAGE DEVELOPMENT IN THE *HILLSBORO ARGUS*, 1901. The former Richard Perkins property sold at auction to the Standard Corporation, an investment and mortgage company. Adjacent to the railroad, the land included the old Plans-Falls Road, today's Southwest Kinnaman Road. The southern boundary was near today's Rosa Road. In the early 1900s, David Wheeler subdivided a 50-acre tract. In 1911, Shaw-Fear deeded a five-lot school site with two roads and sidewalks. They were installed by M.E. Blanton. He built a residence on the road to the school, next to what would become Southwest Blanton Street. The first Aloha-Huber District No. 107 bond election was held in September 1912. A debt of $5,500 was unanimously approved by 32 voters, and a four-room school was completed in time for the 1913 school year. (*Hillsboro Argus*.)

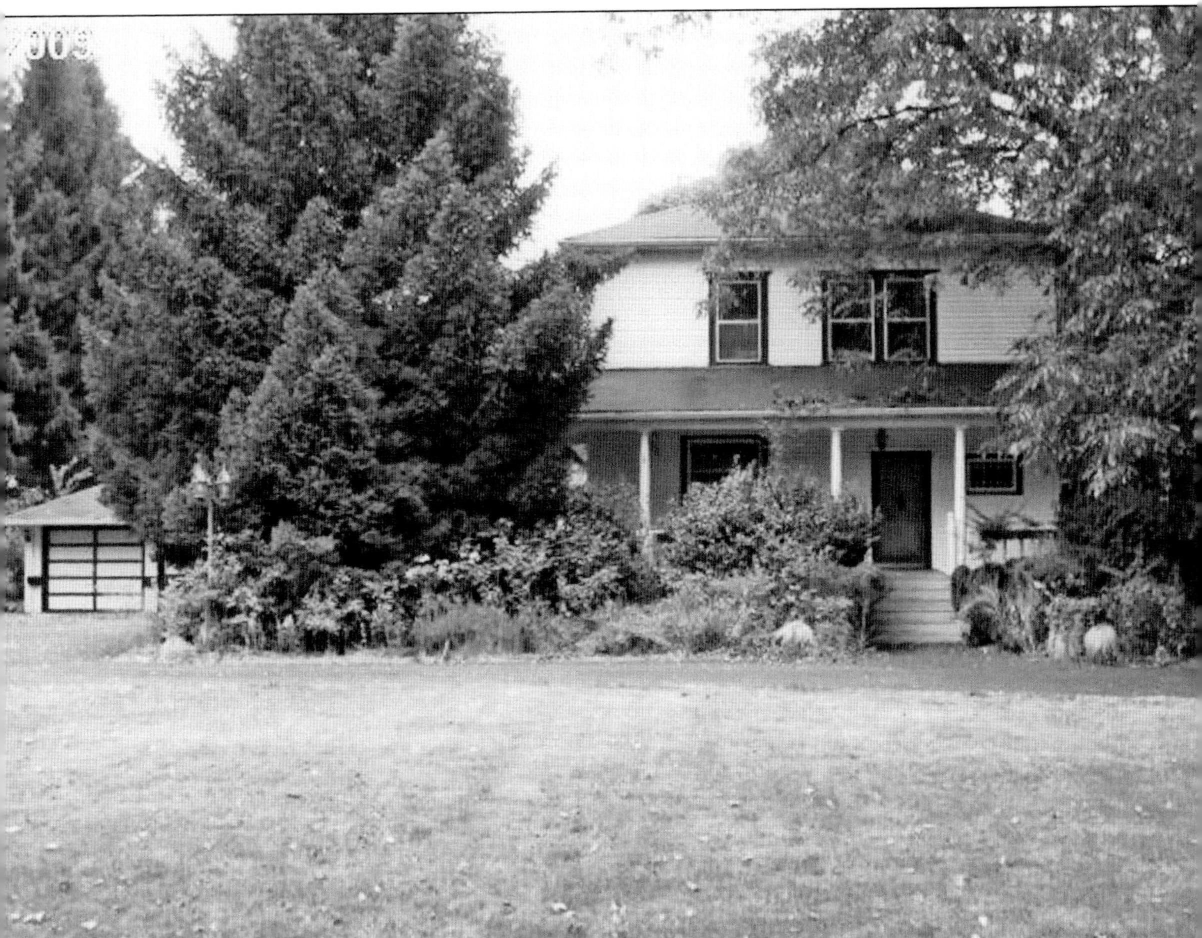

A c. 1901 Residence Still Standing on Southwest Kinnaman Road in Aloha. The two-story, four-bedroom home has a veranda and a detached double garage. It faces the old military road used during the early 1800s, before Oregon was a state. Once part of the original Torney land claim, the property sold to James H. McMillen in 1850 and to Richard S. Perkins and Arthur W. Johnson in 1856–1857. It was part of David and Alice Wheeler's 50-acre subdivision. Wheeler helped Julius Buck and his brothers construct a building for their general store in 1908. Called Buck's Market, it was on Wheeler Avenue. (John L. Scott Real Estate.)

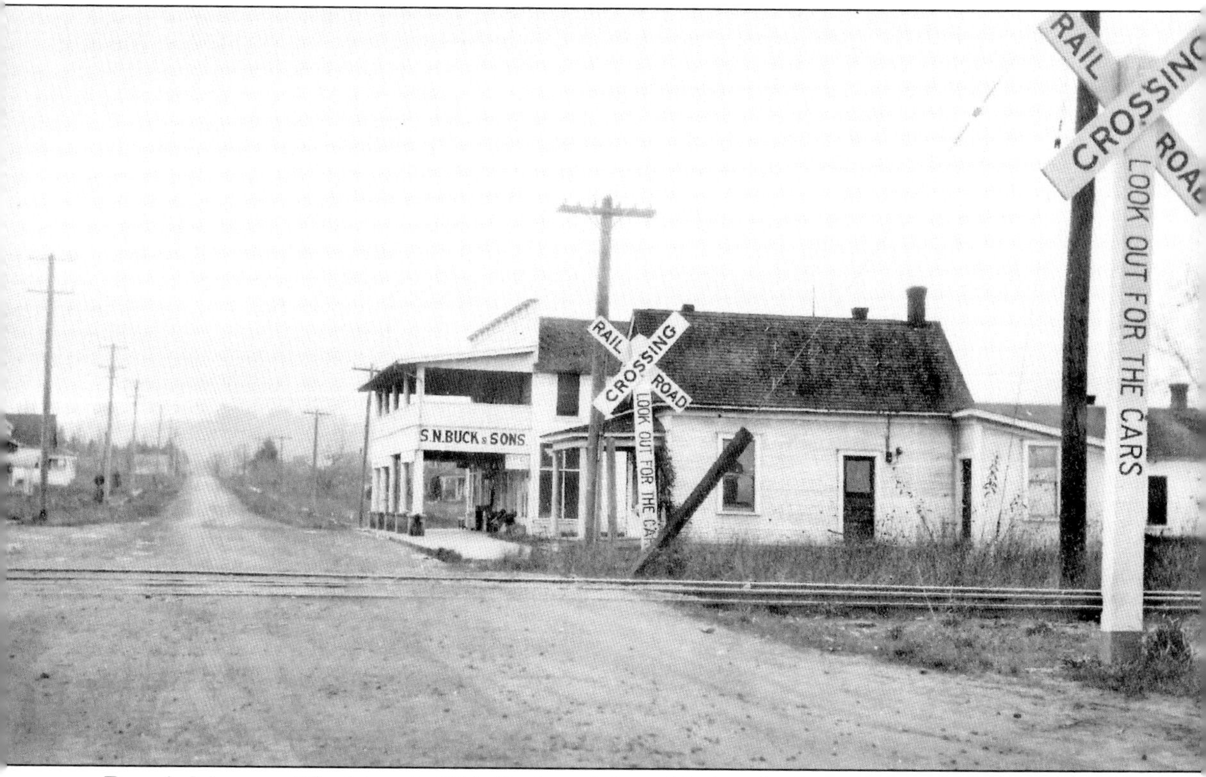

Buck's Market. The historic S.N. Buck and Sons Market, built in 1908, was a general store, longtime landmark, and the first commercial business in what is now Aloha. Once located on Wheeler Avenue, near the corner of today's Southwest 185th Avenue between Blanton and Shaw Streets, it anchored the Shaw-Fear Company's real estate development, Beaverton Reedville Acreage. The building was constructed by David Wheeler and storeowners Silas, Julius, and Joseph "Hawley" Buck, originally from Wisconsin. In 1912, the Bucks opened a post office inside the store and sold tickets for the Red Electric interurban railway. It operated on the Southern Pacific track north of the store. Buck's was renovated in 1915. The second story was sometimes rented as apartments or used for meetings and dances. The field next door to Buck's was sometimes used to play baseball, show movies, or host visiting carnivals. (Oregon Historical Society, No. bb009717.)

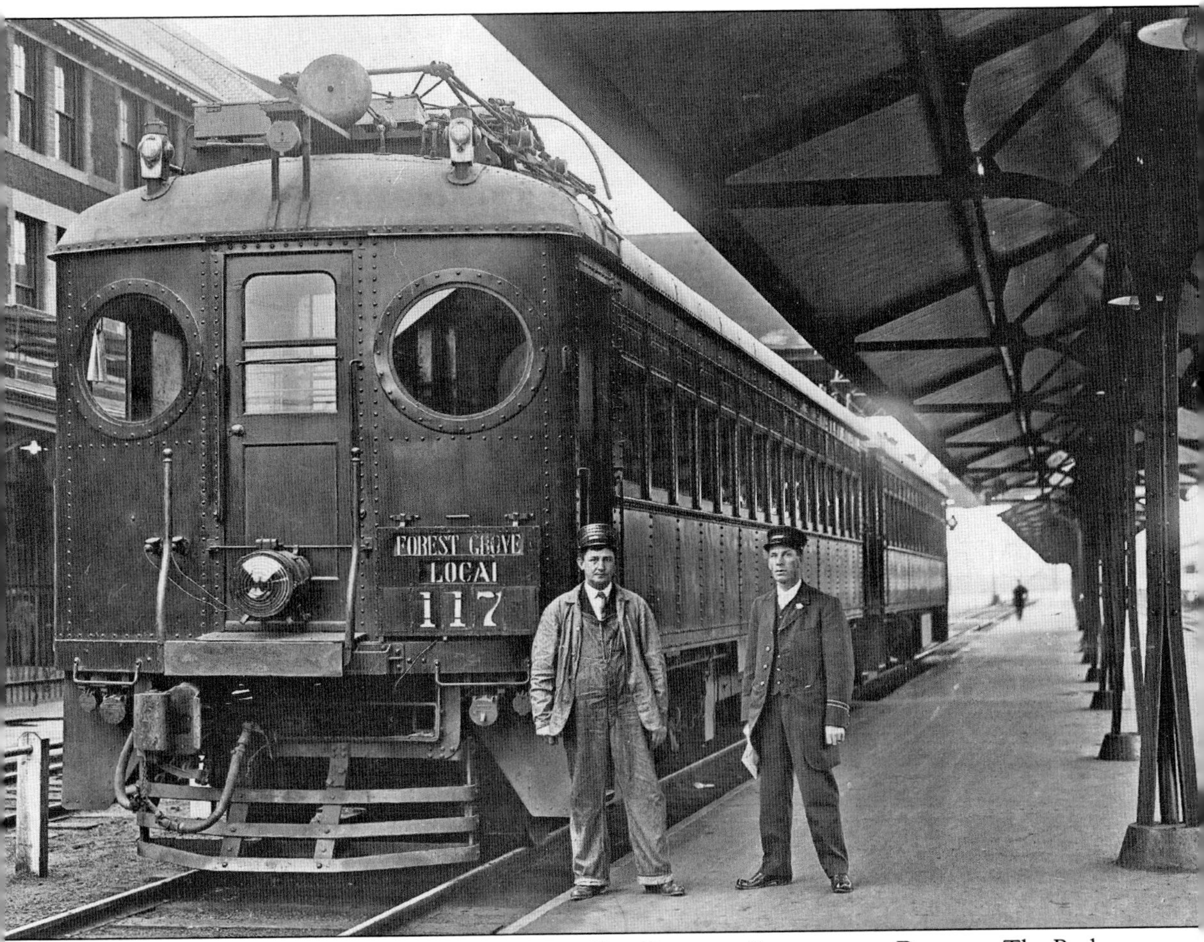

FOREST GROVE LOCAL 117, A STREETCAR ON THE RED ELECTRIC INTERURBAN RAILWAY. The Red Electric transported passengers to and from Aloha from 1912 to 1929. In 1905, the Willamette Valley Traction Company was organized to develop an electric interurban railroad. Service began in 1907. A station at Wheeler's Crossing, today's Southwest 185th Avenue, was added in 1909. Other nearby stops included St. Mary's, Huber, Tobias, and Reedville. Operated by the Southern Pacific Railway, it was one of the only major steam passenger railroads to convert some lines to electricity. Steel trolley cars manufactured by the Pullman Company in Chicago were powered by pantographs that conducted electricity through a contact wire. The Red Electric was one of the last in the nation to be implemented and, in 1929, one of the first to be abandoned. (Washington County Museum.)

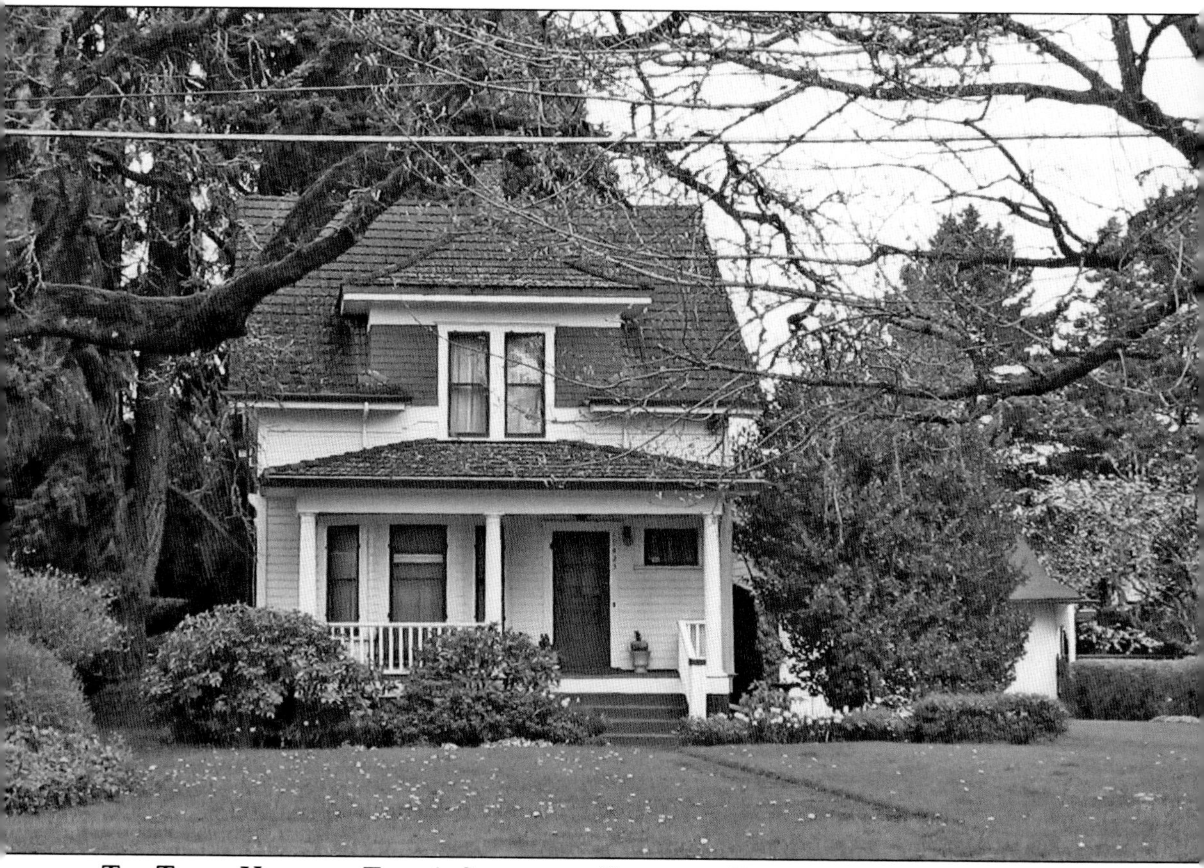

The Twohy House on Today's Southwest Kinnaman Road in Aloha. The Twohy house was built in 1919 facing the old Plains-Falls Road. The one-and-a-half-story residence is a well-maintained Queen Anne transitional-style home with Craftsman detailing. Located in the Beaverton Reedville Acreage development, the structure is rectangular in shape and sided with shiplap and shingles. Ceramic tile covers the medium-pitch gable roof. The front dormer has a slightly bellcast roof, also covered with ceramic shingles. The house has two one-story porches. The front porch is supported by Doric columns. A lattice skirt shelters the bay window. East of the residence, a two-room house has been converted to a garage. There is a large oak tree in the front yard. Significant as an example of early-20th-century suburban architecture, the house was added to the Washington County Cultural Resource Inventory in the 1980s. (Photograph by the author.)

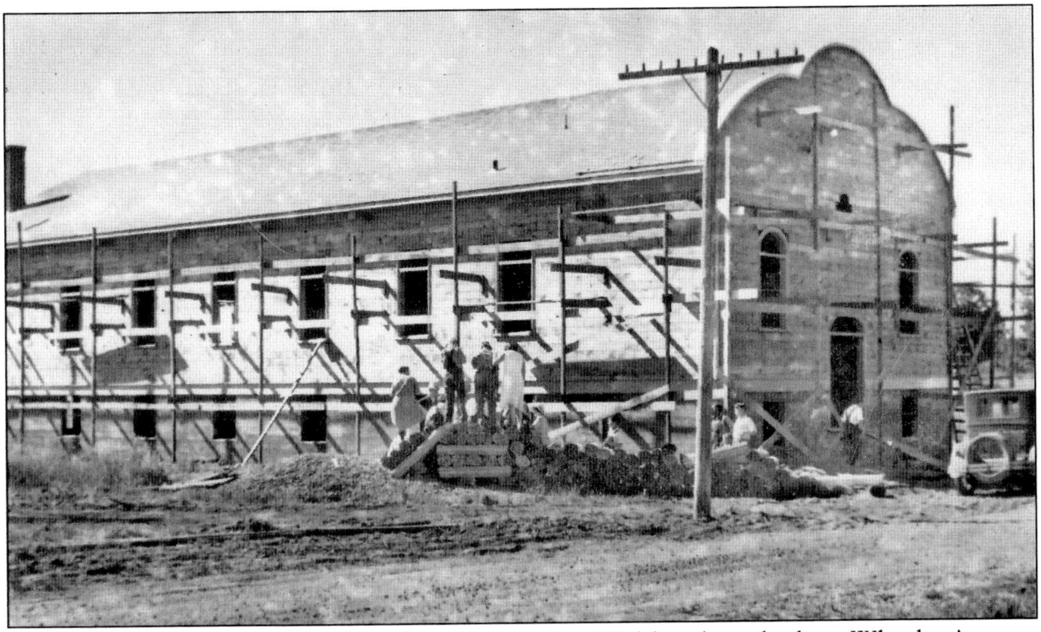

The Aloha Grange. In 1932, the Aloha Grange No. 773 (above) was built on Wheeler Avenue. Initially Grange meetings were held on the second floor of Buck's Market. Below, volunteers helping to build the Grange, which still stands today on Southwest 185th Avenue, are, from left to right, (first row) Mrs. T. Nault, Mrs. H.C. King, and Mary Grand; (second row) Mrs. S. Whitehead, Mrs. E.C. McElroy, Mrs. Jay Frost, Mrs. L.E. Klatt, Mrs. C.E. Barker; (third row) Mrs. A.J. Nault, E.J. Johnson, J.L. Schmid, and Mrs. W.F. Norman. (Both, Oregon Historical Society. Above, No. bb009064; below, No. bb009063.)

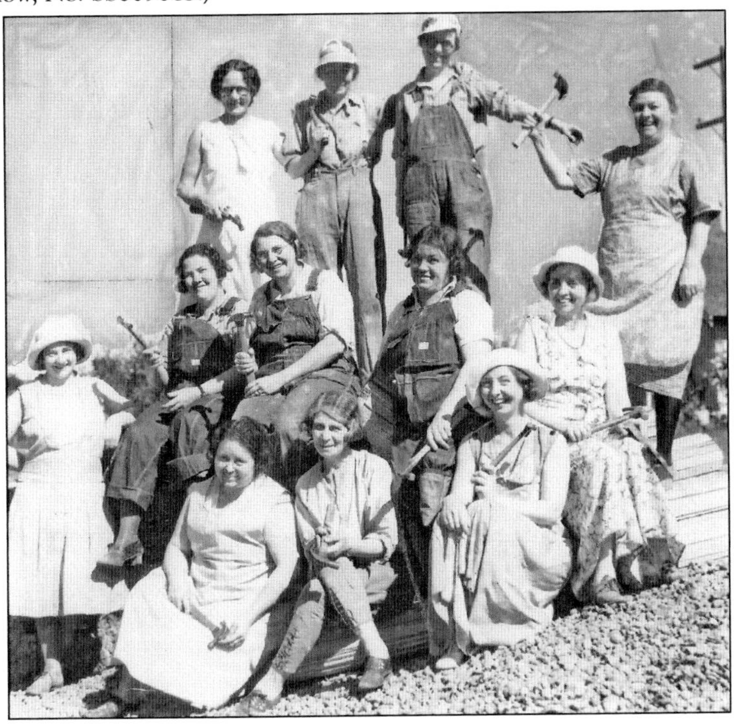

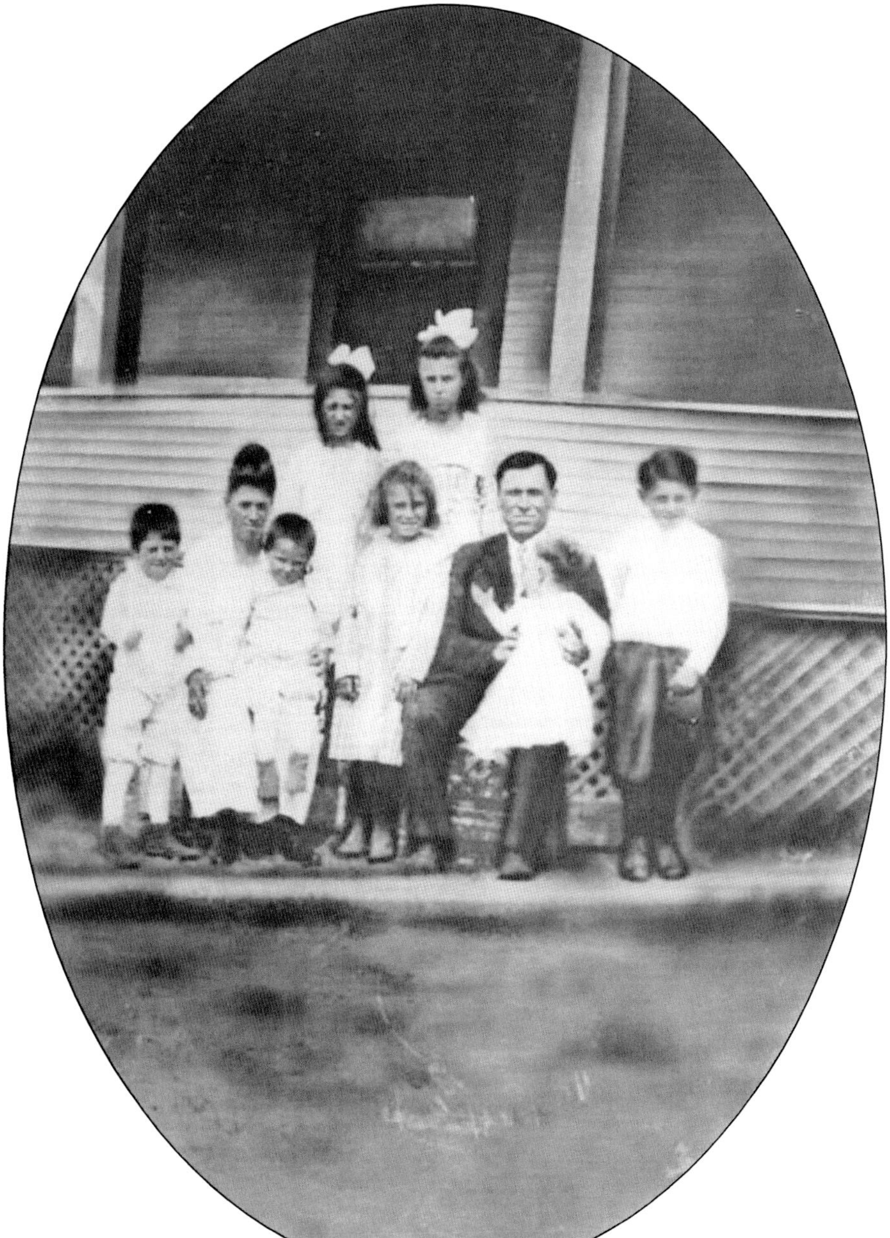

A Dimeo Family Portrait in Front of Their First Residence in Aloha, near Rosa Road, 1922. During the Great Depression, the Dimeos moved to a farm south of today's Kinnaman Road in Aloha. From left to right are (first row) Frank Jr., Teresa holding John, Helen, Frank Sr., Joe, and Peter; (second row) Angie and Rose. In the mid-1900s, the Dimeo farm was located east of Wheeler Avenue, today's Southwest 185th Avenue, between dairies operated by Lon Kinnaman to the east and Dan Shaw at Perkins Corner, the intersection of Kinnaman and Farmington Roads. In addition to raising cows, pigs, and chickens, the Dimeos had an orchard and grew berries and grapes. Frank also planted a large vegetable garden every year. Surplus dairy and farm products were sold at farmer's markets. (Dimeo family.)

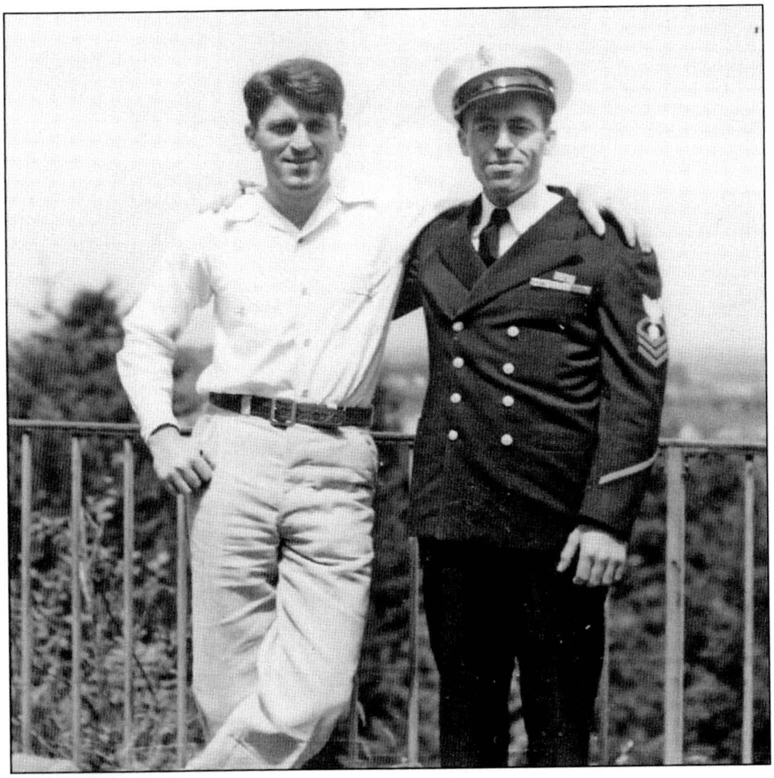

Frank Dimeo (Left) and Joe Dimeo (Right), 1940s. Joe Dimeo enlisted in the Navy after high school graduation. He was a chief petty officer on the USS *California* on shore leave the night before Pearl Harbor was attacked on December 7, 1941. (Dimeo family.)

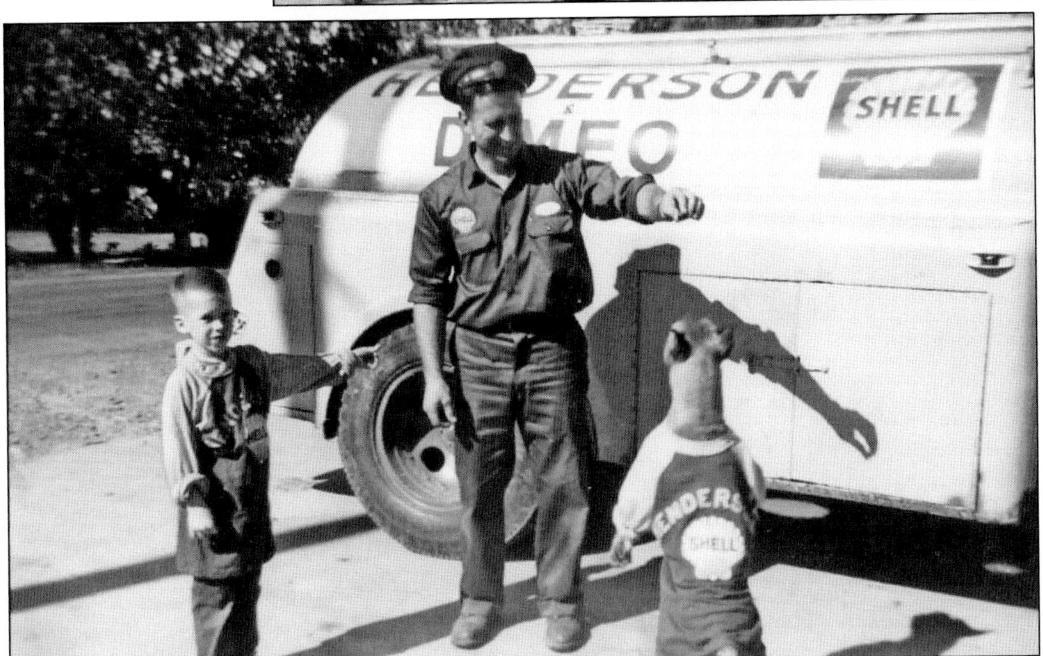

George (Right) and Son John Dimeo (Left) with Their Dog, February 1960. In the 1930s, the Dimeos maintained property on Rosa Road for Mr. Henderson, who owned a heating oil company. George Dimeo worked there in the 1950s and later purchased and operated the business. (Dimeo family.)

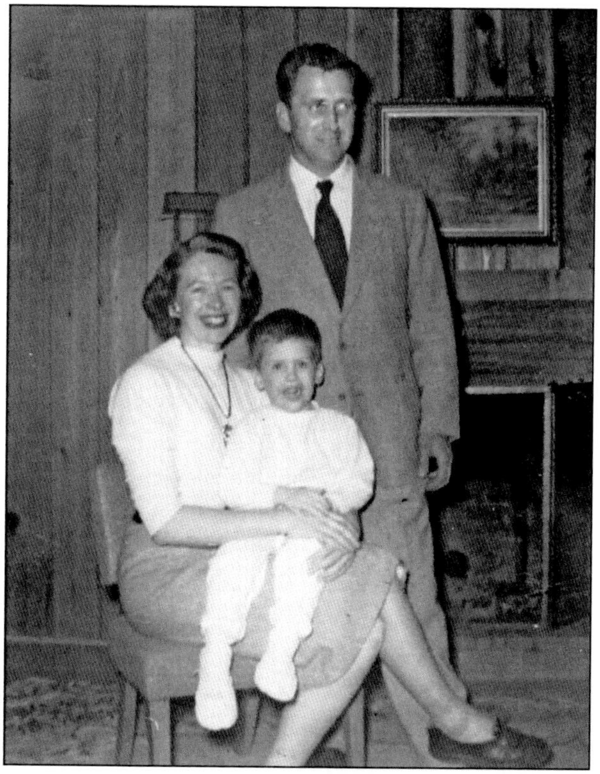

From Left to Right, "Margie," John, and George Dimeo, 1950s. As a teenager in Aloha, George organized and recruited players for Little League. In the late 1940s, they operated the Beaverton Rural Fire Protection District from their home and also helped organize Aloha Days parades and other events. (Dimeo family.)

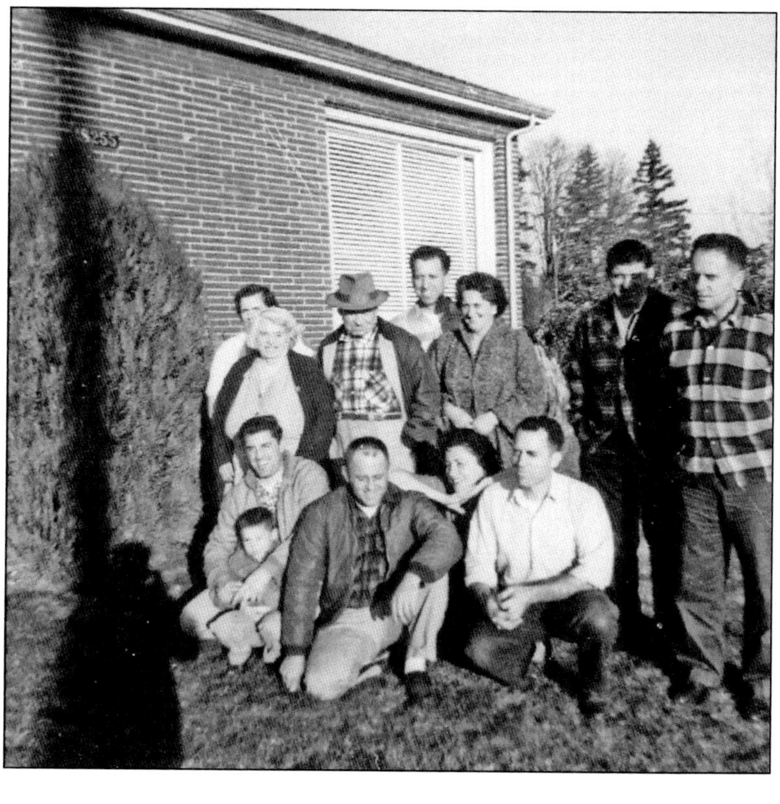

Three Generations of the Dimeo Family, August 1962. From left to right are (first row) Dave and son Gary, Bill, Stella, and Joe; (second row) Theresa, Frank Sr., Angie, Frank Jr., and John; (third row) Helen and George. (Dimeo family.)

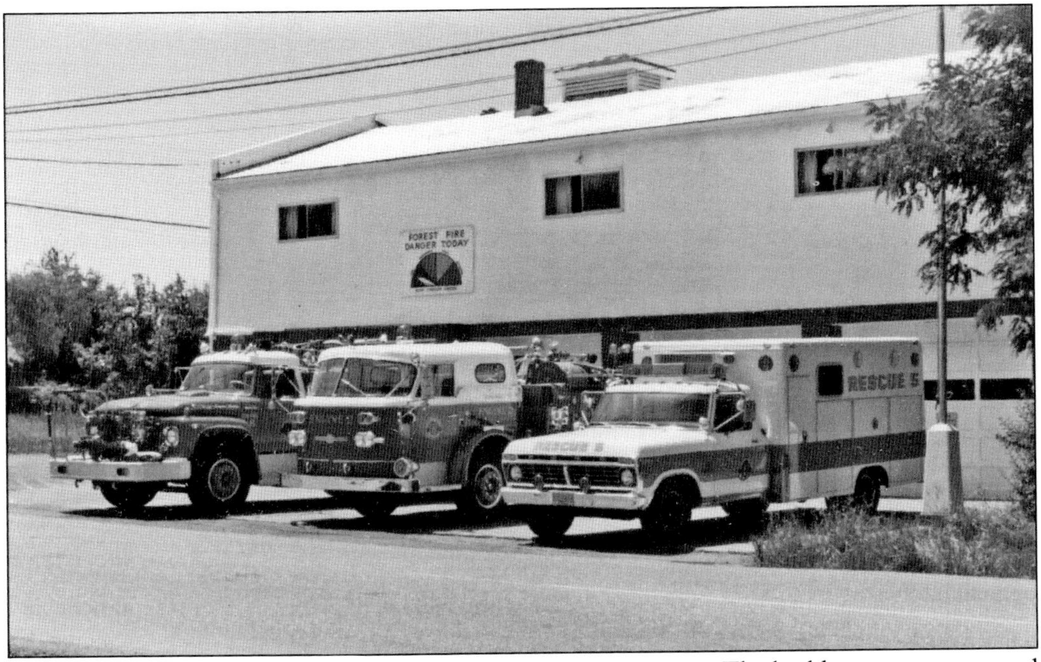

The Aloha Fire Station on Southwest 185th Avenue, 1977. The building was constructed by volunteers in 1950. George Dimeo and others helped organize the Beaverton Rural Fire Protection District, also known as the Aloha Fire Department, in 1947. For three years, George and Marge Dimeo operated the agency from their home in Aloha. When he retired in 1961, Walter "Walt" Platt became the first paid fire chief. From left to right below, volunteer firefighters LeRoy Albert "Bud" Slovick and Platt, ride on an old fire engine in an Aloha Days parade in 1956. (Above, photograph by Harvey Thomas, courtesy of Tualatin Valley Fire and Rescue; below, Slovick family.)

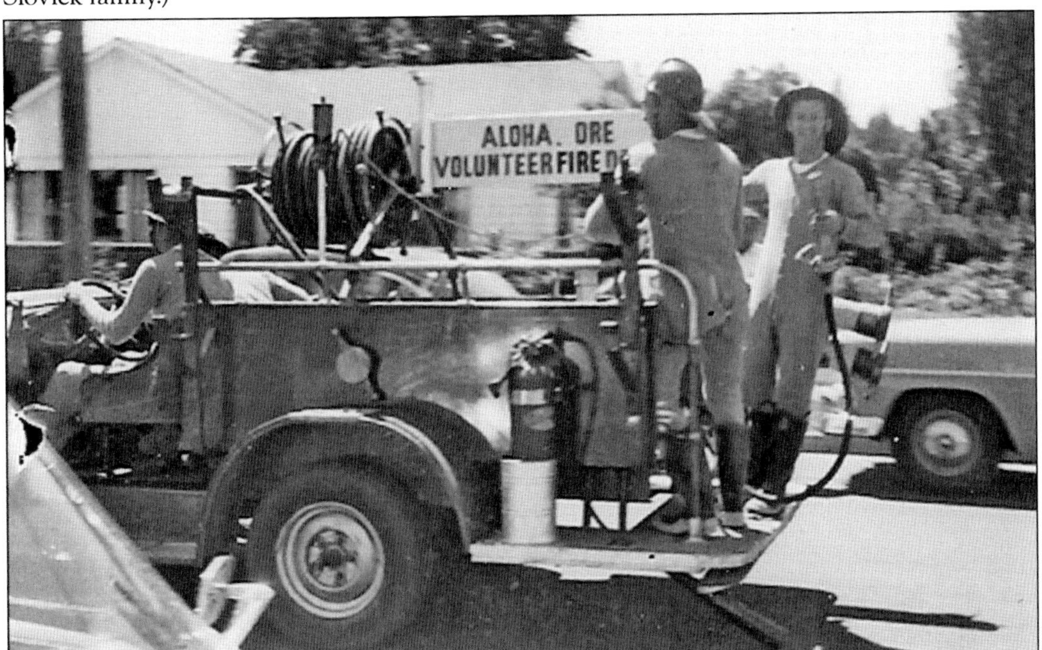

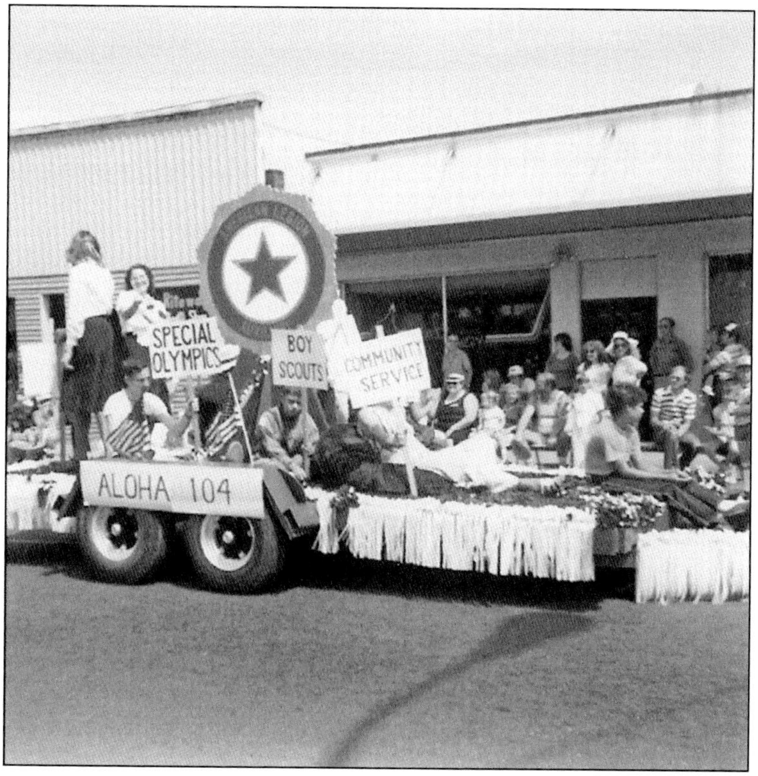

FLOAT REPRESENTING ALOHA POST 104 OF THE AMERICAN LEGION IN THE ALOHA DAYS PARADE, 1980. Now located on Southwest Alexander Street in Aloha, near today's 203rd Avenue, Post 104 was formed in 1934. (Slovick family.)

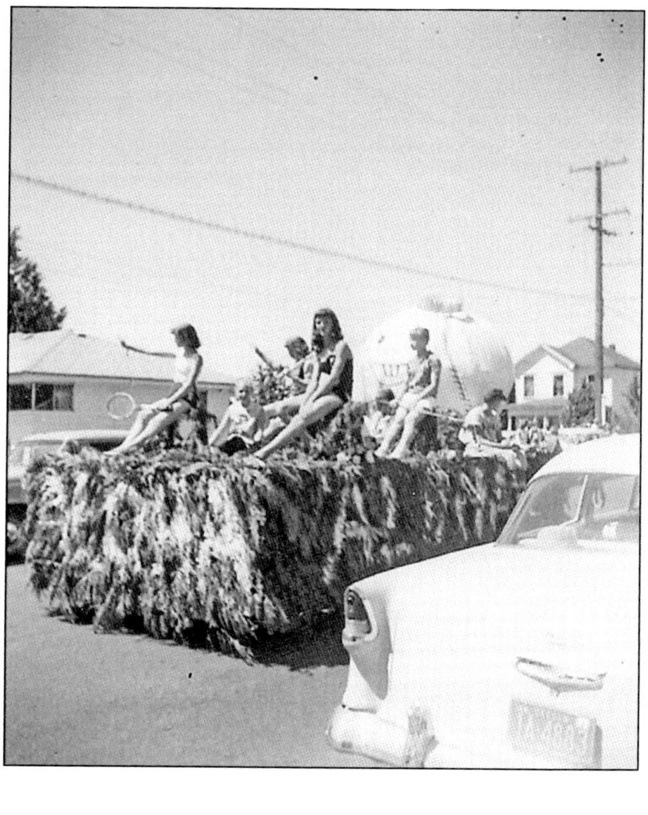

LOCAL CHILDREN AND TEENAGERS RIDING ON A FLOAT IN THE ALOHA DAYS PARADE, 1956. In the mid-1900s, the community organized annual summer celebrations featuring parades and other community events, including an annual history contest. (Slovick family.)

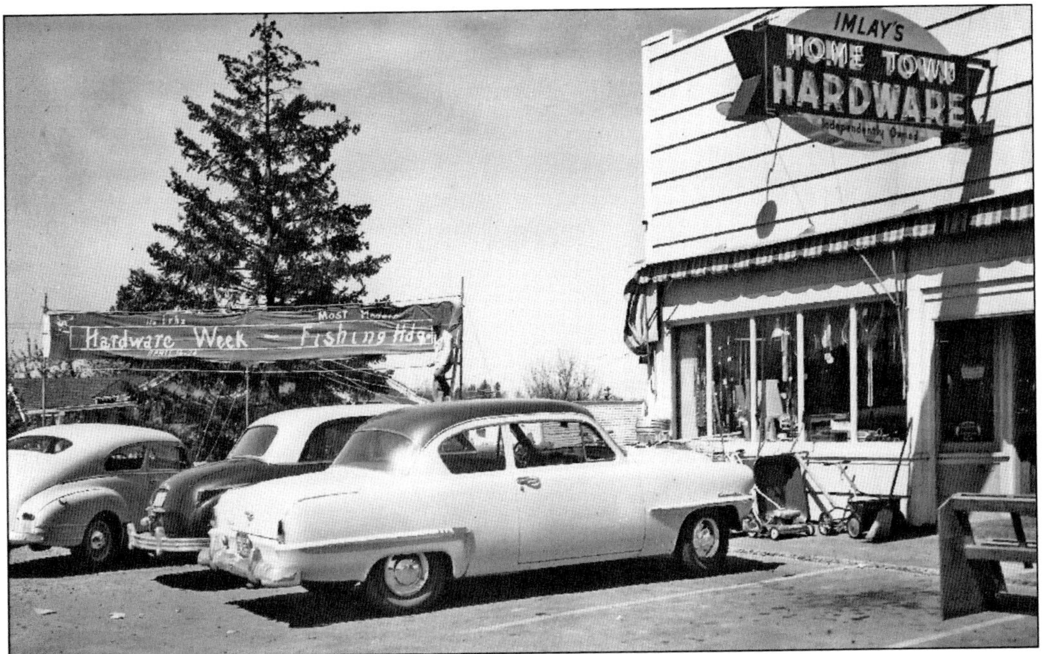

The J.B. Imlay & Sons Hardware Store in Aloha, Early 1950s. The store was once located north of Tualatin Valley Highway and west of Wheeler Avenue, today's Southwest 185th Avenue. It was built in the mid-1930s and managed by Charles Towers Imlay Sr. The youngest son of James Burd Imlay, he graduated from Reedville School in 1906. Beginning in 1933, he was the owner and proprietor of J.B. Imlay & Sons grain and feed mill in Reedville, and he owned Imlay's Home Town Hardware in Aloha. He was also a member of the Reedville School Board. (Both, Kathleen Imlay Eames.)

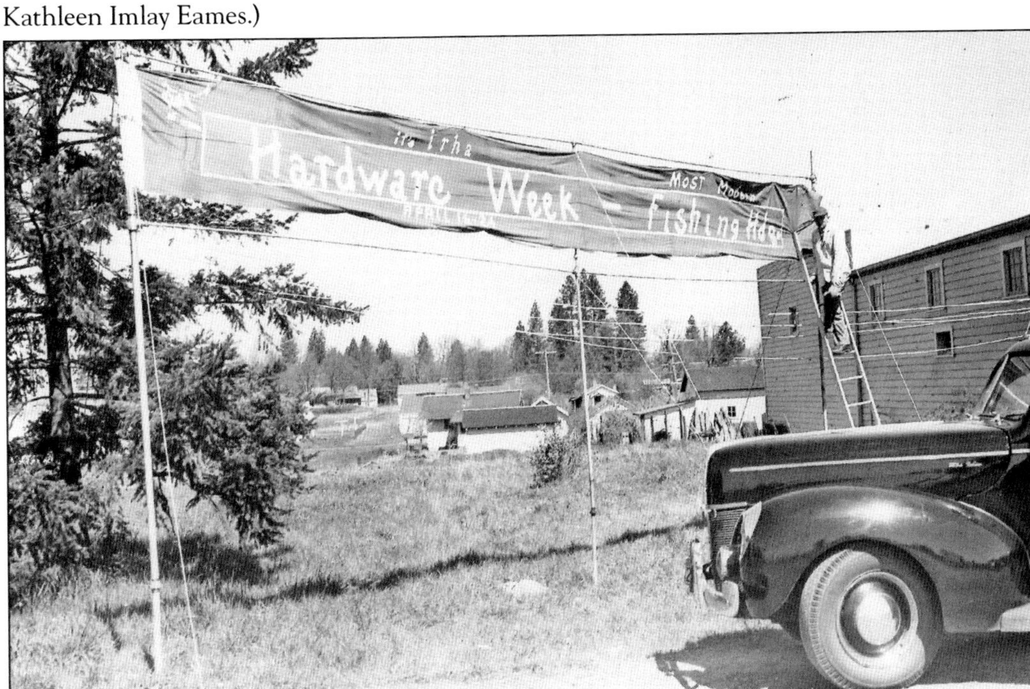

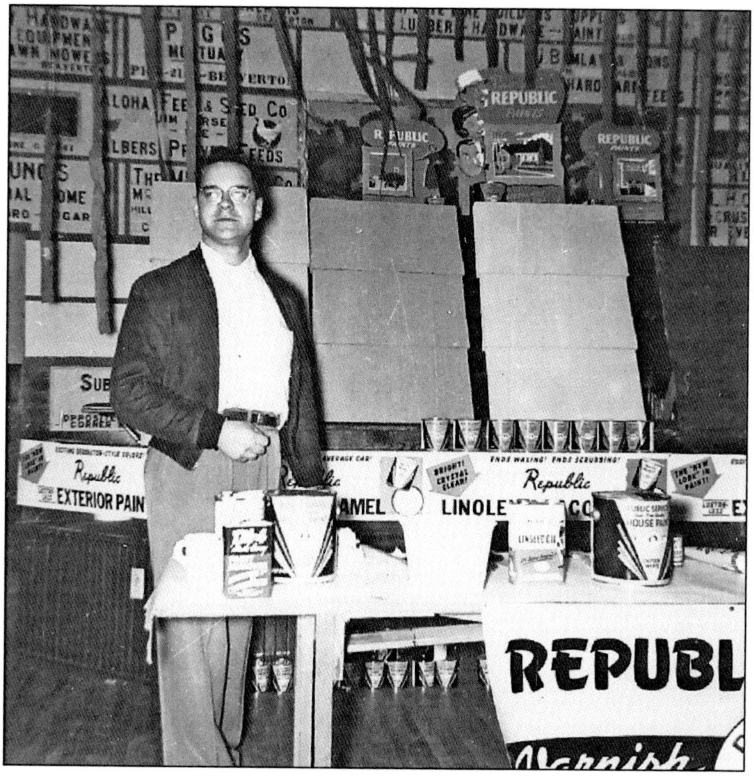

Charles Towers Imlay Sr., Proprietor of Imlay's Home Town Hardware in Aloha. Imlay is pictured attending a promotional Paint Fair the business sponsored at the Huber Grange in the early 1950s. Imlay was president of the Oregon Feed and Seed Dealers and a member of the Northwest Hardware Association. (Kathleen Imlay Eames.)

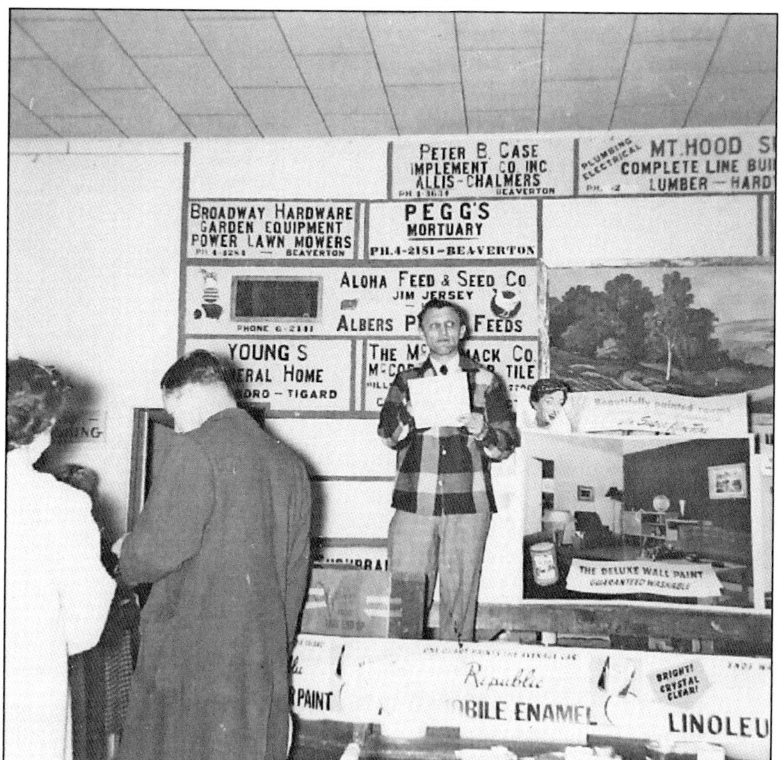

Walter J. "Walt" Eames. Eames was master of ceremonies during the Paint Fair at the Huber Grange in the early 1950s. Employed at Imlay's Home Town Hardware from 1952 to 1954, Walt was the second grandchild of John Nyberg, Tualatin's second mayor and his wife, Ora. Walt married Kathleen Imlay in the mid-1900s (Kathleen Imlay Eames.)

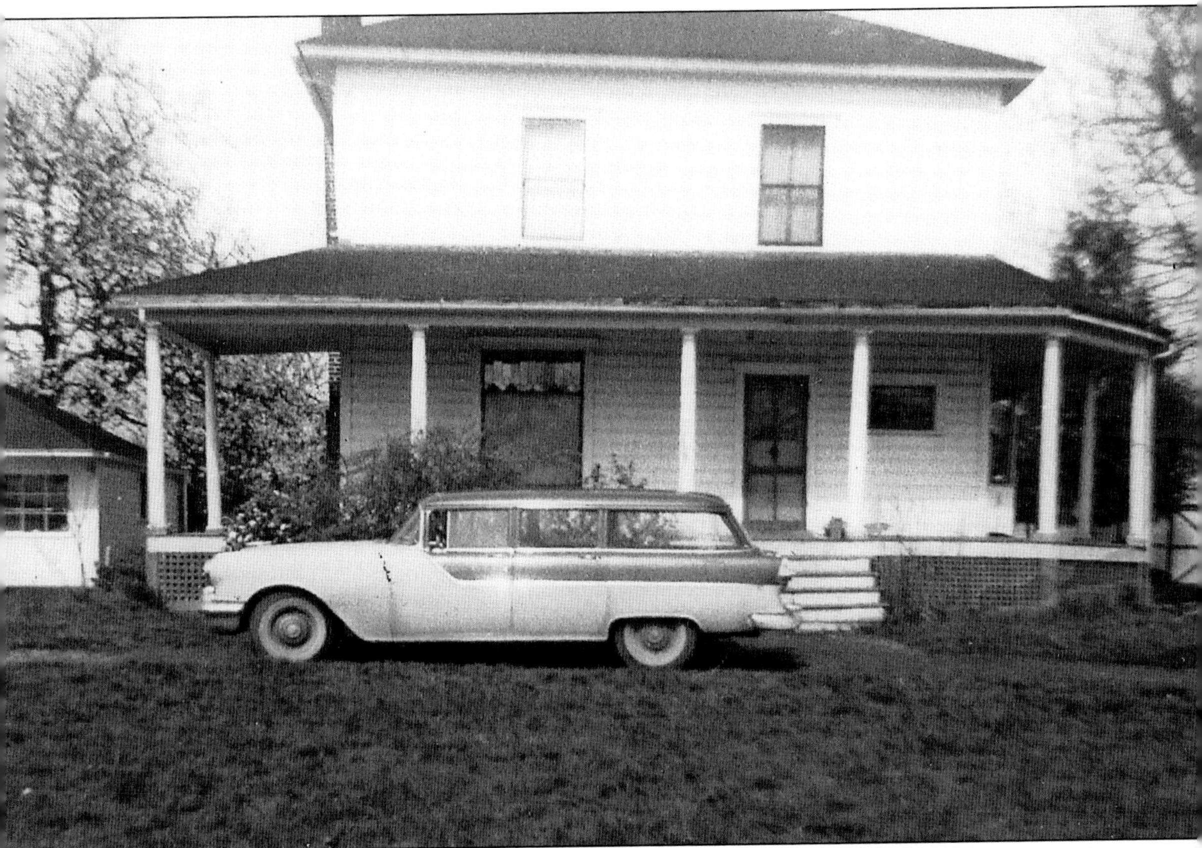

The Louris Family. From 1956 to 1964, Chester "Chet" and Ruth Louris and their family lived in one of the original houses in the Aloha Reedville Acreage development, built at the beginning of the 20th century. There was a large dining room, kitchen, and parlor with a corner fireplace on the main floor and bedrooms on the second story. What had been a carriage house was converted into a garage. Apple, Bing cherry, Bartlett pear, filbert, and walnut trees were also on the property, which was located across the street from the Kinnaman Dairy. Ruth was an artisan and entrepreneur who owned Sylvan Originals, creating and manufacturing handcrafted ceramic earrings. She was also a 4-H leader. After moving to the property, they discovered that the previous owner kept pigeons. During the Columbus Day Storm in 1962, the pigeons flew away and never returned. (Louris family.)

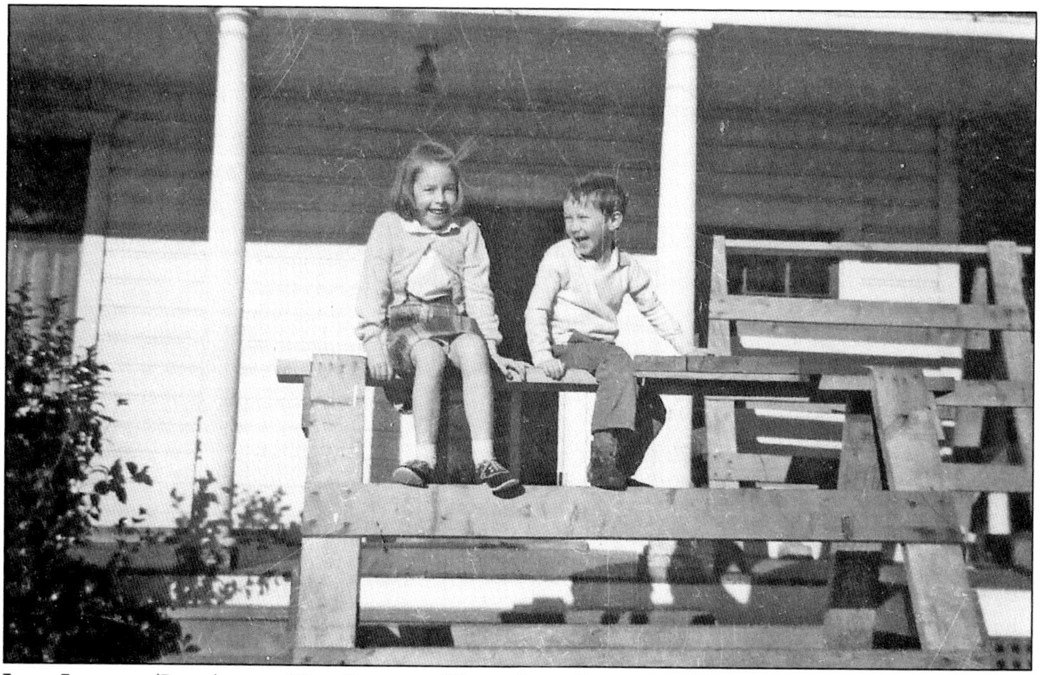

Lisa Louris (Left) and Tom Louris (Right) in Front of Their House on Southwest Kinnaman Road, around 1960. There were three additional Louris children—Marsha, John, and Cathy, not pictured. They lived in the house across the street from Aloha High School from 1956 to 1964 and attended Aloha-Huber Elementary School. (Louris family.)

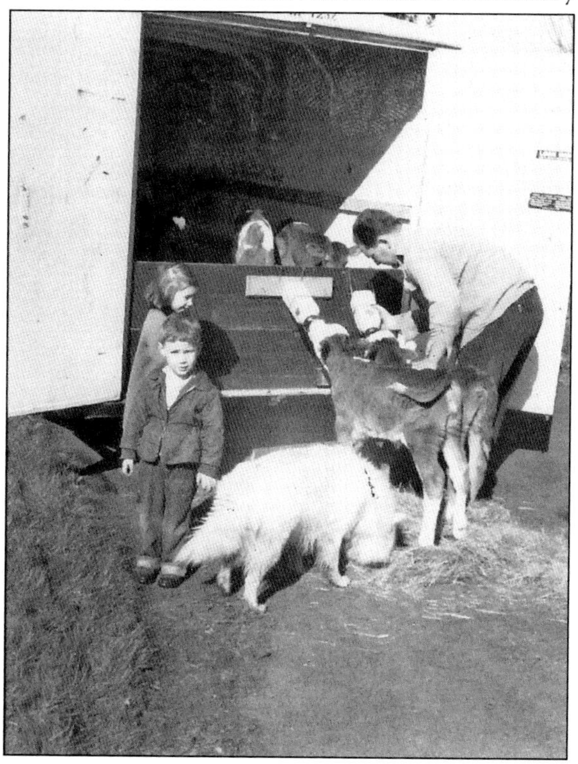

Lisa and Tom Louris. Lisa and Tom (left) are pictured with uncle Don Jahnke (right) near a barn they salvaged from the blueberry farm next door. The family raised and sold calves and competed in the Oregon State Fair in several categories. Ruth Louris, formerly Jahnke, was originally from Minnesota. (Louris family.)

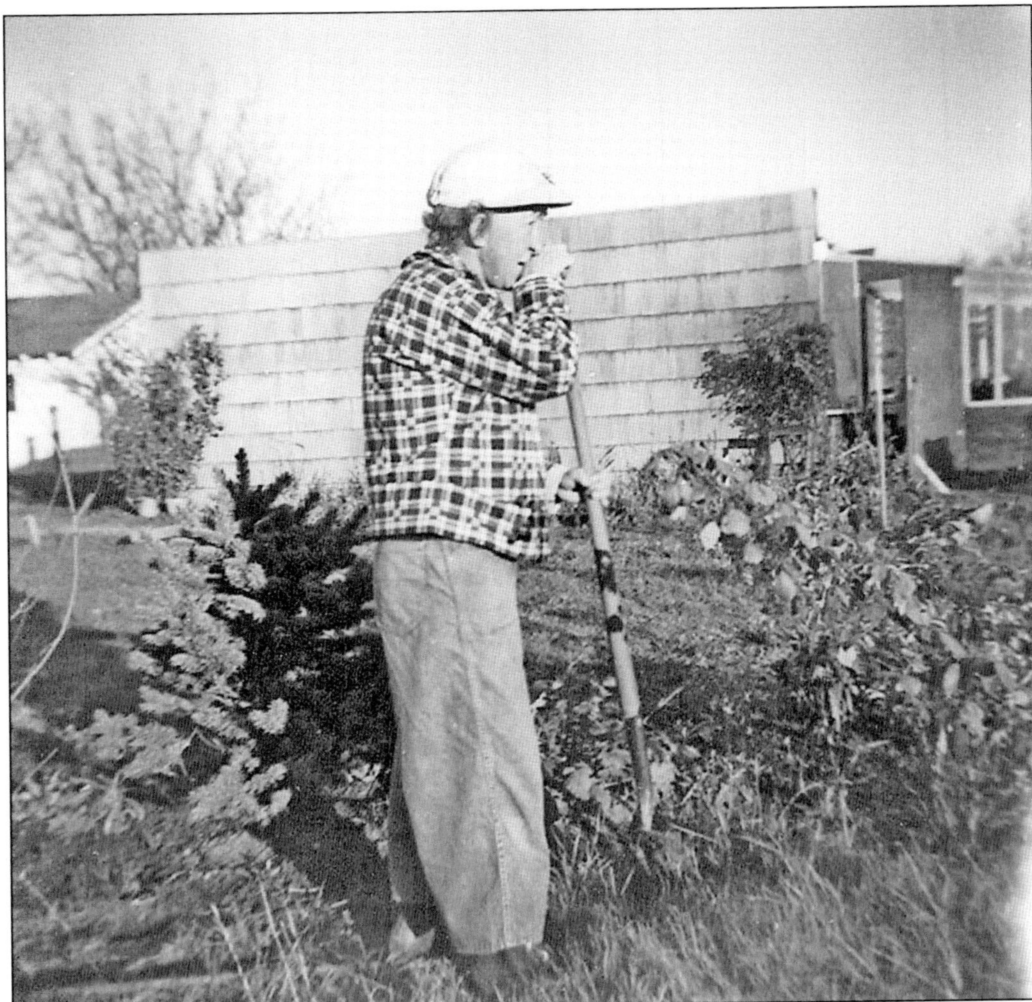

Rosa "Rosie" Halemba, March 1958. Rosie is pictured by her store and residence at Southwest 185th Avenue and Blanton Street in Aloha. In the 1920s, Rosie's parents, Alois and Pauline Halemba, purchased 12 acres on what was then Wheeler Avenue, now 185th Avenue. Alois, who emigrated from Austria, named Rosa Road after his daughter when he made a sign to indicate where a lumber delivery was to be delivered. In 1937, Rosie acquired an old streetcar, moved it next to Noah Hill's Feed Store, and opened a gift shop. In 1938, she bought an abandoned barbershop and opened the Aloha Variety Store. The streetcar was moved next door and used as a greenhouse. Pansies, at three for 25¢, were best sellers. The Halembas built a duplex that is still standing today, facing Southwest Blanton Street. Rosie's Aloha Variety Store, a gift and flower shop, was featured on the *You Asked for It* television program. (John Foster.)

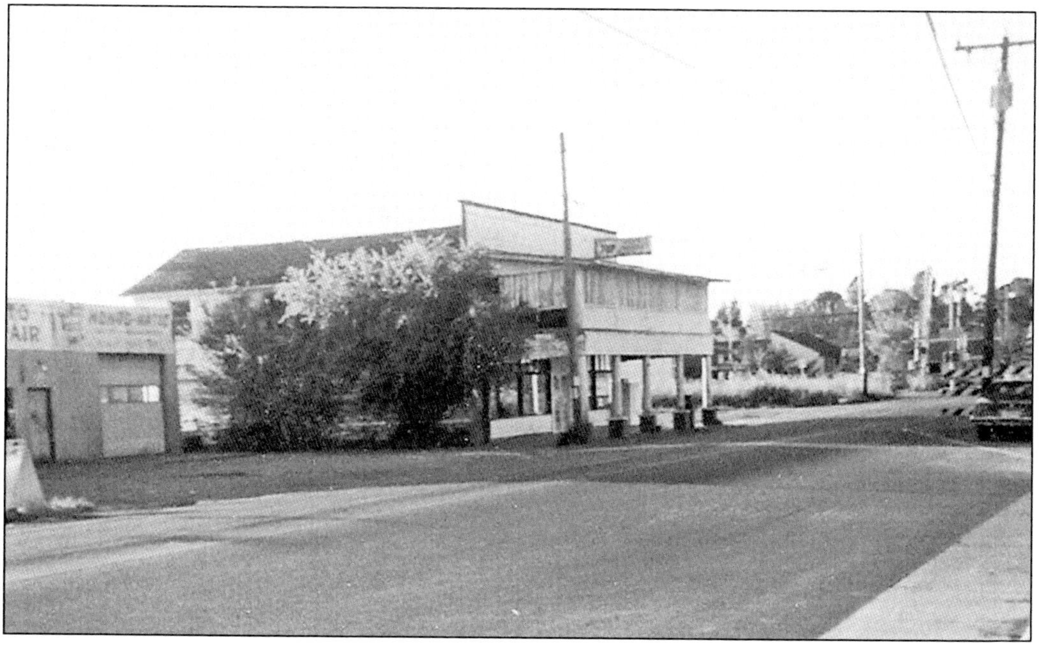

The Former Buck's Market in 1982, When It Was Shopeze Market. It faced today's Southwest 185th Avenue at the corner of Shaw Street in Aloha. In 1957, the Bucks sold to Mel and Avis Watt. They operated the Aloha Market until 1967. Ross Williams bought the store, and it became Williams Aloha Market. It was renamed the Shopeze Market in 1971 and was under the ownership of Plaid Pantry stores by 1977. (Both, Slovick family.)

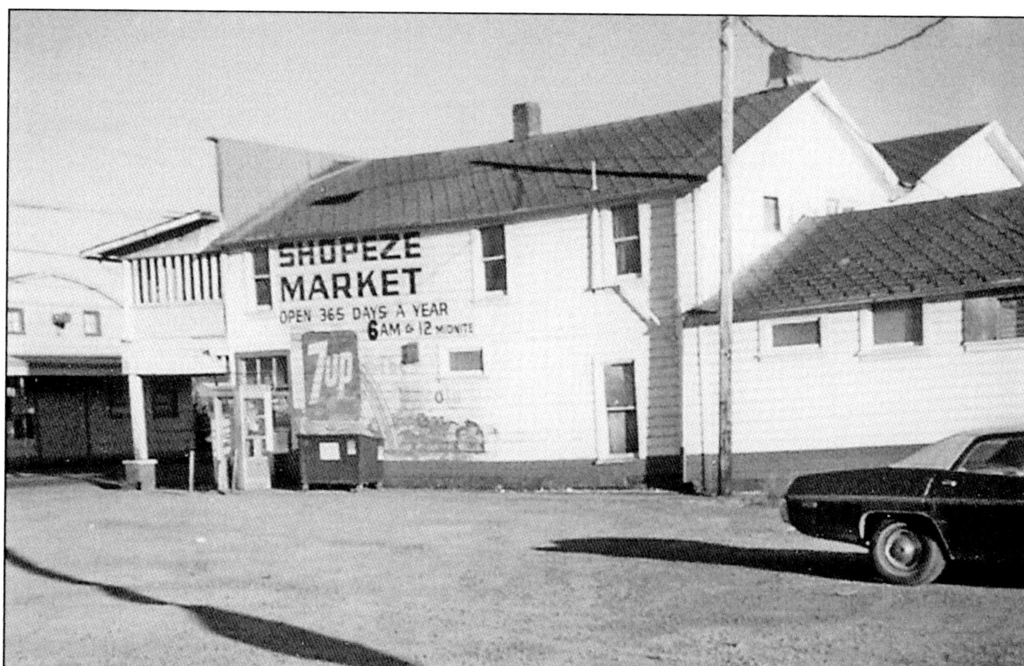

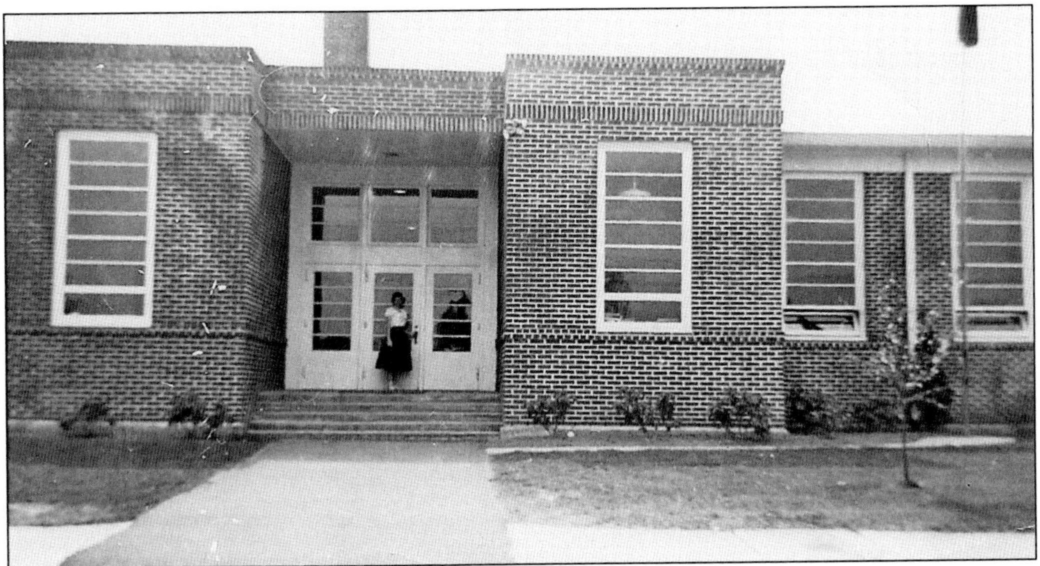

The Entrance to the Aloha-Huber School on Southwest Blanton Street, 1956. Above, the first Aloha public school opened in a private residence in the fall of 1911. Aloha-Huber School District No. 107 held its first bond election in 1912. There were 32 voters present at the Shaw Theater office. In 1913, a four-room school building was completed in 1913 at a cost of $5,545.93. In 1920, there were 141 residents qualified to vote in school elections; there were 247 in 1947. The eighth-grade graduating class at Aloha-Huber School in 1956 is pictured below. Aloha-Huber schools became part of Beaverton School District No. 48 in 1960. (Both, Slovick family.)

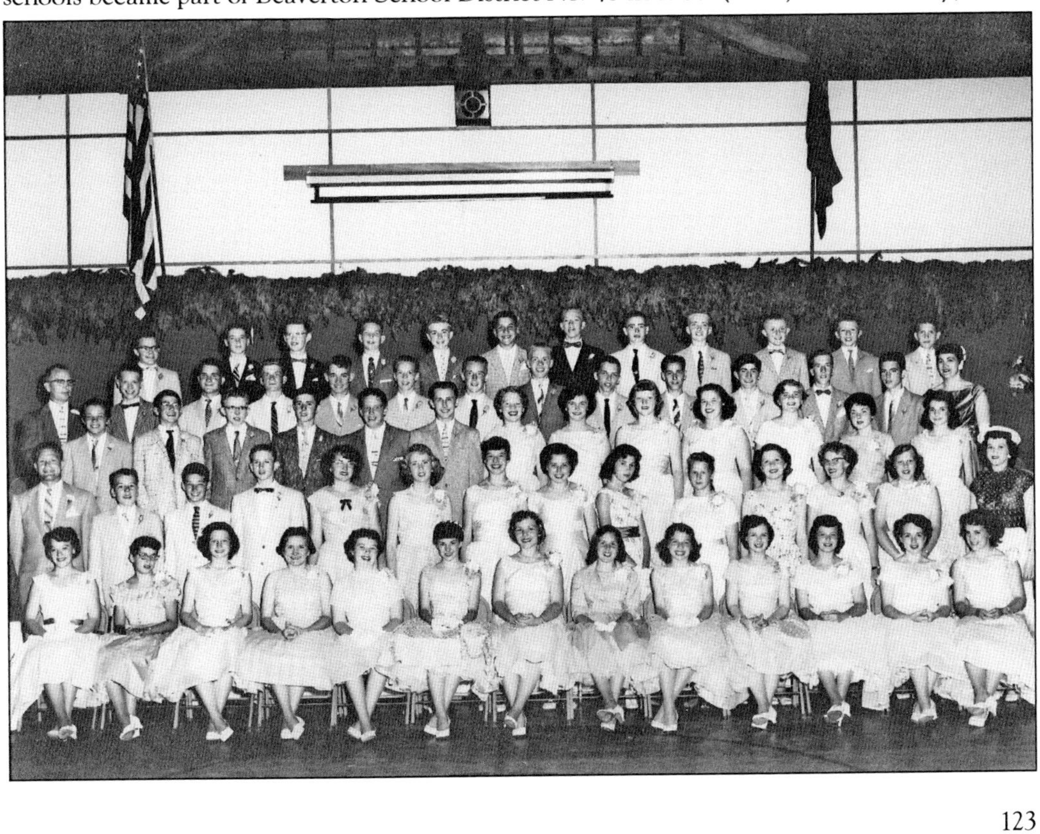

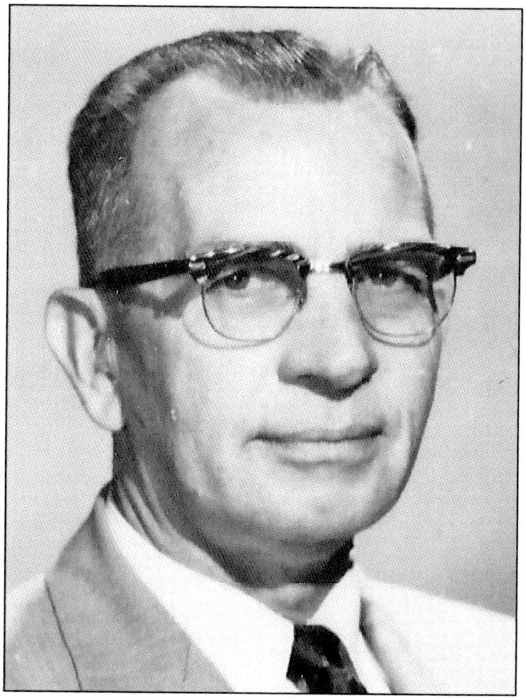

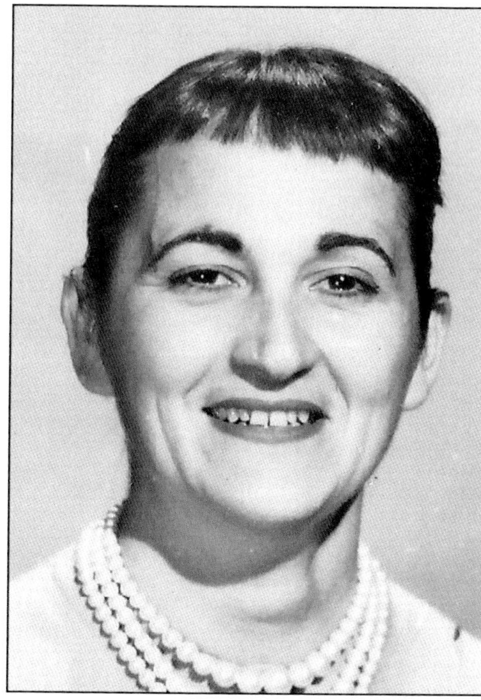

VAL BULLIS AND MAXINE CLOW. V.H. Valmore "Val" Bullis is pictured in October 1959 (left). A graduate of the Oregon Normal School in 1934, he was the superintendent of the Aloha-Huber School District in the 1950s and 1960s. Maxine Clow (right) served in the US Coast Guard during World War II and was principal of Aloha-Huber Elementary School for 20 years. The school is pictured below in 1963. Located on Southwest Blanton Street near today's 172nd Avenue in Aloha, the building is now used by International School of Beaverton, part of School District No. 48. (Above, Art Bullis; below, Louris family.)

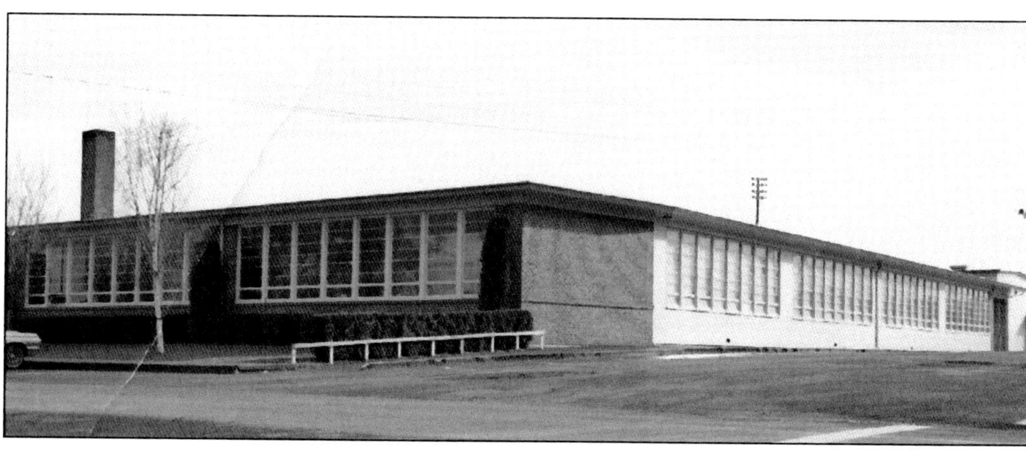

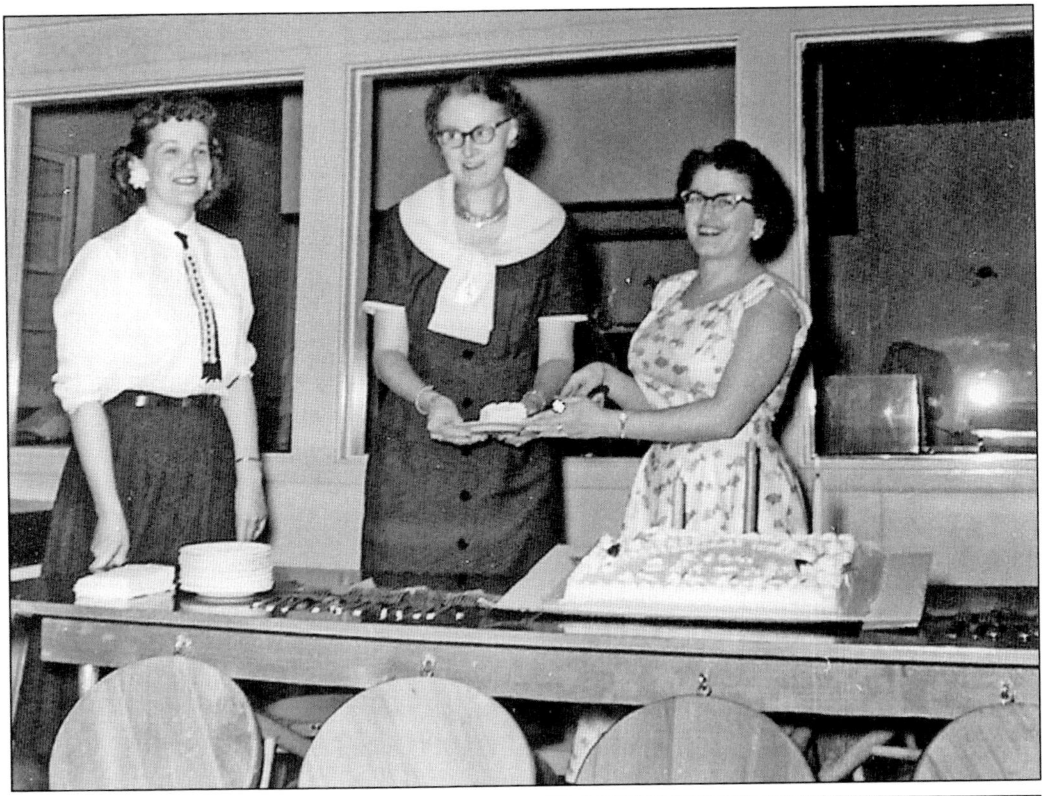

Inside the Cafeteria of the Aloha-Huber School, April 1957. From left to right above are teachers Helen Slovick, Miss Gideon and Mrs. Brown, president of the Aloha branch of the Oregon Education Association, celebrating the National Education Association Centennial. The association, founded in Philadelphia, Pennsylvania, was formed to promote literacy, strengthen public education, and improve credentials. Women were allowed to join in 1866. There were over 700,000 members in 1957. Attending the celebration below are, from left to right, Mrs. Jones, Mrs. Sherwood, Mrs. Helvogt, and Mrs. Gordon. (Both, Slovick family.)

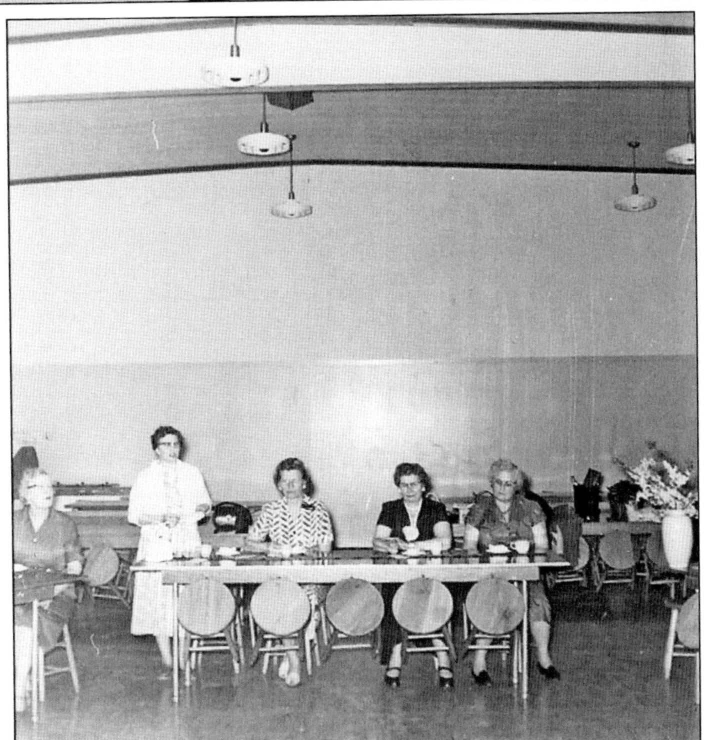

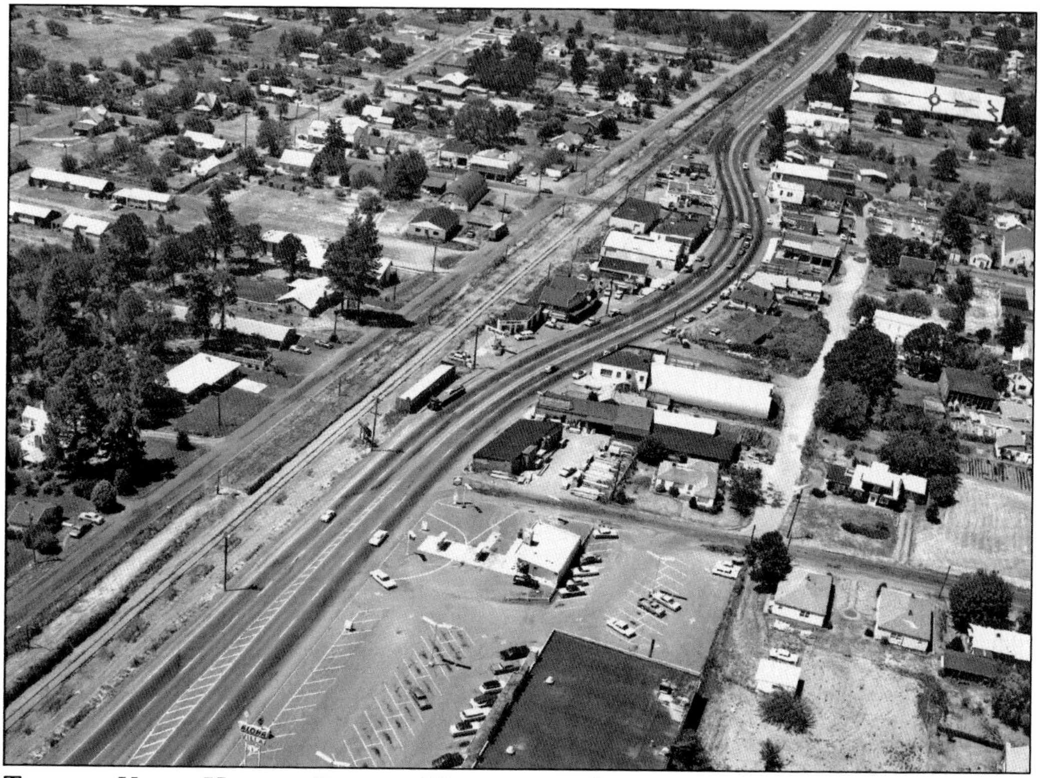

TUALATIN VALLEY HIGHWAY LOOKING WEST TOWARD SOUTHWEST 185TH AVENUE, 1965. The old Piggly Wiggly store, today's Aloha Villa mall, is in the foreground (right). In the mid-1900s, businesses operating in Aloha's central commercial district at the 185th Avenue–Tualatin Valley Highway intersection (below) included Aloha Feed, Earl Fultz's shoe repair, Lenard Farlow's Aloha Pharmacy, Ivan Bernard's barbershop, Nancy Carrol's coffee shop, Stubbs Market and meat lockers, Suburban Hardware, and Mount Hood, later King's Lumber. After World War II, Blue Bus Lines operated Tualatin Valley Stages in Washington County. In 1953, it reorganized as Tualatin Valley Buses, Inc. (Both, Business Services History Center, Oregon Department of Transportation.)

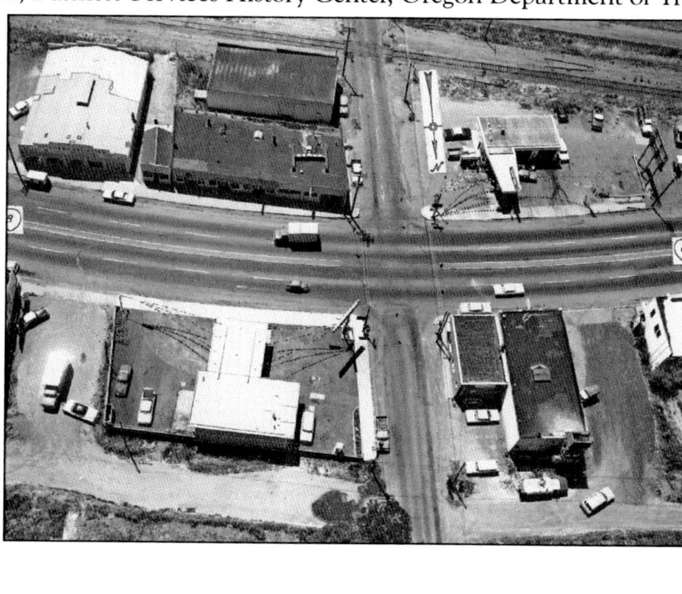

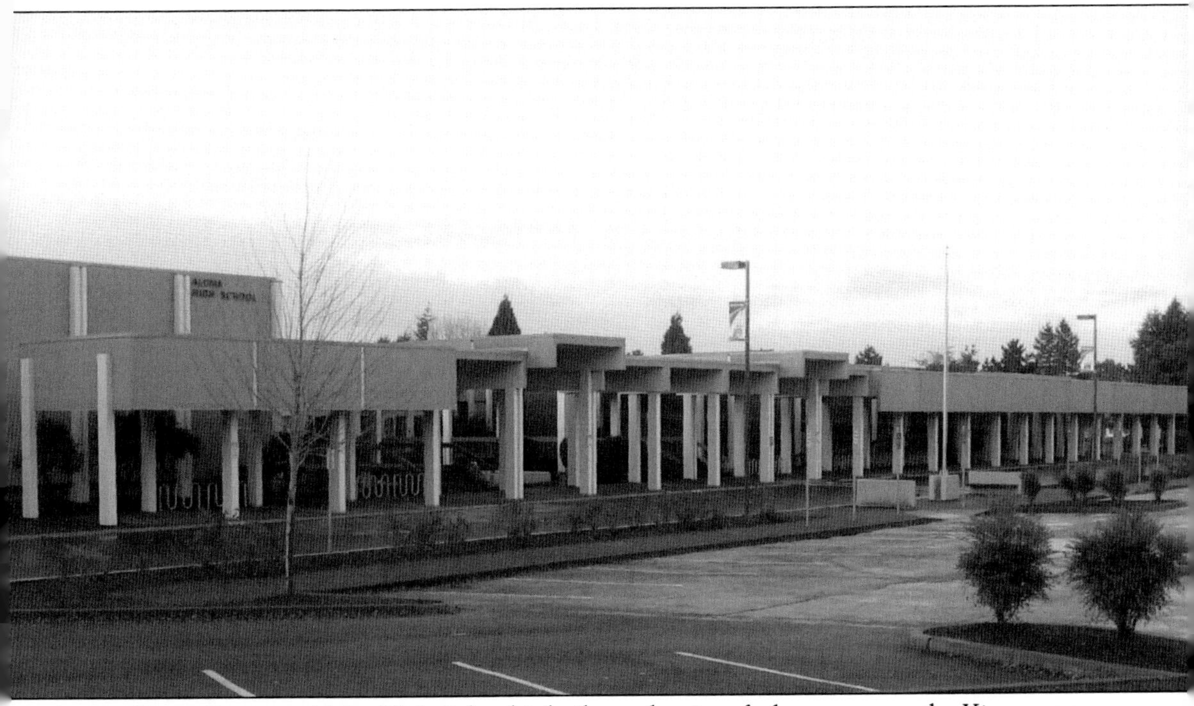

ALOHA HIGH SCHOOL. Aloha High School is built on the site of what was once the Kinnaman dairy on today's Southwest Kinnaman Road in Aloha. In 1962, Beaverton School District 48 purchased the 35-acre dairy farm. In 1966, construction began on what was then the third high school in the district. Because of a building delay, classes were held in the abandoned Merle Davies elementary school building during the 1968–1969 school year. An open house for the new school was held on October 5, 1969. Although not yet complete, the Aloha High School building was opened to students in September 1970. Jack Wood was the first principal. At a cost of around $8 million, the school was designed to include movable walls that readily adapted to fluctuations in enrollment and class size, an innovative feature at the time. Today, Aloha High School is one of 12 high schools in Beaverton School District 48, which was established on May 14, 1874. (Photograph by the author.)